HUMAN GROWTH AND
DEVELOPMENT

HUMAN GROWTH AND DEVELOPMENT

A Psychological Approach

Second Edition

Frank Wesley, Ph.D.
Edith Sullivan, Ph.D.

Portland State University
Portland, Oregon

HUMAN SCIENCES PRESS, INC.
72 FIFTH AVENUE
NEW YORK, N.Y. 10011-8004

Printed in the United States of America
0 987654321

Library of Congress Cataloging-in-Publication Data

Wesley, Frank
    Human growth and development.

    Bibliography: p. 293
    Includes index.
    1. Child psychology. I. Sullivan, Edith. II. Title.
BF721.W385   1986   155.4   86-10530
ISBN 0-89885-316-8
ISBN 0-89885-317-6 (pbk.)

CONTENTS

FOREWORD TO THE SECOND EDITION

Since the publication of our first edition, research and theories in developmental psychology have increased in quantity and quality. Advances in medical technology have made genetic and prenatal counseling more feasible and more pertinent to assure the health of the newborn. There has also been an increased interest in the infant's first social interactions with family members and strangers and more research is accumulating which examines the long-term prosocial and antisocial effects of this interaction.

Developmental psychology is presently experiencing a "cognitive revolution" with attempts being made to unify much of the existing data under the concepts of perceiving and understanding. To convey these new developments to our students we have added the following three chapters to our first edition: Chapter 10, Pre-conception and Prenatal Influences; Chapter 11, Personality and the Social Self; and, Chapter 12, Cognition. We hope our students will find these additional chapters as informative as they have found the previous ones.

F. W.
E. S.

Chapter 1

DEFINITIONS AND ISSUES

In the present century mankind has experienced more developmental changes than in all its previous million years of existence. We live longer than ever before, our infant mortality rate has decreased twentyfold, and a family now needs only two instead of six offspring to keep the population at its present strength. The machine age has made us live more by our brains than by our brawn and the physical work that does remain often taxes our patience more than our muscles. It has become clear that humanity will have a better chance for survival if overpopulation and overproduction are prevented and if child-bearing and work are virtuous only when limited. Bound to fewer biological and existential "musts" we experience more choices throughout our entire development. Whether and when to give birth is now usually a choice and further choices arise through the existence of alternate educational programs and life styles. In order to make the best choices for a child or for ourselves we look to the psychologist with increasing interest and urgency, seeking information about the short-term and, hopefully, the long-term effect of developmental alternatives.

More than Growing

Development means something more than just growing. Our bodies will grow if we eat, sleep, and do some of our daily chores. But in order to *develop* our bodies we need to do more. We need to exert some effort like playing baseball, riding a bicycle, or running around the block early in the morning. This is for the purpose of developing strong arms, strong legs, a good heart, or, in general, a healthy and well-functioning body. When we talk about our minds, we rarely use the word "grow" because we are quite unaware of the existence and the growth of the billions of neurons in our brains by which our minds function. We like to say that our minds (and also our characters and personalities) "develop" because again, we believe that parents and teachers and individuals themselves must make certain efforts so that the mind will develop to best function for the individual's and society's benefit.

There are many aspects to human development. Besides the broad categories of body, mind, and character, we develop more specifically our perceptual abilities, our understanding of quantitative and verbal concepts, and other mental abilities. With respect to our character we develop our emotions, personality, morality, and our attitudes toward people, beliefs, and objects. In all these areas psychologists have accumulated much information and constructed many theories. It is the purpose of this text to survey this information and to examine critically the evidence for the major developmental theories.

Span of Development

For how long do humans develop? Is their development accomplished by a certain age or do they develop as long as they live? When we discuss the body's growth it is not too difficult to agree on the age of 15 for females and 18 for males as the approximate times their bodies have fully developed. There is, however, much less agreement when we discuss the development of the more abstract entities such as the mind and character. In biblical times humans were considered fully developed around the age of 13. Bar mitzvah, confirmation, and other puberty rites marked the entry into adulthood in many cultures. At 13 persons were expected to be fully responsible for their deeds and actions. Even just a century or so ago youth in itself was not a categorical deterrent to success and recognition. Rulers and military men were often quite young. General Howe, who commanded the British forces in the Revolutionary War, was 24 when he became a general. Lafayette was 20 when the Revolutionary Council in Philadelphia commissioned him a general in 1777. In the same year he commanded the American forces in the battle of Brandywine.

During the present century the beginning of adulthood has been progressively delayed. The increase in technology requires longer periods of schooling in some areas, and many people must now prepare themselves until they are in their early twenties before they can begin to function in their chosen vocations and be fully independent. The notion of prolonged schooling has spread to almost all vocational areas whether there is an actual need for it or not. Ironically, our technology has created surpluses in both material and manpower, and the unemployed at all educational levels are told that the chances of employment are better at the next higher educational level. In the 1940s for instance, much psychological counseling and testing was done by psychologists with bachelor's degrees. Twenty years later master's degrees were required for the same tasks, and now, at the end of the 1970s, psychologists and the public are practically convinced that one must have a Ph.D. degree to do these things correctly. It is not that the task has become more difficult, but rather that the supply of personnel with higher degrees has become more plentiful. In 1930 there were about a total of 15,000 master's degrees awarded in the U.S., in 1950 about 50,000, and in 1970 close to 250,000. In the 1980s this number is expected to reach half a million per year (Digest of Education

Statistics, 1978). Whether necessary or not, people in the U.S. do receive prolonged schooling and this fact contributes to the idea that maturity is not reached until the early twenties, and that there is a distinct period of adolescense—a buffer period between childhood and adulthood.

Whatever the cause may be, we do not have a unitary age concept of development. In the U.S. children can open savings accounts as soon as they can sign their signatures—perhaps from 10 years on. But they must be at least 16 before they can open checking accounts. At age 16 we also consider young people sufficiently developed physically, emotionally, and mentally to drive an automobile (perhaps not quite sufficiently because we charge them more for insurance). But in order to enter a tavern they must "develop" five more years until 21. (They are then fully equal because there is no insurance on beer drinking.) Cross-cultural comparisons of various ages of competency show even more arbitrariness. In Germany, for instance, young people can enter taverns and consume alcohol by age 16, but must wait to drive cars until 18. In World War II 18-year-old U.S. Army recruits were told that they were conscripted because they were at an age when their physical and mental development had reached peak capacity and were at their best. At that occasion they were not reminded that they were not considered mature enough to have a voice in their own government, since the voting age at that time was 21. After returning from overseas service at 20, many of these soldiers were surprised that in their hometowns they were still too "young" to buy a glass of beer or a pack of cigarettes, even though they were decorated heroes.

Traditionally, psychologists considered the developmental period to include only childhood and adolescence. They had good reasons for this, because the word "development" implies a process of unfolding, progressing, and improving to a peak capacity. A tree develops until it is fully grown. Few people would consider a fully grown tree as developing and still fewer would label a decaying tree as developing. However, in the

1970s it became fashionable to consider the entire human life span as a developing period. Perhaps this view arose from the changing life styles people experienced in the last decades; perhaps it arose from the advice and counseling that the popular press and psychologists frequently offer, giving us the impression that we can develop in any thing any time, through marriage, through divorce, through work, through retirement, etc.

The life-span view of development, though more encompassing and erudite, raises many questions that are difficult to answer. Is anything we learn or experience a development or must it be an improvement, and if so, who judges whether something is an improvement or not? Is college an improvement over high school? Is work an improvement over college? Is it an improvement if we spend our last months in a nursing home? Perhaps we need not wrestle with these value judgments if we consider the life-span view from an evolutionary standpoint. Even aging, senility, and death may be seen as improvements for the species as a whole in the same way a decaying tree improves the ground and the rest of the ecology and thus fosters the development of new trees. This analogy, however, seems to comfort few of us!

DEVELOPING AND LEARNING

The difference between the "birth to adolescence" and the "life-span" concepts can be more fully understood when we compare the rate of learning. Measured by the capacity to learn, the human mind stops developing after adolescense. This in no way means that humans cannot learn, improve, and have new experiences after adolescence. It means that their innate capacity has reached a limit after adolescence and that thereafter they will rarely be able to increase the amount and the complexity of learning within a given time unit. The average adult, for instance, is able to recall seven numbers after one presentation of one number per second. Some adults can only recall five numbers, others as many as nine, and a rare individual as many as 13. Whatever one's level may be, the chances are that it was reached during or at the end of adolescence. Recalling random numbers is a task that improves very little with practice. It is likely that adolescents who can only recall five numbers (assuming they try their best) will stay around this score throughout their lives, and that those who can repeat 11 numbers will also maintain their high score through most of their lives.

This example demonstrates the concept of capacity to do a task not readily influenced by practice. How can a peak capacity be demonstrated relating to the acquisition of a language, for instance, which depends very much on practice and in which there is always room left for improvement. In this case we can measure the time it takes for an individual to learn a set of words of a given complexity, and we will find again that the maximum capacity is reached at adolescence. Peak capacities cannot be directly demonstrated because people maintain their capacity for a long time and keep on learning and improving —adding continuously to the number of words and to the linguistic skills they already know. Older people sometimes learn faster because they can make use of previously learned material, a process which is called "positive transfer." Persons in their sixties, for instance, who are well-versed in English are likely to learn the French language faster than adolescents at their peak capacity because the older persons who are very familiar with English will have some familiarity with many of the French words. English and French have latin as a common base and much positive transfer occurs. Should the two groups embark on the study of Russian, which has practically no similarity to English, then the older persons would require more time to learn Russian. If we equate development with learning we must accept the life-span view of development because we never cease to learn and to experience new things, although we also forget, and new experiences will not always be an improvement. On the other hand, if we distinguish between the development of a capacity and the acquisition of knowledge we can accept the birth-to-adolescence concept of development.

EARLY DEVELOPMENT

These two views of development are not opposed to each other. It is interesting to note that while psychologists have emphasized the life-span concept when writing about adult development and aging they have at the same time also emphasized more developmental programs for early and very early ages. In the 1960s they advocated preschool programs such as Head Start and in the 1970s day care centers and guidance programs to stimulate and "enrich" the lives of three-, two,- and one-year-olds. Almost all psychologists believe that early childhood is a very important period for the development of intellect and character, but some of them have different reasons for their beliefs which will be discussed in the following.

Concerns about our intellectual development have emphasized early and correct learning. First-time learning or learning something new is much more proficient than relearning or learning new responses to familiar stimuli. Families who move overseas are often surprised how fast and how accent-free their younger children learn to speak the foreign language. Even though the adults have a higher learning capacity than their young children, they learn more slowly, experiencing more interference or *negative transfer* from their long-established habits. For American adults as compared to American children, it is much harder to learn the word "Tisch" because the word "table" will come to their minds first when they see or think about a table. For some reason, that which is learned earlier is remembered better than that which is learned later. There is an almost forgotten rule in psychology (Jost's Law, 1897) which is based on the empirical findings that the *older* of two associations learned to the same degree will be rememberd *better* and longer. All this points again to the importance of the early developmental period.

Development is self-propagating. Experience builds on experience, and we can learn how to learn. For example, with more words we can ask more questions and learn even more words from their answers. Psychologists have been searching for traits conducive to learning. Traits such as persistence and curiosity have been examined, but they have their negative as well as their positive effects on learning. Too much persistence can prevent us from finding new approaches, and too much curiosity may prevent a thoroughness that is also needed for learning. At the turn of the century educators believed that mere memorization improves the mind. They believed especially that the memorization of Latin words and grammar improves our capacity to understand mathematics, chemistry, etc. This belief, called "formal discipline," is no longer in vogue. There are great doubts and also some controversies among psychologists as to whether the mind's capacity can be improved at all, though all agree that there are many techniques, such as specialized instructions, mnemonic devices, teaching machines, etc., that will speed up the learning process. The Italian physician, Maria Montessori (1870–1952), long ago claimed that young children have to learn how to learn. She devised special tasks for her kindergarten curriculum to foster this process. One of these tasks consists of a series of graduated boxes all contained in the largest box. After the boxes are scattered the child puts them back into the large box. If a box is taken out of order it will not fit or it will be left over. Montessori's tasks can be considered the forerunner of our more modern educational toys and teaching machines. Much of our educational and socialization efforts are directed towards this self-development. It is a continuous process. Even in college there are some independent study courses.

The above points have shown the importance to early development. But how early should the various traits and skills be taught? How many mobiles should we hang over a baby's crib and how often should we change them? How many animals, stuffed or live, should there be around and how much time should we spend vocalizing with our infants? There are similar questions all along the developmental path. How soon should we teach walking, talking, reading, writing, etc., to mention a few positive things. On the negative side, how soon should we teach children not to throw things around, not to bite others, not to urinate on the living room floor, not to scribble in our new encyclopedia. "The sooner the better" has been the trend for the last decade. Failures in high school have been attributed to developmental deficiencies in grammer school, failures in grammer school to flaws in preschool experience, and so on down the line to birth itself. Some psychologists now believe that a child's future intelligence, social competence, and general ability to learn are all largely determined before the age of three. New programs have been established to enrich and stimulate the lives of children before the age of three. The directors of one such program, the "Brookline Early Education Project," believe that the most critical period for learning is the short, often neglected span between 8 and 18 months. During these 10 months social workers, psychologists, and pediatricians participating in the project monitor the infants' development and teach parents how to teach children (Pines, 1978).

One may wonder why there is such a rush, since psychologists now also believe that one can develop and progress as long as one lives. What has not been emphasized is the possible detrimental effect of "overstimulation"—stimulating children too soon with too much. In certain instances we may overtax children with visual and auditory stimuli and they may become desensitized toward their environment, be it the parental milieu or the school atmosphere. Children may shut out stimuli of normal intensity and respond only when the stimuli become more and more intense. There is, of course, a balance between deprivation and overstimulation. How much can be taught changes increasingly with age, depending on the individual's inborn capacities—variables which Binet, Piaget, and other notable psychologists investigated. It is easier to know the appropriate training times for physical than for mental tasks. In a way children "tell" us when they are ready to walk—they stand up freely and move along holding on to a table, for example. We have far fewer clues as to their readiness for toilet training, school entry, piano lessons, etc. But, in general, the mental capacities in early childhood go hand in hand with the physical development. Psychologists study this relationship when they deal with "maturation," which will be discussed in the following chapter.

"You can't teach an old dog new tricks," or "A seedling bends, but not a tree" are sayings that indicate the popular belief that character and moral vaues are best taught at an early age. A century ago it was believed that denials, restrictions, and, if necessary, disciplinary actions were childhood essentials so that individuals would learn to cope with them and would therefore experience fewer strains and stresses in adulthood. These developmental trends have completely reversed themselves during the twentieth century and the popular belief now is that love withheld during early childhood will not only delay but actually mar the development of the human, causing more or less permanent deficiencies. Much has been written about the "necessity" of holding and cuddling infants and many clinical psychologists believe that certain character deficiencies in adulthood are a result of insufficient love and contact received in childhood. It is therefore often recommended that children be given an "overdose" of love, assuming that this will protect them from the strains and stresses the future may bring. These notions stem mostly from the writings of Freud, who assumed that all neuroses occurring in adulthood are due to frustrations experienced in infancy and early childhood. These beliefs have found much acceptance in Western societies, particularly in the U.S. and England which are not predominantly Catholic and in which reliance on supernatural guidance has diminished.

In these countries many parents and psychologists assume that if children are loved they will forever be protected from evil and misfortune. Kagan (1978) has pointed out that this "love formula" may put many children into a "parental love trap," giving them the unrealistic idea that they are liked and valued under any circumstances. However, such a "private" conception of love and self-worth can grossly interfere with individuals' socialization processes making them insensitive to the needs of others. Kagan also discusses other well-functioning societies that de-emphasize parental love and that consider genetics and a healthy communal life as the most important development factors.

Research findings suggesting that the parental love role may not be as important as generally assumed have not found their way into the more popular American developmental literature. For instance, Schaffer and Emerson (1964) found that about one third of the babies they investigated were by nature "noncuddlers," resisting any holding, rocking, cuddling, etc. There are also the findings of Kagan and Klein (1973), who observed that Guatemalan children who spend their first year in a moderately isolated environment of windowless huts, but who are allowed to play rather unrestrictedly with older children after they are 15 months old, turn out to be lively and happy. There seems to be a resiliency in infants that psychologists do not like to admit or to advertise, fearing perhaps that some parents may use this knowledge as an excuse for neglect and abuse. On the other hand, the witholding of these resiliency data does nothing to minimize the increasing "mother-blaming" trend in our society. No wonder that 25-year-old Tom Hansen, who thought his parents failed to rear him properly, sued them for $350,000 to cover the cost of psychiatric treatments which he thought he needed for the rest of his life. His attorney stated that the claim involved "malpractice of parenting" (APA Monitor, 1978). If children should win such cases parents may be allowed to countersue for ulcers they developed worrying about their children and for the deafness caused by their children's hard rock records. When this time approaches, human development students had best study law!

In our society mothers are not only blamed for the love they did not give, but also for the love they gave too abundantly. Around the time Gary Gilmore was executed in Utah for the murders he committed, a prison psychiatrist stated on television that Gilmore was incorrigible during his 18 years of incarceration because he was reared by an "overprotective" mother.

Many of these deficiency or excess hypotheses are hard to prove because they involve assessments of relationships that occurred years if not decades ago, and terms like "rejecting" and "over-protecting" are not easily defined.

DEVELOPMENTAL STAGES

Human development is full of stages. A number of psychologists have divided childhood into various stages. Freud's categorization, which divides early childhood into the oral, anal, and phallic stages, has been very influential in Western society. Freud assumed that specific desires must be satisfied in each stage, or else the desires would increase to abnormal dimensions in adulthood, giving rise to neuroses and perhaps psychoses. For example, during the first year of life, Freud's "oral stage," children must be allowed to suck, chew, and bite or else they will develop "oral personalities" and experience abnormal desires to eat, smoke, talk, etc., in their adult years. Behavior, good or bad, must "come out" during the early years. This rationale has fostered much of our parental permissiveness and certain psychotherapeutic notions that neurotics have to "act out," "ventilate," "let off steam," or, in a more sophisticated term, have a "catharsis" before they can get better.

By far the most complicated stage system concerning mental and moral development has been advocated by the Swiss psychologist, Jean Piaget. He postulated the following four basic developmental periods: sensorimotor (0–2 years), preoperational thought (2–7 years), concrete operations (7–11 years), and formal operations (11–15 years). He maintains that certain mental processes and experiences have to take place during each period before the next period can be attained. The name of the first period, sensorimotor, does not imply thinking and various types of logic as do the remainder of Piaget's categories. But the human mind is hard to categorize and Piaget believes that there are six substages within the sensory-motor period.

According to his own definition only the first substage, the "reflex stage" (0–1 month), is a period of pure stimulus-response reactions. In some of the next stages, called "primary circular reaction stage" (1–4 months), "secondary circular reaction stage" (4–8 months), "coordination of seconday schemas and their application to new situations stage" (8–12 months), etc., habits are formed, intentions enter in, actions are prolonged for self-satisfaction, and new environments are explored.

A system simpler to learn, but not simpler in its dynamics, is advocated by the Harvard psychologist Erik Erikson. He postulates that our personality development continued throughout our whole life cycle, which consists of eight stages, each stage having a positive and a negative component. In the first stage, designated "trust vs. mistrust" (0–1 year), the infant is dependent on the help of others; it is then that he learns whether or not the world can be trusted. In the second stage, "autonomy vs. doubt" (2–3 years) children find out what they can and cannot do by themselves. Adolescence is designated by Erikson "identity vs. self-diffusion," middle age as "generativity vs. self-absorption," and old age as "integrity vs. despair."

The above sketch of stages is brief and incomplete. It may serve, however, to show that the psychologists who write about them are guided in their observations by their own attitudes and interests. Both Freud and Erikson were and are concerned about coping with conflicts and the development of personality. Freud had a more pessimistic view, seeing the child by nature as "polymorphous perverse" and as having to go through some of these perverted and antisocial acts in the course of development. Erikson's concept of development is more positive. He believes that children are not "bad" by nature and that humans have positive as well as negative experiences throughout their entire lives. In contrast to Freud and Erikson, Piaget's system deals with the intellectual development, more specifically how the concepts of space, time, and number develop.

Much research has centered around the stages of Freud

and Piaget and some of the research will be discussed in subsequent chapters. Stages are very descriptive and are useful as sources for hypotheses. However, they rarely explain why a certain behavior occurs. Too often they are used for *ex post facto* (after the fact) explanations. For example, first we observe that babies put all sorts of objects into their mouths—so we call it the "oral stage"—and then we say babies put things into their mouths because they are in the "oral stage." Even more misleading are some of the assumptions that underlie certain stages, especially some of those postulated by Freud. There seems to be no correlation between infantile sucking (thumb, pacifier, blanket, etc.) and the amount one eats or smokes in adulthood. It is also questionable whether catharsis is necessary for the cure of neuroses. If one is not careful, the "acting out" of bad feelings can make things much worse.

The approach in this text shall not follow any specific periods or stages. The conditions of the body and mind change continually from birth until adolescence, and rather than describing certain stages, we shall elaborate on various types of learning and on factors that influence it—maturation, imitation, reward, and punishment. The more knowledge we have about maturation and the process of learning, the better will we be able to understand our mental growth and our socialization at any point in our life.

HEREDITY AND ENVIRONMENT

In 1580 the French philosopher Montaigne wondered how he could have inherited gallstones from his father when his father did not have them until 25 years after the son was born and Montaigne himself did not have them until he was 45 years old. Before Mendel's plant propagation experiments in 1866 and before the use of the microscope, heredity was one of the greatest mysteries. To a certain extent it still is. For centuries the "heredity–environment" issue was a controversy of the "either-or" type. Some philosophers in the seventeenth century believed that even the specific words of one's mother tongue and their meanings were inherited and that one would be able to speak it without ever hearing it. On the other hand, the philosopher John Locke (1632–1704) believed that an infant's mind was like a blank slate or a "tabula rasa" where sensory experiences leave their impressions giving rise to knowledge, images, and thought—something like the input into a modern unprogrammed computer. A century later the French politician and philosopher Jean Jacques Rousseau (1712–1778) emphasized again the innate and the natural. He was against all formal education and wanted education to slow down and be free from adult influence, especially the capitalistic variety. He didn't practice what he preached. He sent his own children to a foundlings' home, where in all likelihood they had a very strict upbringing.

The church was opposed to Rousseau and was in general against the idea that "nature shall take its course" during development. Only animals, but not humans, the church maintained, were supposed to live by their natural instincts. Animals could do no "right" or "wrong" and consequently there was no heaven and no afterlife for them. Humans were not supposed to follow their natural instincts. They had free will; it was up to them to sin or not to sin, and they could be judged to go to heaven or hell or such places in between as purgatory or limbo accordingly. The church did not accept any kind of environmental determinism and people could not be absolved from their sins by blaming parents, teachers, alcohol, neuroses, or unconscious motives for their shortcomings.

Around the turn of this century the heredity-environment issue flared up again. Stimulated by Darwin's theory of evolution, some people were no longer hesitant to look at their relation to animals and to natural instinct. Freud based much of his psychoanalytic theory on natural instincts such as "father-hating," "father-loving," etc. In America, McDougall (1871–1938) began to categorize human behavior into instincts. First there were a few instincts like fear, anger, love, fighting, hunting, etc. The list grew longer and there were additional instincts for being orderly, disorderly, gregarious, pugnacious, etc. The lists contained many opposing terms, so that psychologists would have an "answer" for everything, and many instincts were given Greek or Latin names so that the abstract fallacies or the *ex post facto* explanations would not be so readily apparent. When somebody disagreed with McDougall he just added another instinct to his list—"argumentativeness." In 1924 Bernard was able to list over 10,000 instincts that psychologists and others had postulated.

The most popular opposition to the instinct theories came from John B. Watson (1878–1958), the founder of behaviorism. He protested calling everything an instinct. He believed that there were only three basic instincts: love, rage, and fear. He believed that humans were innately capable of these reactions but that specific loves and fears, such as fear of the dark or fear of snakes, were learned. Watson's (1926) famous statement: "Give me a dozen healthy infants, well-formed, and my own specific world to bring them up in, and I will guarantee to take anyone at random and train him to become any type of specialist, doctor, lawyer, artist, merchant. . . ." did not help his environmental cause. It was considered too radically environmentalistic since it sounded like Watson believed heredity had no influence whatsoever. Watson, however, was fully aware of the importance of heredity because he wrote detailed reports on individual differences in constitution, neural tissues, and chemicals. He rejected the term "mind" because it was too abstract and because it implied that the mind is not part of our body. He therefore equated mind with body, and we should therefore assume that Watson's words "healthy" and "well-formed" meant infants with normal physical and mental potentials. Watson was well aware that neither morons nor idiots could be trained to be doctors or lawyers.

Though the arguments about heredity and environment have become more sophisticated, they have not lessened in intensity. It is no longer a question of one or the other. Everybody now recognizes that both heredity and environment are absolutely necessary for any human endeavor, but heated arguments still exist about the degree to which they influence each other. Psychologists who believe that one is genetically predisposed to fast or slow learning have been beaten up and had their offices stormed by Oxford and Berkeley students. The psychologists are accused of being elitists wanting to find excuses for not helping those with lower abilities. They in turn maintain that it is unrealistic to believe that people are born with equal potentials and that this assumption can lead to years of annoyances, false hopes, and unfulfilled expectations during the process of development.

The most recent debates about heredity and environment center around the topic of sex roles. One debate is trying to answer the question whether or not or to what degree our feminine and masculine traits and behaviors are innate or culturally conditioned. The questions are of great interest to all those who believe that sexual equality can only be obtained when both sexes give up some of their "stereotyped" behaviors. Those who advocate sexual equality are generally opposed to the notion of inborn traits and tendencies. It would be most to their liking if there were no biological causes for the various sex-role behaviors such as "male" aggressiveness and "female" nurturance. As will be shown in a subsequent chapter, most sex-role behavior is culturally conditioned, but certain biological influences cannot be ruled out. Since we cannot raise humans in a cultural vacuum, the evidence for either heredity or environment can only be indirectly assessed. For example, it was generally assumed that males die seven years sooner than females because they experience stress in business and because they are providers for their families. To test this hypothesis, Madigan (1957) compared the vital statistics of 9,000 nuns and monks and found that men in this subculture also die seven years earlier than women. He concluded, therefore, that the shorter life span of males cannot be explained by business or family stress and that it is probably biologically determined.

REWARD AND PUNISHMENT

Perhaps even older than the heredity controversy is the reward and punishment issue. The Bible mentions that not only you but also your offspring will be punished for your bad deeds. The Egyptians were punished for not letting the Jews go to their Holy Land and the Jews were punished for doubting that Moses could lead them there. The Bible's reward and punishment system, culminating in heaven and hell, has not been surpassed by any psychological methodologies. For the most part it is verbal and imaginary and neither the actual reward nor the actual punishment ever needs to be carried out. Such a system works best if the conditioning has been carried out since childhood. If that is not the case, or if a conquerer's subjects were raised under a different belief system, then more direct methods of reward and/or punishment will have to be used. Bismarck, the founder of the German Reich in 1871, advised that one should keep a whip in the left hand and a piece of candy in the right. Almost all great men, Christians or not, have had something to say about punishment. Confucious said that each child should be spanked once a day—if the parent doesn't know wherefore the child will!

Reward and punishment are closely linked to learning and therefore permeate our entire lives. In education we speak of grades and honors and in the business world of incentives and merits. In the last decades psychologists have constantly searched for more effective reward methods and have shied away from recommending any type of punishment, although some forms are harmless and very effective. In some situations punishment may be the only effective alternative. It will be discussed in a later chapter how often, in which form, and at which instances we should punish and/or reward so that our action will be effective without being detrimental to the person's development.

MORE CHOICES

Throughout the history of mankind parents have never had as many developmental choices available to them as in the latter part of the twentieth century. Beginning with conception, women and men have a number of alternatives concerning whether or not they want to create a new life. During the first three months of pregnancy women have the additional choice of abortion. Marriage is no longer a social must and some women choose to rear a child without a father. The working mother has become more socially acceptable, although adequate day-care facilities are still lacking in many communities. In terms of schooling there are also alternate programs and there is less urgency to bring up a child in a traditional sex role. In high school a variety of electives are available—some larger schools offer as many as 250 minicourses on diverse subject matter. For adults changes in marital status, jobs, careers, and in life style are more acceptable.

All this sounds like utopia. But are we freer of frustration because we have all these choices? At each junction we seem to wonder whether we are making the correct choices for ourselves and for our offspring. In 1975 over 200 "how-to-parent" books were in print and it is estimated that over 23 million were sold in the U.S. from 1973 to 1978 (Clarke-Stewart, 1978). There is more dependency on advising, counseling, and therapy at all ages. School psychologists counsel pupils how to get along with their teachers and vice versa. Adults seek more vocational, marriage, sex, and even death counseling. Aside from seeking professional help, an increased number of people are joining for example, Scientology, Lifespring, "I found it," and maharishis with mantras in order to find "self-awareness," "identity," and so forth. Are they seeking systems that tell them how to make "correct" choices? It seems incongruous that dependency has increased at the same time the number of choices have. But it may well be that we are often dissatisfied with our choices because we made or think we made the wrong ones. At times people blame themselves for past choices even though they were quite correct when they were made. At other times the decisions were outright wrong and this could have been predicted. There are also those decisions that are difficult to analyze in terms of "right" and "wrong." They often involve conflicts between immediate and delayed gratification—whether to take the cash now or the credit later.

Further uncertainty about our choices is due to changing values in our society. To a large degree we make our choices so that they conform to the attitudes and opinions we have acquired through modeling. But in a society that is changing we can often find as many models on the "pro" as on the "con" side. For example, the number of female and male college students living together unmarried is about equal to the number of those who are married. So whatever one has decided, one meets many who decided differently. It is difficult to know whether more opportunities and more choices must necessarily lead to more insecurities and more frustrations. Values are changing in our society and there is occasional conflict over whether to judge by new or old criteria. Perhaps when we consider such matters as abortions, marriage, and whether or not a mother should work more as practical than as moral issues will we feel less bothered by the decisions we have made.

The many developmental alternatives which our society offers in the 1970s have not made the study of human development any easier. They require not only psychological but also social, economic, and cultural considerations. It is comparatively simple, for instance, to advise parents how to raise a nonaggressive child, should they so desire. But before this advice is given it would be useful to know how some of the neighbors raise their children.

Toward Objectivity

Everybody has some ideas and some knowledge about human development. People remember parts of their own upbringing and certain developmental desires and fulfillments from adolescence and adulthood. This "subjective" knowledge contributes to our individualism and becomes part of our personality. Occasionally we encounter difficulties communicating our subjective feelings. We can best describe our toothache to somebody who has had one. Otherwise we must describe it by analogy. We must find some ache we had in common, perhaps an earache, and then piont out that is is like an earache but it is in the mouth and elaborate further on other communalities.

Subjective knowledge is of limited use in finding causes for our own behavior and feelings. Many of our likes and dislikes were taught to us in early childhood, often in minimally noticeable increments, so that we remember only the end effects but not the actual causes. For example, most Americans like steak, but few remember the gradual process by which we were taught to eat it. It happened most likely in our early childhood with our mothers applying some "tricks" to make us eat our first bite. In adulthood we may think that we always liked steak and that this desire is innate. In other instances our subjective knowledge may be based on some misinformation our parents or others have given us. We may have heard "Ever since you had that mean third-grade teacher you have hated arithmetic" for so long that it has become our subjective belief. In actuality we may have hated it from the beginning but our sentiments were not noticed because they had occurred so gradually. It is difficult to be critical about developmental information our parents may give us because in most cases we cannot disprove it. We are equally unable to disprove some of the causes and explanations the experts give us when they base them on a single case history. If, for instance, a psychologist or psychiatrist tells a single parent, a mother, that her six-year-old son wets the bed because he was raised in a fatherless home, she cannot disprove it. Had she raised the son with a father present he may have also wet the bed. But nobody can be raised twice and the experts know that.

If the subjective method is unreliable to assess the causes of our own behavior, it can be quite misleading when we use it to explain the behvior and the feelings of others. In order to become more certain about the events we subjectively suspect as causes, we must observe or examine a larger number of people and/or incidents. To follow our previous example about the "mean" third-grade teacher we should look at other of her or his former pupils and find out how many of them also hate arithmetic. Is it only our child or are there ten or twenty more who were in the same class? We should also find some kind of a control, some "nice" teachers, and see how many of their pupils hate arithmetic. With regard to the causes of bedwetting, we would also have to examine a large number of bedwetters. We may want to look at the family status of 100 bedwetters and tabulate what percentage of bedwetters come from fatherless homes and what from homes where the father is present. Only if a significantly larger (larger than chance) proportion of bedwetters comes from fatherless homes can we infer a causal relationship between bedwetting and paternal absence How large must a proportion be before we can make a statement one way or the other? Perhaps 70, 80, or 90 percent? There are no definite answers, but the larger the proportion the surer or the more objective we can be about our assumption.

Before we begin to collect objective data we must define that which we are looking for by concrete or *operational defini-tions*. For example, if we want to find out whether children who attend a Montessori kindergarten learn better than children in a conventional one, we must define "learn" and "better" in operational terms. What must the children do in terms of observable behavior to be given a "plus" for "learning" and a "plus" for "better?" Will they have to solve a jigsaw puzzle, name colors, operate a mechanical toy, learn a poem, and what will be our critieria for better? Learning faster, making fewer errors, remembering longer? The adherence to operational definitions minimizes the chances that the experimenters will change their criteria during the observation—something that is otherwise difficult to avoid. For example, we are likely to overlook incorrent answers if a child smiles and is physically attractive.

Perhaps the most important reason for operational definitions is their objectivity in telling other experimenters and the public what exactly has been observed. If, for example, experimenters want to find out whether married persons are "happier" than single ones, they must first list which of their subjects' behaviors or attitudes they will count as happy. Some may list smiling, singing, getting up early in the morning, having two cars, or much money. Others may list sleeping in late, riding a bicycle, or having no money. Operational definitions are neither "right" nor "wrong." They merely tell the reader in a more or less concrete way what the experimenter has measured—and "money" is, of course, as concrete as "no money." An operational definition need not be made so that the response needs to be measured with a yardstick or an oscilloscope. The subjects' "yes" or "no" responses may suffice. One can only be critical if one knows the measure by which data were obtained.

How far back should we look for causes in our own behavior; or how long shall we wait to see whether a certain condition in childhood has an effect in later life? If we let our babies cry for a while before feeding them, what personality might we expect in adolescence? How will children who are frequently punished relate to their own children thirty years hence? Will they be just as strict, more strict, or less strict? These are typical developmental questions and they present a difficult problem because in order to find answers we must often wait ten, twenty, or more years. Such long-term or *longitudinal* studies are usually carried out by university research institutes that supply funds and continuous staffing.

Terman's study of genius (1925–1959) is one of the best known longitudinal studies. In the early 1920s he and his associates at Stanford University began to examine the physical, mental, and personality traits of over 1,000 intellectually superior children in order to find out what sort of an adult the typical gifted child becomes. The same subjects have been examined at ten-year intervals since 1922. The most recent survey was taken by Sears in 1977 when the average participant was 62 years old. The various surveys showed that there was much consistency over the entire life span with respect to their somewhat superior health, professional satisfaction, and marital status. Somewhat unexpectedly it was repeatedly found that the geniuses lived very normal lives. The males were in no way eccentric and the housewives were as satisfied as the female professionals—that was in the survey taken in 1959!

There are ways to get around the long-term planning and the extensive financing that longitudinal studies require. If, for instance, experimenters are interested in studying the effects of breast- and bottle-feeding on adult personality they need to start out with infants now and follow them into adulthood. They can sample adults and find out from their mothers whether they were breast or bottle fed, although this method introduces an error of memory. At the same time, the adults can be tested as to their health, mental, and personality status and in this way it can be found out whether and in which way the breast-fed group differs from the bottle-fed one. Such studies should be "blind" studies—meaning that the experimenters who test the individual must not know to which group an individual belongs, since such knowledge may prejudice them in their assessment. Incidentally, no adult behavior or personality pattern seems to be related to the breast or bottle variable.

There are other shortcuts to longitudinal investigations. For example, the cross-cultural study by Kagan and Klein mentioned earlier researched the childrearing environment of one-year-old infants in Guatemala and also the personalities of older Guatemalan children. These results were compared with those of American children of similar ages and in this way inferences about the effect and the importance of early stimulation were made. The cross-subcultural study of Madigan has also been mentioned. Here the subculture of monks and nuns was investigated to isolate the effect of family and business life on longevity.

A historical perspective often can be useful to evaluate developmental studies. Television, for instance, is often considered the cause of aggressive and criminal behavior in our present society. Our recent history, however, shows that the most aggressive and cruel acts mankind ever experienced were committed by the Nazis before the advent of television. Because human behavior is so manifold and can occur in an endless number of situations, there is rarely a single study or a single methodology that gives us decisive results. It is hoped that the studies selected for discussions in the following chapters will illuminate some developmental areas and will tell the reader why there is still uncertainty in others.

Chapter 2

MATURATION

We ask again what does it mean to develop? To develop is to grow, to mature, to learn. Growth generally refers to physical changes, changes of quantity that involve addition rather than transformation, changes such as enlargement of body structures or changes in height and weight that can be directly measured. *Maturation* refers to the changes occurring with age, independent of environment, that can only be assessed if the environment is factored out. Maturation manifests itself through prenatal and postnatal sequences that follow the instructions built into the genetic code. Todd (1937) has discussed the various meanings of "growing," pointing out that growing up is different from being grown up and from growing old. Maturation, he believes, represents a progressive growth— which implies development until adolescence. Changes in adulthood and senescence can perhaps be called "dematuration."

Maturation is the physiological substratum on which experience imprints itself. This is best exemplified in Carmichael's (1926) classic experiment with salamanders in which he demonstrated that maturation alone provides lower organisms with practically all that is necessary for the development of their behavioral repertoire. Carmichael placed a control group of salamander eggs in a tank of pure water and another group in a chlorotone solution, an anesthetic which paralyzes the animal's movements, but not its breathing. After five days the control group of salamanders in the tank of pure water had learned how to swim—seemingly by a long process of wiggling and squirming. But, when the experimental group was freed from the chlorotone solution after five days they began to swim in about a minute or two—apparently as soon as the anesthetic wore off. Within one hour they could not be distinguished from the control group which had been moving freely for five days.

In some lower animals the maturational process is so predominant that it cannot be modified by learning. The moth has matured in such a way that it flies into the light of a candle (helioptropism) even though repeated contacts with it will be fatal. It cannot learn to stay away from it. The wall swallow builds its nest in a very specific manner without ever having seen another swallow build one. Humans have no such built in tropisms or instincts. With the exception of the simple reflexes, more extensive behaviors have to be learned or modeled. The higher organisms need longer maturational periods and also longer learning periods. From conception on the human needs to mature about two years before speech begins; about two further years of maturation and learning are needed before a basic conversational level is reached. In this chapter we shall discuss the prenatal development and some of the reflexes that are present at birth, as well as some of the interactions between maturation and experience that take place from birth to adolescence.

PRENATAL MATURATION

Within the first 24 to 36 hours after conception, the single cell splits in two (mitosis) with each of the new cells containing the 23 pairs of chromosomes. Mitosis continues rapidly until the whole cell mass is about the size of a pinhead. Within two weeks the fertilized ovum has traveled down the fallopian tube to the uterus and implanted itself in the uterine wall. The ovum up to this time has been on its own as far as oxygen and nutrition are concerned. It is at this time, when the ovum is gradually descending the fallopian tube, that identical twinning could occur. Timing is critical since after the seventh day the ovum cannot feed off its cells and must have an adequate supply of oxygen and nutrients. At the time of the implantation the surface of the uterus has become thick and spongy, engorged with blood. It is difficult to explain why this small body of cells (ovum) does become attached since it represents a foreign protein and normally the body is programmed to reject such an invasion. In fact, 50 percent of fertilized ova fail to make this life-giving attachment (Kennedy, 1975).

The implantation marks the beginning of the period of the embryo. The total group of cells divides into two groups, one of which forms a sort of sphere around the inner group of cells; then the sphere develops rootlike structures, villi or tendrils, which attach themselves to the wall of the uterus in order to absorb nutrients from the maternal blood supply.

The major event of the next eight weeks is the development of the placenta. The outside layer next to the uterus is the *chorion,* which is covered with thin hairlike villi that penetrate the surface of the uterus. The middle tissue or *lumen* is the filter layer of the placenta. The *amnion* is the inner layer that is attached to the embryo through the umbilical cord. Through the permeable placenta to the child's bloodstream flow components such as proteins, sugars, and vitamins, as well as some drugs, including alcohol and nicotine. Only certain chemicals, but not the blood, cross the placenta. There are no direct neural connections. For the unborn infant the placenta does the work of the lungs, kidneys, intestines, liver, and hormone-producing glands. To the mother the placenta contributes hormones essential to the maintenance of pregnancy and for the production of milk after childbirth (Apgar & Beck, 1972).

Growth during the embryonic period is extremely rapid. About 95 percent of the body parts are differentiated, and there is a 2 million percent increase in size. In this eight-week period the embryo is first differentiated into three specialized tissue layers: an outer layer, the ectoderm, of baby skin and surface tissue such as sweat glands, hair, and nervous system; a middle layer, the mesoderm, that is the rudiment of the skeletal, muscular, and circulatory systems; and an inner layer, the endoderm, that for the most part becomes the viscera or internal organs. By the end of eight weeks the embryo, which is now about two inches in length and weighs less than 1 ounce, has relatively large and oversized eyes, ears, a mouth that opens and closes, and a nose. It has an undersized body with a liver, a heart with rudimentary heart beat, arms with elbows, legs with knees, fingers and toes webbed rather like a duck's foot, and a tail. These odd size relationships make the embryo at various stages look like various animals—a fish, a lizard, a pig, and a chimp. It seems that the development of the individual (ontogeny) goes through the various developmental stages through which the species (phylogeny) went in the millions of years of its development. At the turn of the century the motto "Ontogeny recapitulates phylogeny!" was sometimes heard as a drinking toast among univeristy students who were liberal and daring enough to proclaim Darwin's theory of evolution.

It is during the embryo's rapid growth period that the majority of birth defects are formed. In general, the greater the defect the earlier it is formed since the embryonic period is a time of great shifts in cell division, cell differentiation, and changes in biochemistry. It is a period when the mother should take the greatest care with regard to her nutritional and drug intake; unfortunately, the whole process may occur without the mother knowing she is pregnant. In fact, a woman who is anticipating pregnancy should regard her nutritional and drug consumption long before conception. Prepare for the optimal uterine environment long before the guest arrives!

During the third month, the beginning of the fetal stage, the human infant now weighs about one ounce. It is surrounded by amniotic fluid which acts as a shock absorber and prevents fluid loss through the porous skin of the fetus. The intestinal tract and kidneys are beginning to function and the muscles are developing with spontaneous movements of arms and legs, the "quickening." Sex becomes distinguishable and many of the organism's major systems begin to function at the end of the fourth month. The nervous system is an exception. Its major growth does not occur until the last three months of pregnancy and its myelination, the growth of a fatty sheath around some neurons, is not complete until six to twelve months after birth.

Prenatal development is regular and predictable, occurring in a fixed order in a fixed time period. Even though biologists have unlocked the genetic code with the discovery of deoxyribonucleic acid (DNA), it is not known how the individual cell "knows" that it is to become a particular body part. We do know that the *sequence* itself is affected by only quite extreme environmental influences and that it seems to be universal for our species. Birth normally occurs at the optimal time for the infant's development, approximately 266 days after conception. It is then ready to live independently of the stimulation of the biochemical system of the mother.

Maturation in Infancy

At birth, what can the infant do? The newborn can hear a whole range of sounds but is especially sensitive to sounds with the pitch range of the human voice and to rhythmic sounds that appear to have generally soothing qualities. Not only can the newborn react to visual, auditory, and tactile stimuli, but it can learn after only a few conditioning trials to substitute one cue for another and to anticipate cues in procedures. These are discussed in more detail in the following chapter.

Newborns are able to focus both eyes on some point, follow a moving object, and discriminate colors and brightness. They react quite violently to certain odors but details about their smell perception are not known. Engen et al. (1963) attempted to measure infants' olfactory sensitivity by observing activity and breath rate. It was found that babies breathed faster and moved more in response to some odors than others, suggesting that infants perceive certain odors with different intensities than adults. The infants' sense of taste is less impressive (Pratt, 1954). The distinctive tastes of salt, sugar, citric acid, or water do not elicit different responses, even when placed directly on the tongue, although by the end of two weeks most infants react more greedily to sugar than to salt—and that stays with most of them for quite some time! Although infants are very sensitive to touch, particularly around the mouth and hands, their tolerance for pain seems remarkably high (McGraw, 1943). Perhaps the processes of birth and circumcision are not quite as painful as adults imagine.

Most of the behaviors that the neonate can perform are reflexive. They do not require learning and can be readily elicited in the normal child by presenting the appropriate stimulus. The sequential appearance of certain reflexes and their gradual suppression by more complex responses are important as indicators that maturation is progressing in an orderly sequence. Dennis (1934) listed some of the reflexes and their respective stimuli that are common to newborns in the accompanying table.

Probably the best known reflex of survival value is the *sucking reflex* and those related—rooting, swallowing, hiccoughing, sneezing, and vomiting. These all can be elicited by the appropriate nourishment-related stimulation. Therefore they are referred to as the *vegetative reflexes.* Other reflexes demonstrate emergency reactions. When an infant is exposed to

Reflex	Stimulus
Sucking	Object in mouth
Head turning (rooting)	Stroking the cheek or the corner of the mouth
Swallowing	Food in mouth
Sneezing	Irritation in the nasal passages
Moro reflex	Sudden loud noise
Babinski reflex	Tickling the middle of the soles
Babkin reflex	Thumb pressure on palm of hand
Toe grasp	Tickling the soles just below the toes
Palmar grasp	Placing object in the infant's hand
Swimming reflex	Infant horizontal supported by abdomen
Stepping reflex	Infant vertical, feet lightly touching flat surface
Sphincter reflex	Full bladder or full colon

a sudden loud noise or sudden loss of support it shows a startle reaction by throwing out its arms and feet symmetrically and by pulling them back toward the center of the body. This reflex, labeled the *Moro reflex,* ordinarily disappears about three months after birth and is often used as a reflex marker to test the neurological development of newborns. In cases where there is impairment of the motor centers of the brain the Moro reflex is weak or absent. Another reflex used to determine neurological damage is the *grasp reflex.* When a baby's palm is touched with an object the baby will grip it firmly. Newborns have been known to sustain their own weight while being picked up out of bed by an adult who places his index finger in the palm of the infant's hand. This reflex subsides gradually and disappears around the twelfth month whereafter it can be executed as voluntary action.

When a neonate's foot is stroked its toes will fan outward in what is called the *Babinski reflex.* It begins to disappear six months after birth when certain neurons, mainly in the pyramidal tracts, have become myelinated—covered with cells that act as insulators of the neurons facilitating neural conduction. After the sixth month the same stimulus, stroking the sole of the foot, will cause the toes to curl downward. This opposite reaction to the same stimulus is called the *plantar reflex* and stays with us throughout our adult lives.

The swimming reflex is a perplexing one to observe. It occurs in infants under six months of age and provides them with the ability to swim without training. The infant swims head down, and does not breathe except to exhale slowly through the mouth. This mobility, which lasts for some minutes, and the ability to keep water out of the lungs make the rescue of children younger than one year more possible. One of the authors remembers her six-month-old son lunging off the steps of the pool and proceeding to swim. Needless to say, the mother was much more frightened than the young swimmer, who incidentally made swimming one of his favorite sports.

An extensive study investigating swimming movements as a function of age was conducted by McGraw (1943) who trained raters to identify three types of actions: reflex swimming movements, disorganized or struggling activity, and deliberate or voluntary swimming movements. The raters observed 42 infants from 11 days to two and one-half years of age, making a total of 445 observations. McGraw found that reflexive swimming was at its peak at birth and then fell off rather steeply, disappearing after about 250 days. At about 100 days after birth a disorganized, struggling activity began to appear, reaching a peak at 175 days, whereafter it declined for the remainder of the study. About 200 days after birth deliberate or voluntary movements began to appear, reaching a peak at 300 days after birth and remaining constant throughout the study. Thus, if parents want to make use of the natural swimming reflex it should be done before the child is one year old, as the evidence seems to indicate that children can make a smooth transition from reflexive to voluntary swimming at that time.

Toilet training is of much concern to many parents. Initially urination and defecation are controlled by *sphincter reflexes* over which the infant has no control. The signal of a full bladder or a full colon is sufficient to set off the reflex which releases the sphincter muscles. Voluntary control of sphincter muscles must occur in a roundabout way that involves additional muscles (see "Toilet Training"). Just how early these additional muscles can be trained to function is a question of maturation. McGraw (1940) investigated this maturational process by starting one twin in an early toilet training program soon after birth. She waited to start the other twin until the first one showed evidence of 90 percent success in bladder control, which occurred about at age two. At this point the second twin's training was started, and the twin reached the 90 percent success level within a few days. Her data show that sufficient maturation must take place before toilet training can be successful, supporting the recommendation that it should be started when the child is about two if the greatest advantage is to be taken of the neurological development.

MATURATION IN EARLY CHILDHOOD

In the history of child study, Arnold Gesell (1880–1961) has been the most articulate spokesman for maturation as the central concept of developmental psychology. Through observations by eye and camera Gesell et al. (1940) studied the maturational changes in children from 16 weeks to 10 years of age, discovering a number of developmental principles. One of these principles is the *spiral effect* of development, which relates to the observation that growth does not proceed at a uniform rate and that there are apparent regressions. For instance, even those children who eventually established a clear-cut right-handedness changed their preferences several times during the first years of life. Around one and one-half years they tend to be markedly bilateral; at two a dominant preference appears; from two and one-half to three and one-half bilaterality is again exhibited; and by four, the dominant hand is usually determined, although at seven a transient period of bilaterality may reappear.

Gesell also described the principle of *cephalocaudal* (cephalo = head, caudal = tail) direction, which refers to the fact that head movements come under the infant's control long before the movements of legs, feet, and toes. There is also the *proximo-*

distal (close-far) direction, which describes the fact that the more central parts of the body, e.g., torso and arms, come sooner under coordinated control than the distal parts, e.g., the hands or fingers. Gesell also described the principle of *self-regulating fluctuation,* which refers to the relapses that occur as a child progresses to more and more complex behaviors. For example, as children begin to become preoccupied with speech, a sharp regression in their motor development occurs frequently. Another one of Gesell's principles, that of *functional asymmetry,* refers to the bilateral nature of the infants. For example, when they try to reach for an object, even for a very small one, they reach for it with both hands. With increasing maturation this bilateral response changes into a unilateral reaching. A final principle is that of *individuating maturation,* which Gesell uses to explain individual differences, attributing developmental differences to inherited maturational programming. In summary, Gesell (1954) believed that maturation is a progressive organization of behavior forms. Maturation is the name for the regulating mechanisms of the growth process which are so intricate and sensitive that nature needed to preserve and stabilize them by internal regulating processes. Gesell was so impressed by the predictability of the maturational process that he gave little credence to learning as an important factor in behavioral change. It should be emphasized that Gesell's principles are descriptive terms; they tell us how maturation proceeds but not why.

When will a child learn to walk, to talk, or to ride a bicycle? Not until the cortical development required for the task is completed. The fine coordination necessary for walking, for talking, or for riding a bicycle is quite impossible before the motor cortex and cerebellum have matured sufficiently. We can make this statement because we know, in general, that the cortex controls finer movements and the cerebellum coordinates movements, especially those necessary to keep a balance. However, we do not know where in the cerebellum this balancing is controlled, whether there is a certain place for balancing walking and another for balancing on a bicycle, nor do we know what happens in the cerebellum when balancing can be accomplished. In spite of these neurological unknowns we have many pyschological experiments that show that a mere growing of the neural tissues (mostly myelinization) is a prerequisite for learning certain tasks. An excellent example of this was shown by Dennis and Dennis (1940), who investigated the walking behavior in Hopi children. These children spent much of their first two years on a cradle board and had almost no practice in standing, creeping, or crawling. Yet they walked at a normal age. Following the principle of maturation that Carmichael demonstrated with salamanders, early training or practice is also of negligible importance for humans with respect to walking.

While maturational changes influence much of a child's behavioral repertoire during the first year of life, environmental influences become more important during subsequent years. This has been shown by Dennis (1960), who compared the motor development of children living in different orphanages in Tehran. One of these orphanages was in a very impoverished condition. The infants there spent almost all their time lying in their cribs on their backs. They were seldom placed in a prone or face-down position. They were fed by means of a bottle propped up on a small pillow while they were lying in their cribs. Later, when solid foods were introduced, they were either held for short periods by one of the attendants while being fed or they were fed sitting up in their cribs. They were only occasionally taken out of their cribs, when bathed or when put on a linoleum or stone floor in a room devoid of toys or children's furniture. There was one staff person to eight or more children. The other orphanage was established mainly to demonstrate improved methods of child care. The ration of attendants to children was one to three and the children were held during all feeding and frequently at other times. In their cribs the children were often placed into prone position, and toys and ample opportunity for play were provided.

   Dennis examined various motor activities after the children had been in both orphanages from early infancy until they were between the ages of 2 and 3. As the following table shows, almost all the children in the improved orphanage could sit, creep or scoot, stand, and walk alone. At the impoverished institution not even half of the children could either stand or walk with holding. Hardly any could walk alone, but many of the children were capable of some other means of locomotion, mostly by scooting, propelling themselves with their arms and legs while in a sitting position. (See table on page 46.)

   Given Dennis' data, it appears that it is necessary for infants to lie prone as well as supine if they are to learn to creep. The children in the impoverished orphanage did not remain handicapped for life. Testing them a year later, during their fourth year at the orphanage, Dennis found that 90% of them could stand holding on, 63% could walk while holding, and 15% could walk alone. The more general conclusion supported by the Dennis' experiment is that locomotor skills involved in sitting, standing, and walking are not solely the result of genetically predetermined maturational processes, but may be severly retarded by experiential factors; it is reasonable to suppose that they can be accelerated by experiential factors as well.

HORMONES AND GLANDS

   The endocrine system consists of various glands which have no ducts and secrete directly into the bloodstream. Throughout life they regulate growth, metabolism, reproduction, and many other vital functions. They are of special interest to our understanding of maturation because they regulate our growth rate and influence our sexual development. Since the secretions of our endocrine glands, the hormones, go directly into the bloodstream they influence other glands and neural tissues that are chemically susceptible to them. The *pituitary*, a small structure attached to the hypothalamus at the base of

Activities at age 2–3	Impoverished orphanage	Improved orphanage
Sit alone	95%	100%
Creep or scoot	75%	100%
Stand holding	45%	100%
Walk holding	40%	100%
Walk alone	8%	94%

the brain, has been called the "master" gland because its secretions stimulate other glands, the target glands, namely the adrenal cortex, the thyroid, the pancreas, and the sex glands, the ovaries and testes. Thus an adrenocorticotropic hormone, abbreviated ACTH, which is produced by the pituitary, stimulates the *adrenal cortex*, the outer shell of a gland located at the upper end of the kidney. This stimulation produces cortisone, androgens, and estrogens which promote male and female sexuality, respectively. Another trophic hormone produced by the pituitary stimulates the *thyroid* gland, located at the neck's front, to produce its own hormone, thyroxin, which in turn regulates our metabolism. Pituitary secretions also influence the pancreas gland and promote the conversion of fats and proteins into carbohydrates. The pituitary also produces gonadotrophin, particularly during the time of adolescence. This promotes the secondary sex characteristics (development of breasts, Adam's apple, pubic hair, etc.) and stimulates the ovaries to produce eggs and the testes to produce sperm.

Aside from the trophic (feeding) hormones indicated above, the pituitary secretes a growth hormone that regulates bone and muscle growth. Deficiencies of this hormone produce dwarfism; excesses produce gigantism. In certain cases these conditions can be medically corrected or ameliorated with additional hormone injections or neutralizing agents. In certain instances hormonal dysfunctions can be somewhat more easily corrected than neurological ones since a hormone can be injected anywhere into the bloodstream, while neurological dysfunctions often occur in specific pathways and brain centers which cannot be reached without damaging closely interwoven functioning tissues. Even though some of the hormones can be chemically analyzed and their functions can be observed, it is generally not known why the pituitary secretes its own growth hormone or its various trophic hormones when it does. Because the pituitary has neural connections with the base of the brain, it is not surprising that its hormone production can be influenced by thought processes in the brain, correlates of neural activity.

The independence as well as the interdependence of the endocrine-neural system has been demonstrated in various experiments with animals and humans. Dogs from which the testes have been removed after puberty have continued copulation almost as frequently as before the operation. Nach (1978) who has reviewed endocrine-neural relations with respect to sexual functions cites human cases where an apparently normal sex life was continued for thirty years after castration. He also refers to *The Arabian Nights* (not to the nursery version), which mentions that some eunuchs were accomplished performers and that some women preferred intercourse with them because the act was enjoyably prolonged since there were no ejaculations and periods of quiescence. Nash mentions other data which indicate that the secretions from the adrenal cortex are almost as important for the sexual functions as the ovaries and the testes. Thus, sexuality in the human seems to be influenced, perhaps somewhat redundantly, by secretions of the gonads (ovaries and testes), the adrenal cortex, and the pituitary, which in turn is stimulated by thought processes and other bodily activities.

Other glands that regulate and relate to sexual activities are the thymus gland, which atrophies after adolescence, and the adrenal medulla, the inner core of the gland at the upper end of the kidney. In contrast to the adrenal cortex (the outer shell of this gland), the adrenal medulla is directly controlled by the nervous system, which stimulates it to secrete epinephrine and norepinephrine (also called adrenalin or noradrenalin), substances related to emotion and aggression. These substances reinforce the sympathetic nervous system to prepare and to act during emergency situations through an increased heart rate and an increased blood clotting capacity and through increasing sugar output and muscular strength. Aggression is frequently a component of sexuality and other character traits related to dominance and submission. Since the prominence of the glands and their secretions are a matter of maturation it is likely that some of our character traits are influenced by this genetic determinism, a subject which will be discussed again (see "The Intellect"). It should be emphasized that glands and hormones influence basic urges and desires but not the direction or the mode in which these desires will be satisfied. As mentioned again later (see "Sex Roles"), testosterone given to homosexuals does increase the frequency of their intercourse, but does not change the objects of their intercourse, but does not change the objects of their affection.

MATURATION IN LATER CHILDHOOD

Whatever the mechanism of maturation, are there individual as well as sex differences with regard to the rate and the ultimate level to which we mature? There are many statistics available describing the average height and weight and the onset of puberty for boys and girls at various ages. From the psychological point of view we are interested how early and late maturation affects socialization and character development. We must discuss the sexes separately because their growth rates are quite different. From ages six to nine girls are slightly taller than boys. Thereafter the sexes remain about equal in height, until around thirteen when the boys begin their adolescent growth spurt. Sexual development, not necessarily linked to mere height, begins also in the early teens with a wide range of onset and completion spans. It is quite normal for boys to begin their pubertal development any time from 11 to 16 and girls

from 10 to 14 years. While these spans are normal in the physiological sense they may not be without consequences as far as an
individual's socialization is concerned. First, because our society puts some premium on good looks linked with tallness and
second, because our school systems primarily use age rather
than physical and mental maturation as a base for instructional
grouping. Moreover, we have coeducation so that, for instance,
14-year-old boys generally just beginning their pubertal stage
are in the same class with girls who on the average will have
finished their pubertal development. In this situation a fast
maturing boy, one who is already mature at 14, will be in an
entirely different social milieu than a slow maturing one.

For *early maturing* boys almost all of the consequences of
early physical maturation appear to be favorable during the
time of adolescence and for about 15 years thereafter. Early
acceptance into athletic programs and recognition by girls of
their own age seem to give the early maturing boy a "start" that
is often maintained throughout life. Kinsey et al., for instance,
mention that early maturers report consistenly higher levels of
sexual activities from adolescence on until their fifties, although
this difference between early and late maturers tends to decrease with age. In contrast, *late maturing* boys are rated by
adults as lower in physical attractiveness, less masculine, more
animated, and more attention seeking. However, as Jones and
Bayley (1950) report, late maturing boys, in comparision to
early maturers, do not differ in their ratings of popularity,
leadership, prestige, cheerfulness, or social effect on the peer
group. These evaluations seem somewhat incongruent, but apparently there seems to be a fine line between the social behavior
of the early and late maturers. Both interact socially, the early
maturer in a matter-of-fact style, the late maturer through seeking attention more actively.

Late maturers have equal and sometimes superior phy-
siques in their late adolescence, but they also have a greater
number of delinquents among them. Glueck and Glueck (1950)
concluded that late maturation and its accompanying antisocial

feelings contribute to and encourage delinquency. Jones & Bailey suggest that late maturing boys are more prone to delinquency because they try to overcome the immaturity with which they are treated by adults: unfortunately, this compensation occurs often in socially undesirable ways.

For girls the effects of early and late maturation are still unclear. In general, longitudinal studies have shown that girls are more resilient toward their social and physical environment than are boys. Bayley (1968) found that girls were much less influenced than boys by the maternal behavior (warm or cold) they received in infancy and Stein et al. (1975) found that a severe starvation period in Holland during the winter of 1944–1945 affected girls less than boys. Hence, it is not surprising that the social stigmata and preferences towards late and early maturing children affects girls less than boys. There may be some temporary advantages for the early maturing girl—being able to attract boys earlier and being more desired socially. But the late maturing girls soon catch up, and that perhaps may be another reason why long-lasting positive correlates have not been found for early maturing girls.

Tanner (1968) estimates that in the past one hundred years the age of puberty has decreased by as much as 3 years, and in some regions by as much as 5 years, and that, concurrently, growth now ceases earlier than it did. Earlier maturation and tallness have advanced together, but in the United States they have leveled off during the last decade or so. Nash (1978) believes that an optimal environmental level as far as physical growth is concerned has or may soon be approached in the United States and that an improvement beyond this point will have no further effect on growth. Once the environment exists at an optimal level, variation in growth will depend solely on the hereditary factor—on maturation. Such a "threshold" effect may also hold true for our intellectual development (see "The Intellect"), as our present society may be close to an atmosphere of maximum mental stimulation. There is an interesting relationship between physical growth and IQ, with the early maturing individuals scoring somewhat higher on standardized IQ tests and in scholastic performance. This advantage cannot be attributed to mere growth or diet since early and late maturing persons reach the same height around the twentieth year, but the intellectual advantage remains for those who matured early (Bee, 1978).

The maturational data discussed above are general trends revealed by research and it should be emphasized that there are always glaring exceptions to these general findings. As mentioned before, we recognize the existence of certain maturational variables, but we do not know their underlying causes, and are therefore at a loss to explain why one individual matures early and another one late. Nevertheless, it is useful to know the extent to which maturation exists because it forms a basis for much of our learning.

Chapter 3

LEARNING

Learning is central to human development. Maturation accounts for our physiological urges and capacities to act and to think, but how our actions and thoughts are carried out is determined by what we have learned. Even such a basic bodily function as eating is influenced by what we have learned to eat and how we have learned to eat it. We begin our learning at birth, or perhaps before, with simple reactions and continue it with increasing complexity throughout most of our lives. What exactly happens in our brain when we learn, store information, forget, or remember has so far eluded all physiological research. The brain contains billions of microscopic nerve cells and the average one interconnects with as many as 100 other nerve cells. Psychologists have circumvented these neuroanatomical complexities by using the "functional" approach, which means they try to investigate the circumstances under which learning takes place. In the study of development they examine an individual's growth and maturation in relation to learning as well as to the factors of awareness, intention, and motivation. They are trying to find out what is best learned alone, what needs to be taught, and what the various methods of teaching are. The present chapter addresses itself to these questions.

NONAWARENESS

We have a tendency to minimize the importance of learning since much of it took place during our own childhood in processes of which we were never aware or which we have since forgotten. We can demonstrate this to ourselves by performing two simple handfolding tasks the following way:

> Please fold your hands. Note which thumb is on top. Unfold your hands. Fold them again, but this time with the other thumb on top and with all other fingers changing places corresponding-ly. Press down firmly with all fingers in this "new" position and note how it feels.

The new position feels strange to most people because rarely, if ever, did we fold our hands this "other" way. We do not know how long we have been folding our hands "our" way, nor do we know if we acquired our way suddenly or gradually or whether we copied a parent or did it coincidentally.

The way we fold our hands is rather unimportant. Do we know more about the origin of events more important to us? How do Americans learn to like coffee, steak, and ice-cold drinks; and how do Britons learn to prefer tea, kippered her-ring, and a tepid drink? Why does one family member learn how to smoke and another one learn how "not to" smoke? Perhaps we are unable to answer these questions because we are unable to point to any single causal event. We acquire many of our desires and skills in prolonged and gradual processes. The stimulation at each instance may have been so minimal that it escaped our attention. A favorable word about a teacher heard at the age of four, a friendly teacher's deed experienced at six, an unexpected "A" perhaps could exemplify hundreds of such stimulations, all appearing unimportant at the time, all forgotten by the adult, but all having contributed to an individual's desire to become a teacher.

As adults we are not aware of these learning details and we fancy that we have logically reasoned out our professional choice. If students are asked why they are taking this course in human development they will first answer that they have to take this class because it is required for certification. When asked further why certification is wanted, the answer is usually "Because I want to be a teacher." If asked again "Why do you want to be a teacher?" then "Because I want to make a living" is the usual answer. Such an answer, however, explains very little, because the vast majority of the population also makes a living, and often a much better one at that, in hundreds of other vocations all outside the teaching profession. In other words, "Because I want to make a living" does not tell us why the teaching profession was chosen above the medical, carpentry, or plumbing professions.

> While each step in the above question and answer game appears logical, the final answer has probably no connection to the actual, gradual conditioning or learning process by which the desire to become a teacher was formed. The answers are probably all "pat" phrases that we (nonteachers included) have learned in order to satisfy people who ask us too many questions. Everybody has found out that answering "I don't know" is considered stupid, impolite, and does not land us jobs if put on application forms. For years we have been rewarded for such answers as "I love children," "I feel it is my calling," or "I would like to make a living."

We are taught to give pat answers and are rewarded for it. If we do it long enough we begin to believe our own words and everything they stand for.

Being unaware of our own learning processes is not only related to our childhood. There are several experiments with adults as subjects which investigate "incidental" and "intentional" learning. In an intentional learning task, for example, the subjects are asked to memorize a list of words and are offered a prize. For the incidental task the subjects are asked to cross out all e's as fast as they can and are likewise offered a reward. As expected, the subjects who intend to learn the words will memorize a good portion of the list, but the subjects who were busy crossing out all the e's and had no intention of learning the words also remember some of them, though not as many. We apparently have only a limited control about that which we learn and about that which we remember as we repeatedly find out during final-exams weeks.

SOME DEFINITIONS

The psychologist talks about learning and means thereby any modification of behavior that does not come about merely through the body's growth, or through drug or fatigue. Learning to the psychologist is something that is acquired by practice. This practice, however, can vary from the lengthiest and most tedious to the shortest, one-trial imitation. It is also important to realize that both wanted and unwanted behavior are learned. We call the learning of wanted behavior "education." It implies the formal learning of socially accepted things, a goal, and a subject matter. Teachers are hired to teach us the three Rs, but who teaches us to punch other kids around or to roll spitballs? We tend to believe that bad things are not learned, that they are just "picked up." We fail to realize that the rolling and throwing of spitballs may also be learned in many practice sessions.

There are many more popular words that suggest various types of learning. One may suspect, for instance, that brainwashing or indoctrination is much different from learning or education. This is not so. In discussing the mechanics of indoctrination and thought control, Sargant (1961) shows that brainwashing is closely related to educating. Brainwashing seems to be a more condensed form of learning, different in quantity, not in quality. The terms "brainwashing" and "indoctrination" generally imply that the subject matter is bad, that the teacher supplies most of the effort, and that the student is unwilling and innocent. Such distinctions, however, are difficult because teachers and parents must often muster much effort to teach "nice" things to "unwilling" pupils.

As different as all these terms may seem, we have no evidence that there is anything different going on in a person's brain when he or she is "briefed" rather than "brainwashed." Words in their connotative (emotional) meaning can be misleading. They may convince us, for instance, that our soldiers, who are "briefed" by our "intelligence" corps, are better and smarter than the enemy soldiers who are "brainwashed" by "espionage" agents. There are plenty of words around in the social sciences. They can enlighten us, but they can also deceive us if we do not search for their more concrete and operational meanings.

THE FIRST EXPERIMENT

For those students who are allergic to Pavlov's dog, we can start our learning story with the German eye specialist, Raehlmann, who experimented with babies (Wesley, 1968). In 1890, in Raehlmann's time, psychologists believed that children were not able to perceive colors until they are about four years old. They believed this because they observed that children under four made frequent mistakes when naming colors. When shown green, they would often say blue or red. Raehlmann thought it may be possible that children see and consistently recognize color differences much earlier in their lives, perhaps before they have learned to talk. To test his idea, Raehlmann took opaque milk bottles and painted some of them red and some green. At feeding time he approached infants with a red bottle in one hand and a green one in the other. The red bottle was always filled with milk, the green one always empty. During the first trials the infants chose the filled red bottle about as often as the empty green bottle. Gradually they learned to move their heads and hands only toward the red bottle. Almost all infants learned to do this with 100% correctness by the time they were six months old. Some learned when only three months old.

Raehlmann was a very careful experimenter. He equalized the red and green colors for brightness. He also changed the red and green bottles' position in his hands. Thus he was reasonably sure the infants discriminated by color only. Raehlmann also tested another group of infants for whom the conditions were reversed, with the green bottle filled with milk and the red bottle empty. These infants learned to turn and make movements toward the green bottle only. Thus Raehlmann showed clearly that infants can learn to discriminate colors. That they can see colors was of great interest to the eye specialists. That they can learn so readily, simply, and reliably while only several months old should have been of interest to psychologists, educators, and parents (Raehlmann, 1890, 1903).

Raehlmann, however, was a busy eye surgeon and did not pursue his learning experiments. He reported his work in a journal for eye specialists where it escaped the attention of psychologists. Investigations of infant and child learning lay dormant for several decades until the American psychologist, J. B. Watson (1878–1958), and his followers began experimental work at Johns Hopkins University in the 1920s. Watson (1919, 1924) tested many rules of learning that Pavlov had discovered while working with animals. Watson found that many of these rules also hold true for human learning.

SIMPLE LEARNING

Newborn infants cry; suck; move their heads, arms, and legs; close their eyes; sleep; open their eyes; and so on. We say they do all this by nature, by instinct, or by reflex. Again we have fancy names but little knowledge as to the exact cause of those actions. Babies cry when hungry. They also cry sometimes when not hungry. Perhaps there is pain, or some other physical cause that comes from inside the body. Some parents let their babies cry, believing that this strengthens the lungs and is healthful. Their neighbors may have an entirely different opinion!

Whatever the cause, the parent is interested in directing certain of these self-occurring or natural behaviors. For instance, we want sucking at bottle, but not too much at thumb. We want a child to move when we say "Come here," but not to move when we say "Stop." We want the child's eyes to close when we say "good night," when we think our day is done. In other words, we want actions (also called *reflexes* when specific and *responses* when more general) that happen naturally to occur when we give the cues (signals, commands, suggestions, or stimuli). How can psychologists help us to solve some of these problems?

As early as 1928 Aldrich conducted such a simple cue-substituting experiment with a three-month-old girl. This infant failed to respond to stimuli of sudden noises and was believed to be deaf. Aldrich had some doubts and wanted to find out whether the girl was able to sense the noise but unable to respond to it in the usual way by head turning or crying. He therefore introduced another stimulus, scratching the sole of her foot, to which the girl would readily respond by leg withdrawal and crying. He now accompanied this sole-scratching stimulus by ringing a dinner bell. After about 15 such pairings the infant began to draw up her leg and cry when the bell was rung and the foot was not touched. For some reason this infant was not able to indicate hearing through the usual head turning, but she was able to indicate hearing by leg withdrawal after a conditioning sequence in which the foot-scratching stimulus was replaced by the sound of a dinner bell. In more technical language, the infant learned to substitute an auditory stimulus for a tactual one.

In 1931 Dorothy Marquis conducted extensive experiments at Ohio State University and showed again that infants learn fast to substitute cues. She fed eight infants six times daily by bottle from the first day to the tenth day after birth. A buzzer was rung each time before the bottle was inserted in the infant's mouth and again for 5 seconds after the infant started to suck. Seven of her eight infants learned within 3 to 6 days to expect the bottle on the buzzer signal. They showed this by starting sucking motions and by opening their mouths as soon as they heard the buzzer. The bottle did not have to be present. They also reduced their general activity and their crying as soon as they heard the buzzer.

In both of the above experiments a sound could bring about the same response that a touch had before. A sound could make the infant withdraw its leg. A sound could make the infant move its lips. In Aldrich's experiment infants would start crying when they heard a sound, in Marquis' experiment they would stop crying. Is this surprising? Not at all. The sound in one experiment was the signal or cue for being stroked on the foot; in the other experiment it was the signal for food.

The vast behavior possibilities that simple learning (cue substitution or conditioning) offers us should now be readily apparent. We may add to this the fact that a child receives many commands or suggestions by hearing. By nature, for instance, children would withdraw their hands as soon as they *touch* something hot. However, we want to safeguard them and need to teach them to withdraw to a *sound,* to such words as "stop" or "no." Thus in childrearing we depend very much on cue substitution as shown in the above studies.

At the first International Congress in Child Psychiatry held in Paris in 1937, there already existed 1,500 conditioning studies relating to infants and children. This number has increased by the thousands. There is absolutely no more doubt that humans of all ages can be conditioned to learn new cues and/or new responses. Now the reader may ask if conditioning can be obtained so readily in the laboratory, why do we have so much trouble in life situations in which Johnny is just as likely to touch something whether we say "yes" or "no." The whole story has not been told. Even in the laboratory we must take care of certain very important details that can make or break simple learning. Let us look at some of these details.

THE IMPORTANT MOMENT

Pavlov (1849–1936) spent a lifetime working out the finer details involved in the conditioning process. He found that a new stimulus is learned fastest if it is presented one-half second before the old stimulus. If you want to train a dog to come for its dinner when you ring a bell, you will train the dog in the fewest number of training trials (in perhaps five to ten trials) if you ring the bell just one-half second before the dog can see or smell the food. You will also get results, though not so quickly, if you increase this interval to 30 seconds, 1 minute, and so on, or if you narrow it and ring the bell at the same time you present the food. This type of conditioning is called *Pavlovian* or *classical conditioning.* Strangely enough, you will not be able to train your dog if you ring the bell after the dog starts to eat. Krestoff-nikoff (1913), one of Pavlov's students, could not condition a dog to salivate to a bell within 374 trials when he presented the sound after the dog had gotten the food and had salivated, a methodology called *backward conditioning.*

Though humans vary much more in their responses than animals, many conditioning experiments as summarized by Hilgard and Atkinson (1967) have shown that the half-second interval is also the best time span for conditioning children as well as adults. We need not go to the laboratory to realize that timing is of utmost importance. We can look at events occurring in the average household. There are no buzzers in our homes by which we make sounds for babies, but in many homes the sound of the mother's footsteps is likely to precede each feeding. If this is so, the infant will learn to take the sound of the mother's footsteps as the cue for the bottle. Suppose that the mother warms the bottle regularly by placing it into running, hot water before bringing it to the infant. In this case the sound of the running water will replace the sound cue of the footsteps. Later on, the running water cue may be replaced by the sound of the refrigerator door. As soon as it is opened or closed the infant will become quiet and will start some sucking motion.

We have now seen how infants anticipate events. As time goes on they learn to anticipate their own anticipations. Much of our adult behavior depends also on anticipation. Bernard Baruch became one of America's richest men because his stock market cues were the earliest. For poor men, empty box cars were the cues for selling certain railroad stock. For richer ones, the harvest report. For Baruch it was the spring weather conditions. Like infants, millionaires depends on cues, although on more subtle ones, of course.

From laboratory and daily observations we can state that learning is fastest when the new cue comes one-half second before the old one. The practical importance of this rule in the upbringing of children will be shown in the following example.

Some fine morning a child may start crying when the father or mother leaves for work. Whatever the cause, we are likely to observe that on the following days crying will start a little sooner, perhaps when the parent puts on a hat. A week or so later, the child may already begin to cry when the parent puts on his coat or leaves the breakfast table. The child starts crying a little earlier each day. If the mother or the baby sitter is anxious to divert the child from crying, it would be best to be one or two jumps ahead of the child's conditioning or anticipation process. Suppose that in our leaving scene the child is at the stage of "crying-when-hat-is-put-on." If the baby sitter wants to prevent crying, the intervention should start when parent gets up from the breakfast table. At this point of the game the child will still be calm, and the chances are still great that a toy, some candy, a hug, or some playing will be accepted. This in turn will enhance the chances that the child will pay less attention to the parent's departure. Even if the child sees the parent depart while being hugged or played with, he or she is likely not to cry as hard, if at all.

All this sounds, of course, very logical. One only needs to be a moment or so ahead of the child. Parents who do not realize this will work against themselves. They will pay all the attention to the one leaving and none to the child until it begins to cry. Then they will try to calm the child. But a crying child is not so easily diverted from crying. Some mothers will shout or spank their children at such moments and will tell them not to cry. This, of course, will make the child cry longer and harder. Some parents will try it in the friendly way. They may offer some candy or consoling words. But who feels like eating candy while crying? The crying child is likely not to care for candy and may even throw it down. Now even the friendly mother will be annoyed and is likely to start shouting, and the child will keep on crying. Reward and punishment and their effect will be discussed in the next chapter. From the above, however, we can already guess that it is not so important what we give as reward or punishment, but that we give it at the right moment.

How Learning Spreads

We can best see how learning spreads by looking at an experiment performed by John B. Watson and Rosalie Rayner (1920). These experimenters tried to condition Albert, a nine-month-old infant, to fear a white rat. Albert was the son of a wet nurse living at Johns Hopkins Hospital and the experimenters were reasonably sure that Albert had no previous experiences with rats. Like most other infants of his age, Albert was not afraid of a rat when it was first shown to him; to the contrary, he made noises expressing pleasure and he reached for the rat. The experimenters had also found out that loud and sudden noises make most infants, including Albert, cry. Now there were two cues—the rat that made Albert smile and the loud noise that made Albert cry. Watson and Rayner wanted to see if the cue value for the rat could be changed from smiling to crying. Thus, while Albert was playing with or reaching for the rat at different occasions, a loud noise was made that made Albert withdraw from the rat and cry. Note that the rat was there *before* the noise. This assures that the new stimulus, the rat (new for the crying response), was there one-half second before the old stimulus, or the old cue, the noise. (The noise here is called the old or *unconditioned stimulus* because it already produced crying before conditioning was started.) After about seven pairings of rat and noise, the presentation of the rat alone would make Albert cry and make him move away from the rat. The child was now conditioned to make the response to the rat that he originally made to the noise. The rat with respect to crying is called the *conditioned stimulus* because only after conditioning did it make Albert cry.

Watson and Rayner went further with their experimentation. They wanted to see whether the crying cue had spread to other objects, objects similar to a rat. They showed Albert separately a rabbit, a white piece of fur, and a Sanata Claus mask with beard. Albert cried and withdrew from each one of these objects. This additional testing showed clearly that cues can transfer to similar cues with which the child had no previous experience. Pavlov had called this spreading of the cue *stimulus generalization*.

Many other experiments have been conducted since Watson and Rayner's experiment and we can safely say that "generalization" does occur in humans of all ages. To give another example we should mention the study of Diven (1937) who investigated the development of fears and phobias in adults. For this purpose he administered shocks right after pronouncing the word "barn." Thereafter the word "barn" produced certain electric currents measurable on the skin's surface. (These currents are called "galvanic skin responses." They compose part of the lie detector test and are indicative of fear and anxiety states. They also occur during excitement caused by pleasurable events; a circumstance that may make the lie detector "lie.") Diven found that other words that had never been paired with shock such as "hay" or "pasture" produced similar electric currents. Though his subjects may have never been hurt in a pasture or by its word, the shock cues of the word "barn" had spread to "pasture." This is, of course, quite similar to Albert's fear of the white fur, the rabbit, and the Santa Claus mask in spite of the fact that he had never been hurt by them.

Though we can be fairly sure that learning generalizes by spreading to other cues, we cannot always predict what these other cues will be. In Albert's situation, for instance, the fearfulness transferred to whiteness and/or furriness. It is quite possible that another child with poorer vision being tested in a less well-illuminated room might have generalized on furriness or liveliness rather than on whiteness, on the touch sensations rather than on the visual impressions. In such a case a rabbit of any color may evoke crying, while a lifeless piece of white fur may not.

Now the parent may ask what good it does to know about generalization if one cannot tell what other cues will or have become involved. In that respect childrearing is still an art. But it may help the parent to realize that there are causes for a child's behavior which come via generalization. Let us show this through an example. A father wanted to surprise his child with an Easter rabbit. The child cried upon seeing the rabbit, though he or she had never seen a rabbit before. A father who is not aware of generalization may label the child's behavior as negativistic or stubborn. The father who is aware of the consequences of generalization will take the matter less personally. He may search and wonder if the child has ever been bitten by a rat or had large amounts of cotton applied to a wound. Even if this father will not find a reason (and very often we do not find the reasons), he will be less likely to blame the child, the neighbors, the devils, or what not.

In many respects generalization helps us in our socialization process. A child who has been scratched by one cat is likely to stay away from other cats. The burnt child fears the fire, all sorts of fires. Fearful cues, however, are not the only cues that generalize. Mary Cover Jones, one of Watson's students, tried to make a small child lose his fear of a rabbit. After showing the rabbit repeatedly at feeding times the child's fear disappeared. Once the fear of the rabbit had disappeared, the fear of similar objects or animals had also disappeared.

There are other useful aspects of generalization. Much of human thinking and speech is based on the formation of categories, general classes, or concepts. When a poodle comes along, we tell the child it is a dog. To a fox terrier we say "dog," also to a German shepherd. We need not show the child every kind of dog. We expect that cues will spread to other types of dogs not previously seen by the child. But what has happened when at the next county fair the child sees a pony and calls it "dog"? Then generalization has spread too far, further than we adults, or the zoologists, wanted. And here we have come to the negative side of generalization. Unknowingly, this negative side is often supported by the parent. Over a period of time we may say, for instance, "Don't touch daddy's book." "No, no, these earrings belong to mother!" "This is your doll; hold on to it." With all that we may have established a generalized concept of "nonsharing." Should we wonder then when our child refuses to give up a toy to a visiting playmate?

Some generalizations stay with us for the rest of our lives. They form the bases for our stereotypes and prejudices when they elicit feelings and actions in us that are detrimental to others. We generalize when one member of a certain class, profession, or race treats us badly and we then believe that all members will treat us badly. Unfortunately we need not even experience a single bad treatment in order to become prejudicial, since words are such strong conditioners we can often form strong prejudice by merely being told that the "other" people are bad. Once this belief has become established we are likely to stay away from the object of our prejudice and unlikely to learn to discriminate who among them is good or bad. Generalization has its advantages and disadvantages. We can support the advantages and counteract the disadvantages through discrimination training.

DISCRIMINATION

While generalization is a natural by-product of learning, discrimination often requires the help of others and more prolonged experiences. It is one of the most important aspects of our socialization because it teaches us the rights and wrongs dictated by our culture. For example, for one group of infants in Raehlmann's color-testing experiment the red milk bottle became the "right" one. It was always filled with milk. The green bottle was wrong; it was always empty. Raehlmann's infants learned fast to discriminate and made no mistakes after they had learned. They learned so well because there was a 100% regularity in associating red with milk and green with no milk. Each time they chose red they were immediately rewarded with milk. Whenever they chose green, nothing happened. Pavlov called this type of learning *discrimination learning*. We may think of it as two simple learning experiments going on alternately. One simple learning process is that red means to reach for; and another one teaches that green means not to reach for.

Now the reader may think that Raehlmann's experiment was rather artificial and that his selection red to indicate "right" and of green to indicate "wrong" was rather arbitrary. Indeed it was, but many of the hundreds of differentiations that we must make daily are just as arbitrary. For red we stop; for green we go. It could have been the other way around. (Red, by the way, is not the most noticeable color. Yellow is seen as brighter in twilight and at longer distances.) In England one must drive on the left side of the street in order to give survival a chance. In France one must first insert the coin and then lift

up the receiver in order to make a telephone call. Social ameni-
ties are just as arbitrary. When you sneeze in America you say
"Excuse me." When you sneeze in Germany the other person
says "Gesundheit," and if you say anything you say "Thank
you!" Also, in Germany mothers permit their children to urinate in the street; in America they do not. From the global point
of view quite a few things are arbitrary, but unless we travel to
other countries we are rarely reminded of this fact. Even if we
do travel we often fail to realize arbitrariness because our socialization has become so natural to us that we think the others are
wrong or at least unaesthetical if they, for instance, drink warm
beer and urinate at the roadside.

The difficulty with discrimination learning, however, does
not lie in the arbitrariness of our "right" and "wrong," but
rather in the irregularity with which cues associate with right
and wrong. Let us take an example, a dog story. A child was
bitten by a dog and is now afraid of all dogs. The child would
now be quite safe from all dogs, but somehow we parents hesi-
tate to leave well enough alone. We are worried that the child
may develop abnormal fears of dogs or may never become a
great dog lover. Trying to balance this fear we will make efforts
to teach our child to like dogs again. When an unusually tame
one comes around, we may get on the floor and play with it,
trying to show our child that this dog does not bite. All this
would be very simple if biting dogs, for instance, were German
shepherds, and nonbiting ones were boxers. Nature, however,
has not made things that simple for us. There are no such
obvious cues. The parent is really at somewhat of a loss to find
good discrimination cues. We may teach our child to stay away
from barking dogs, but often barking dogs do not bite and biting
dogs do not bark. Perhaps teeth flashing or no tail wagging are
better cues? These are more subtle, more difficult for us to
analyze, and more difficult to explain to others, especially to
children.

Our culture requires us to make increasingly finer and
more complicated discriminations as we grow from our child-

hood to adult competency. A one-year-old, for instance, has to learn "Sidewalk, yes; street, no." At age two or so, if the child goes for a walk with the parent the discrimination will become finer. It will become "Street with parents, yes; street without parents, no." After a few more years have passed this rule is likely to change again into "Street without parents but with school patrol, yes; street without parents and without school patrol, no." In this fashion our survival and much of our social adjustment depend on our ability to make discriminations between rules or cues that become more and more involved.

INSTRUMENTAL CONDITIONING

We have now discussed *Pavolovian* or *classical* conditioning with its ramifications of generalization and discrimination. Pavlovian conditioning is also called *respondent* conditioning because in this type of learning we make responses to specific stimuli which nature or other people present to us. Watson and Rayner made Albert cry by striking a gong. The heat of a candle makes us pull our finger back, and the sight of a shiny toy makes a child come to us. These kinds of unconditional or natural stimuli have been called *"forcers"* because they force or bring out the individual's reaction needed for learning. The loud noise that made Albert cry was made while he played with the rat so that the fear of the noise would transfer to the rat. When parents let a child touch a candle they say the word "hot" so this word will become a cue for not touching. On the positive side, when a child comes to us to get a toy we can say the words "come here" and these words will become associated with coming towards us. In all of these examples the stimulus-response relationship, *the S-R,* was predictable. We knew which unconditioned stimulus to use to bring about the response we wanted to pair with the new stimulus, mostly a word.

There are, however, many behaviors we desire from others and from ourselves for which there seem to be no ready-made forcers or unconditioned stimuli. No loud noise or no piece of candy, for example, will make children say "Thank you." Neither are there any known stimuli that will make adolescents clean up their rooms or that will make us study for three hours on Sunday afternoon. For such behaviors there are no buttons to push, and we must therefore use the *instrumental* technique, waiting until the individual performs the desired behavior, or at least part of it, and only then giving the reward. We may have to wait a long time until the wanted behavior occurs, until a three-year-old says "Thank you," or until 14-year-olds clean up their rooms on their own incentive. But there are some shortcuts. Though we may not know the exact stimulus to bring about a certain response, we can prepare the environment so that the wanted behavior is more likely to occur. We can give a child plenty to drink, put a potty chair and perhaps a toy close by, and thereby increase the likelihood that a child will sit on the potty chair and urinate. We, ourselves, can say "Thank you" more often and increase the chance that the child will say it. We can ask teenagers to clean up their room at a time when they are bored rather than at a time when they are about to rush off to a movie. In all these examples we are increasing the likelihood that the response will occur, but ultimately it must come from the individuals themselves. The individual is instrumental in carrying out the response, hence the name *instrumental* conditioning. We may also say that the individual must carry out the initial operation, hence the name *operant* conditioning—these terms are synonymous.

There are other shortcuts that can be applied in instrumental conditioning. The final response need not occur in its entirety. Steps in the right direction can be rewarded in a series of *successive approximations.* Toddlers can be rewarded for attempting to go to the potty chair even though they do not reach their final goal, teenagers can be praised for just cleaning up one corner of their room, and on the first Sunday afternoon on which we succeed in sitting down to study we can already reward ourselves with a cup of coffee or tea after the first half hour, extending this study time on successive Sundays. In instrumental conditioning we can also make use of the fact that behavior fluctuates naturally. Even the most hyperactive children will have their calmer moments when we can begin to reward them. But we must wait with a second reward until they become more calm, etc. *Modeling* or imitating is another process that facilitates instrumental conditioning. It is not clear why humans model, whether it is an innate drive or whether it is a learned desire that has generalized (Bandura, 1971). But in any event children's modeling behavior can be rewarded if they model the right actions. Sometimes this generalization is carried too far, especially when children model their parents' smoking or driving when they are, for instance, only 10 years old.

From birth on we act and our actions receive pleasant, painful, or neutral consequences, or *contingencies*, from our natural or social environment. This instrumental conditioning continues throughout human life. Frequently neither the receiver nor the giver is aware that contingencies are applied. Several experiments conducted to investigate the establishment of sex roles, discussed in a later chapter, have shown that parents are often quite unaware that they react differently to boys than to girls. When mothers were asked to watch an infant dressed in pink with the name "Beth" they smiled more often than when they were watching the same infant dressed in blue and called "Adam." Our entire language development is instrumentally conditioned. If a baby makes a sound similar to a word or a syllable in our language, such as "da," we smile and repeat the syllable in the hope that it soon will be "dada" and later "daddy." In other countries other syllables are reinforced. In Germany "da" is likely to be ignored and "pa" and "papa" will elicit parental smiles and repetitions.

Though instrumental or operant conditioning was first mentioned by Vladimir Bekhterev, one of Pavlov's contemporaries, in 1886 it did not become an important part of psychology until B. F. Skinner and his collaborators worked out many of its details in the 1930s and 1940s. Therefore, instrumental or operant conditioning has a third name—*Skinnerian* conditioning. Skinner worked with animals and constructed teaching machines for humans whereby he investigated how responses are best shaped and whether it is best to reward continuously or intermittently, an issue which will be discussed in the following chapter.

Another comparison between Pavlovian and Skinnerian conditioning may be useful. In *Pavlovian* conditioning, also called *classical* or *respondent* conditioning, we *elicit* a response by applying a specific stimulus. In *Skinnerian* conditioning, also called *instrumental* or *operant* conditioning, we wait for a response to be *emitted* from the individual and we reward it as soon as it occurs. We assume that every response, Pavlovian or Skinnerian, has its stimulus, just as we assume that every effect must have a cause. But for some, if not for most, human responses the stimuli are not known to us and in these instances we must use instrumental procedures. Our ignorance about the specificity of stimuli is a matter of degree and so is the difference between Pavlovian and Skinnerian conditioning. We know, for instance, that the intake of liquid will cause urination, but we don't know exactly when. It may be five or thirty minutes later, and there are no immediate indicators when it will occur. Thus the intake of liquid cannot serve us as a very useful training device, because the formation of associations, as pointed out previously, is limited to brief time intervals.

It should also be pointed out that the reward, also called *reinforcement,* plays an important role in both types of conditioning. In Pavlovian conditioning it often serves two functions. It is usually used as the unconditioned stimulus (the forcer) as well as the reward. The candy that is held up to make the child come to us is usually given as the reward after the child comes. In Skinnerian procedures there is no forcer. Rewards such as foods, praise, tokens, or any other kind are only given after the desired action, or part of it, has occurred.

Successive approximation and its facilitating effect on Skinnerian conditioning has already been mentioned. It also has been successfully used in Pavlovian procedures to uncondition fears and phobias. For example, Mary Cover Jones (1924) tried to condition Peter, two and a half years old, to lose his obstinate fear of rabbits. While Peter was eating, the rabbit was placed in a wire mesh cage about 20 feet away. This distance was the closest the rabbit could be brought to Peter without causing him any upset. At mealtimes, on successive days, the rabbit was brought closer and closer. After about six weeks Peter was no longer afraid. He would actually seek direct contact with the rabbit. Had Jones conducted her experiment in a Skinnerian fashion the rabbit would have remained stationary, but Peter would have been allowed to move around freely. During the first days he would have remained a good distance from the rabbit, but any time he came closer he would have received a reward. Instead of the rabbit being brought closer and closer to Peter, Peter hopefully would have come closer and closer to the rabbit. In circumstances where both Pavlovian and Skinnerian methods can be used, it would be less time consuming to use the Pavlovian methods, since the experimenter can bring out the wanted behavior and is less dependent on chance factors.

As already mentioned, conditioning is all-pervasive in human development. Our entire development can be seen as an interplay between our innate physiological capacities and our various and continued learning experiences. There are many individual differences in the rate of conditioning. Personality differences such as extraversion and introversion seem to have a marked influence on the rate with which subjects can be conditioned. Franks (1953) conditioned the eyeblink reflex using a bell as the conditioned (to be learned) stimulus and a puff of air as the unconditioned one (the natural) and found that after 18 trials introverts responded 80% of the time to the new stimulus, but extroverts responded only 40% of the time. Eysenck (1971) has repeated this experiment obtaining similar results. He believes that extroverts build up more inhibition during an experiment—a tendency to get "tired" and want to do something else.

Chapter 4

REWARD AND PUNISHMENT

There is hardly any learning or conditioning without rewards or punishment, and without them our activities are rarely sustained after they have been learned. But one man's meat is another man's poison and psychologists have wrestled for decades with the definitions of rewards and punishment and with their effects on human development.

Types of rewards: Psychologists differentiate between innate *primary rewards* and learned *secondary rewards.* The primary rewards are pleasures derived from satisfying basic physiological needs such as hunger, thirst, sleep, warmth, sex, exercise, and the alleviation of pain. It is relatively simple to satisfy infants because their drives are still primary ones which can be satisfied with food, some touching, and the ridding of pain. The older child is more sophisticated. It does not appreciate many primary rewards unless they are of a particular nature —such as preferring a hamburger over meat loaf or blue jeans over cotton pants. By definition, secondary rewards are not originally satisfying, but become such through associations with primary rewards, through parental urgings or social imitations. Smoking is a good example of a secondary reward. Almost every smoker detested his or her first cigarette. However, a second or third one was attempted, because one had learned that it was the "thing" to do. Efforts which we make to obtain secondary rewards are called *secondary drives* or *motives*. If we are hungry and want food we follow a primary drive, but if we want money to buy food our want is termed a motive, implying that something is wanted to obtain something else.

Due to the interaction between primary and secondary rewards it is sometimes difficult to distinguish them. Our primary hunger drive is often enhanced or diminished by the secondary reward value of a certain food—by our learned likes or dislikes which psychologists call appetite. Some people may lose their hunger when we suggest a dish of raw oysters, liver, or tongue, while these suggestions would stimulate others to eat extra portions. At times secondary drives may become as powerful as primary ones. During his imprisonment in a Nazi concentration camp one of the authors observed some inmates exchanging their last bit of food for a cigarette. Others refused to drink from a mud puddle or eat meat from a cadaver, even while their death from thirst and starvation was imminent. In a normal functioning society where the basic wants are satisfied, secondary rewards take on overwhelming proportions. It is interesting to speculate how much of the daily strivings of an average American adult are directed towards the satisfaction of secondary rewards—of rewards not needed for our physical well-being. In the supermarkets we walk through aisles of nonessentials before we reach the essentials—the bread, the milk, and the meat in the back of the store.

While we can more or less accurately predict the effects of primary rewards, it is difficult to know which secondary rewards will appeal to people. We will come closer to predicting their preferences if we know their culture, social class, and family background. Even then we will be incorrect frequently.

One of America's most famous educators, Edward Lee Thorndike (1874–1949), spent a lifetime investigating how reward and punishment effect learning. He formulated the *Law of Effect,* which states: "Organisms tend to repeat those responses that are followed by satisfying state of affairs." In an experiment, he asked graduate students at Columbia University to read aloud a list of words and he rewarded them with a quarter after they pronounced certain words. According to his Law of Effect, he expected that his subjects would remember the words for which they had been rewarded better than those for which they had not. Contrary to his expectations, his students did not remember the "rewarded" words as well as the unrewarded ones. In retrospect Thorndike asked whether the quarter might have been an embarrassment for the students—a social punishment rather than a financial reward. Since Thorndike's days our picture of what constitutes a secondary reward has not become clearer. In a society with changing values it has perhaps become even less predictable.

To bring more objectivity to the definition of reward and punishment, Skinner (1938, 1974) proposed a foolproof and self-correcting system. He avoids classifying anything as a reward or punishment until its effect of the behavior in question has been observed. For example, he may put a typewriter in a room and observe how often a child depresses the keys. The rate of this activity he calls the *operant level.* It is the base rate of a behavior before learning or additional learning has taken place. He may now add a bell to the typewriter that rings every time a key is depressed. Is this bell ringing a reward, a punishment, or a neutral stimulus? Skinner need not define it because he gives it a neutral name, he calls the bell a *contingency,* contingent (dependent) upon the pressing of a key. If the typing rate, the operant level, increases under the bell-ringing condition, then bell-ringing in this case and with this child would be called *positive reinforcement* (synonymous with positive reward). Should the typing rate decrease, then bell-ringing would be called a *punishment.* It often happens that one and the same stimulus (a bell, for instance) acts as a positive reinforcement for one person and as a punishment for another.

To give a more practical example of Skinner's approach we can mention a child's tantrum behavior that the parent is trying to eliminate. As a contingency, one may recommend that the child be scolded as soon as a tantrum behavior starts. If after a few days the tantrums become fewer then scolding in this particular case would be considered a punishment and its continuation would be recommended. If scoldings increase the tantrums for another child, then they would be considered a positive reinforcement and they should be discontinued. Even spankings or any other form of physical punishment is considered a positive reinforcement (reward) if its repeated application increases the occurrence of tantrums.

There is the confusing term *negative reinforcement* in Skinner's system. It does not mean punishment. Like positive reinforcement it signifies an increase in the operant level, but that increase was obtained not by adding a reward, but by taking away a pain or punishment. When we take off a shoe that is pinching we are reinforcing ourselves negatively because we are more likely to do so again, and quicker, the next time a shoe pinches us (Skinner, 1974, p. 46). We are also negatively reinforced when an expected punishment is not received. For example, we park our car at a parking meter and have no change and expect to find a ticket upon our return. If we do not find a ticket we will be more likely to park again without paying. Negatively, here, means not getting a ticket and reinforcement means that we are more likely to repeat parking without paying. On the punishment side Skinner distinguishes also between punishment directly received and the punishing effect of an expected reward that is not received. If we visit a friend expecting a good meal but do not receive it we will be less likely to visit this friend again. Although Skinner writes about these two types of punishments he has no separate term for the latter, calling both types punishment. Though this terminology is somewhat confusing, Skinner's approach plays a major role in the modification of a wide range of human behaviors.

WORDS AS REWARDS

We reward and we punish. When we do it verbally we praise and we scold. Through words humans influence each other more than through any other means. Though it is seldom realized, the rewarding and punishing qualities of words are solely established through learning. When a word is first spoken it means absolutely nothing to a child. It has no emotional content and it is neither a cue for good nor for bad. The word "gift," for instance, means "poison" in German. For the German child it will soon become a sign or cue of unpleasant feelings and withdrawal movements because loud noises, frightening facial expressions, hand slapping, and many "nein, nein" will accompany it. Needless to say, an English-speaking child is likely to hear the word "gift" in very different circumstances, mostly in pleasant situations: before receiving a candy bar, a shiny toy, or while going to a birthday party. Pronounced and written the same, the word "gift" will acquire quite a different meaning for the two children.

Parents begin to teach their children the meanings of words as soon as they begin to talk to them. They will say the word "good," for instance, while they cuddle or pat their child, or while giving a favorable food or toy. After a sufficient number of such pairings the word "good" alone will put the child into a mood similar to the one created by a hug or a piece of candy. As the children grow older they will continue to hear the word "good" in pleasant situations, and this word will also be paired frequently with such words as brave, unselfish, recommendable, altruistic, etc. Once a word has been conditioned it can serve as a stimulus to condition the meaning of other words. In the vernacular we may say that the meaning "rubs off." Pavlov was successful conditioning dogs to a stimulus eight times removed from the originally rewarded one. After he had conditioned his dog to salivate to the bell he paired the bell with a light and the light with a touch on the flank, etc. Pavlov called this *higher order conditioning.* To what order humans are capable of being conditioned is not known, perhaps to the hundredth order or more. Needless to say, words have also many positive features. We use words as cues to signify actions and we also use them as rewards. We say "Come here," and after the child has come we say "Good." We ask our neighbor to do an errand for us and after it is done we express our gratitude in words. As with any other secondary rewards, the pleasures we can give with praise and honors are limitless. President Hoover had over 70 honorary doctor degrees. In a society affluent with primary rewards, secondary rewards, especially words, become even more important. Many people who call mental health clinics express the urgency "just to talk to somebody."

Some people have the notion that a verbal reward like "good" is morally better than candy, a material reward. They may call the candy a bribe. Actually both "good" and candy are bribes, if one wants to use this word. The candy is the more efficient one. There can be no moral differences because all words are secondary rewards and are based on primary rewards. There is a technical difference, however. The child who responds to "good" has received more training than the child who responds only to the actual candy. Many adults become moralists when they evaluate children's behavior. They do not apply these same morals to themselves. How many adults would work for the word "good" alone, without getting paychecks enabling them to buy material goods.

Schedule of Rewards

We can hardly imagine our society functioning without social and monetary rewards. Psychologists have studied rewards to make them even more effective. B. F. Skinner (1938) was trying to find out whether or not we must reward an action every time it occurs in order to maintain it at a high operant level. After much research Ferster and Skinner (1957) found out that *partial reinforcement,* also called *intermittent reinforcement,* can be more effective than rewarding every response. They trained a pigeon to peck at a disk to obtain a grain of food. In the initial training it was best to reward the pigeon each time it pecked at the disk. After this response was well-learned, the investigators started to cut out some of the rewards. For instance, they would reward the pigeon with a piece of grain only for the first, third, fourth, fourteenth, seventeenth, twenty-ninth, and so on, peck. The pigeon kept on pecking just the same. More and more rewards were eliminated while avoiding a regular pattern between food and no food. In this fashion pigeons can be trained to peck at a disk about 6,000 times per hour while obtaining only 10 or 20 rewards in that hour. It looks as though a pigeon keeps on working furiously if it is kept on guessing when the reward will come.

Comparing animals to humans is problematical. But anybody driving through Reno can hardly help comparing the persistence of the slot machine players to the persistence of Skinner's pigeons. Bijou (1957) was one of the first investigators to test intermittent reward on young children. He used trinkets as rewards and a ball-placing task as a response. He found that 20 percent reward was more resistent to extinction than a continuous or 100 percent reward. Ryan and Moffitt (1966) tested children with a marble machine. Children in their partial reward group worked faster than those in their constant reward group. It was also found that older children benefit more from partial reward than younger ones. Jane Fort (1961) instructed 144 preschool children to press the nose of a manikin clown to receive a piece of candy delivered from the clown's mouth. Fort had one group that received a piece of candy after each pressing response, the 100 percent reward group. She had another group that received the candy only half of the time, the 50 percent reward group. During subsequent extinction or unlearning trials neither group received any candy. The group that had 50 percent reward kept on pressing the lever three times as long as the group that had received a reward each time.

Applied to a practical situation, we might predict that a child who has been rewarded each time after tidying up his or her bedroom will not keep on cleaning it when the parent is out of town or when rewards are discontinued. On the other hand, a child who had been rewarded here and there for cleaning the room will be more likely to continue. Partial rewards can be thought of as functioning midway between spoiling and extinction. If a response is rewarded 100 percent, we may not only learn to do the job, but learn also to do the job only when rewarded. A child who receives praise and/or a quarter regularly for going to the store will be greatly disappointed the first time the reward is omitted. Younger children may throw tantrums on such occasions. Older ones may refuse to go the next day. Adults will complain to their shop steward.

We may compare the function of partial reward to the "pain/pleasure principle." A meal will simply be more satisfying after a previous one has been missed. Physical health is seldom appreciated while one is well. Even the most feeble walk feels rewarding after one has been bedridden for some time. Too many rewards, particularly if they occur concurrently, may lead to conflicts. Observe the frustration of a child at a birthday party receiving 10 gifts at one time.

SHAPING BEHAVIOR

Rewards do not cause an initial behavior, but they increase the likelihood that the rewarded action will be repeated. But we would have to wait forever to reward the correct construction of a French sentence or the solution of a mathematical problem involving calculus. All complex learning problems must be learned and rewarded in a stepwise fashion. How difficult should the individual steps be and how often should they be rewarded? This answer depends on the learner's age, intelligence, and on his or her previous knowledge. It also depends on the material to be learned. In designing programs for teaching machines, which have been advocated by Skinner (1963), psychologists have developed optimal steps for different ages and different instructional materials. Optimal steps are at a difficulty level where they neither bore nor discourage the learner. A new step can only be obtained if a correct answer has been made to the previous step. It is the immediacy by which the reward follows the correct answer that makes programmed instruction a very effective learning tool.

After rewards have shaped and maintained our behavior for years, the behavior often becomes habitual. We keep on performing some tasks even though there is no detectable social or monetary reward. This phenomenon has been called *functional autonomy*. It seems that the rewards have become "internalized" because the individual will work in the absence of any external primary or secondary rewards.

INEFFECTIVENESS OF REWARDS

We know that rewards are powerful motivators and we are usually suprised if they do not produce the desired behavior. However, both primary and secondary rewards are limited because sooner or later they satiate the individual. If the final response has to be learned by stepwise increments, frequent and continued rewards may be necessary. For example, if we reward pupils with an ice cream cone for arithmetic problems correctly solved within an instructional hour we would soon satiate them and the ice cream would no longer be a reward after the second or third problem. If we reward with smaller amounts, bits of chocolate, for instance, pupils may be annoyed that they get so little. Both large and small amounts of primary rewards have the disadvantage of disturbing the learning process—large amounts through satiation and small amounts through repeated distractions. There are, however, exceptions to this. With the help of "M & M" candy, Lovaas (1976) taught very withdrawn and autistic children how to pronounce words. These children were around age ten and some of them had never spoken.

Secondary rewards are usually more effective than primary rewards because they rarely satiate us. Our stomachs, for instance, will only hold limited amounts of food, but we can deposit unlimited amounts of money in our bank accounts. But secondary rewards have other flaws. Due to the fact that they are originally established by being paired with primary rewards they may lose their rewarding effect if this original bond is not occasionally re-rewarded. Money keeps its high secondary reward value because we buy food and drinks with it, pairing it daily with primary rewards. Words, however, are less stable and they will occasionally lose their reward value, particularly during the early developmental years.

How often will a child respond to our cue "come here" without being given food, a hug, or a toy? How long will we work for a "Thank you?" When a child no longer responds to the words "come here" the parent may say that the child is disobeying. The psychologist will say that the child has unlearned. Pavlov called such unlearning *experimental extinction.* He showed in many experiments that any new cue will eventually lose its effect if it is not occasionally paired with the original cue or similar ones producing the original response. Since Pavlov's work, Skinner has shown that infrequent rewards can be very effective if they are randomly mixed with nonrewards, and that intermittent reinforcement is much more resistant to extinction than 100 percent reinforcement.

Rewards, especially words, often become ineffective because we counter-condition them. We counter-condition when we say "come here" to a person engaged in a pleasant task who is not likely to come, or when we say "come here, clean up this mess!" We begin to make the words "come here" less effective each time we link them with something unpleasant. Some parents will call their children out off the street and will scold or spank them right after they have responded to the words "come here." No wonder some children run away when they are called.

There are many other occasions when we confound reward with punishment without intending to do it. We may take a child to the doctor for a shot and say repeatedly "it will not hurt," just before a more or less severe pain will be felt. If the pain is severe and if the words "not hurt" are given just before the pain is felt, then the words "not hurt" become cues for being hurt. Such a pairing will not help to establish trust and confidence between parent and child. It may even have contrary effects. On the next doctor's visit the child may start crying as soon as the parent says "It will not hurt." The doctor may not even be in sight. The parent, of course, was merely concerned about the child's comfort and had no intention of lying to the child. But before we can expect the calming effect of "not hurt" or any other such words, we must first condition the child to expect pain when we say "It will hurt" and to expect no pain when we say "It will *not* hurt," Only after this discrimination is learned can we do a little fooling, suggesting, or influencing. We can then say "It will not hurt" even though we think it will. We can still leave the back door open and say "It will not hurt too much." We can only expect our words to have a relaxing or soothing effect if we have used them previously in relaxing or soothing situations. If a child does not follow our instructions and continues to disobey us, we should suspect that we have disobeyed some rules of learning or their closely linked rules of reward.

A number of experiments have been conducted in which punishment for incorrect behavior lead to faster learning than rewarding for correct behavior and in which a combination of reward and punishment was no better than reward alone (Walters & Grusec, 1977). In most of these studies the word "right" was used as reinforcement and the word "wrong" as punishment. These results are somewhat suprising because for decades teachers have been told to emphasize the positive aspects of learning. It has been postulated by Paris and Cains (1972) that "right" is less effective than "wrong" because children hear the word "right" and similar social rewards daily in many unspecified situations, while the word "wrong" is usually linked to more specific actions. Some classroom observations supported this hypothesis. "You are doing well" and similar phrases are more often said in nonspecific situations, while "That's wrong" or "You are doing badly" refers usually to more specific events.

ATTITUDES TOWARD PUNISHMENT

Punishment has and will always be the most effective way of changing certain behaviors. Yet since World War II punishment has become very unpopular in America and in other Western countries. Its use is tainted with thoughts of brutality, child abuse, authoritarianism, and other bad things. Many psychologists have fostered these thoughts by accepting Freud's ideas, believing that bad behavior such as aggression needs to be expressed and that it would become worse if inhibited by punishment. This belief has generated much literature recommending nonauthoritarian socialization methods with almost unqualified amounts of love and understanding. For decades psychologists have not even dared to hypothesize that it might, for instance, be effective to bite children back when they bite, or to hit them back when they hit. Perhaps it is much safer to give advice that children should only be rewarded than to recommend any punishment at all. Even the worst overdose of love will show no immediate detrimental consequences; while an overdose of punishment wrongly applied can cause immediate bodily injuries, prolonged crying, or revengeful aggression.

The Freudian psychologists who were against any punishment were joined by the Skinnerian psychologists who believe that adults should not use any physical punishment because children will model it. Modeling does take place and some studies have shown that there is a relationship between the punishing parent and the aggressive child. But studies have also shown that children with nonpunishing parents become more aggressive toward other children after they have viewed aggressive cartoons. They bit, pushed, kicked, choked, or threw things at other children, although their parents had never treated them like this (Steuer, et al. 1971; Grusec, 1972). Since there is plenty of TV around, children will model aggressive behavior whether or not their own parents or anybody else treat them aggressively. Thus, many parents who have hopefully followed the "no-punishment" advice find that their own children hit, push, and kick other children and at times even their own nonaggressive parents.

The psychologists' advice of no punishment has never been fully accepted. Almost 100 percent of 379 kindergarten mothers interviewed by Sears et al. (1959) reported that they had spanked their children at least once. This percentage did not change during the following two decades in spite of the millions of "how-to-parent" books sold in the meantime. In 1979, 98 percent of the parents still report the use of physical punishment, however mild. Among them are 20 percent who hit with objects and 4 percent who give severe beatings (U.S. News & World Report, Jan. 15, 1979). Child abuse is also increasing, and some psychologists believe that this is caused by the fact that we allow any beatings at all (Sage, 1978). However, it would be interesting to find out whether child abuse is as frequent in countries where painful but physically nondamaging punishment is socially accepted, as compared to the U.S. where the belief is prevalent that any punishment may have damaging and irreversible psychological effects. Under such conditions parents may inhibit all punishment until they become extremely emotional, losing all self-control—something which is often reported from parents who have abused their children. It is difficult to say whether the permissive childrearing theories of the postwar decades are here to stay. The number of psychologists who believe that children should be raised with definite rules and limits in the household has been increasing in the 1970s (*U.S. News & World Report,* 1976).

TYPES OF PUNISHMENT

"Sticks and stones will break my bones, but words will never hurt me." This old saying shows that people made distinctions between *primary* and *secondary* punishment long before psychologists were in vogue. Similar to the classification of rewards, primary punishment is natural and unlearned. It consists of pain and related discomfort and unpleasantness and it manifests itself through avoidance. Secondary punishment likewise produces avoidance, but the stimuli involved are learned. Similar to secondary rewards, secondary punishment consists mainly of words, facial gestures, hand motions, and intonations directly or indirectly associated with pain. It also consists of events that have been associated with the loss of reward such as the taking away of food or of obstacles that have prevented the obtaining of rewards. For example, a time-out procedure prevents the child from making responses (noise in the classroom) for which he or she expects to receive positive reinforcement (giggles and smiles from the classmates).

The aversion responses caused by primary or secondary punishment can be of two different types. We can *escape* displeasure after it has occurred, like leaving the house after unpleasant company has arrived; or we can *avoid* this displeasure altogether by leaving before the unwanted company appears. For the avoidance response we need a learned cue that signals the expected unpleasantness—like a telephone call early Sunday mornings which may signal the arrival of our guests. In animal experiments *avoidance conditioning* procedures have been extremely effective. Hundreds of years before Pavlov demonstrated it in his laboratory, the gypsies trained their bears to dance using avoidance conditioning. They would scatter hot coals and ashes on the ground and then pull the bear so that he had to stand on them. Feeling the heat, the bear would soon rear up and begin to lift up his hind legs in an alternate fashion — similar to us juggling a hot light bulb from one hand into the other. While the bear made these motions, a tambourine was sounded to serve as a cue. Only one such avoidance trial was generally needed to make the bear a reliable "dancer." Thereafter the tambourine could be sounded many more times without the hot coals and the bear would immediately begin to dance. Anyone who watches a bear making these motions as soon as the tambourine is sounded will be convinced that the bear is dancing. However, knowing the antecedents we realize that the bear is not dancing at all—he has not added anything positive to his behavior, but has learned to avoid the heat by *not* leaving his forefeet on the ground and by *not* leaving either of the hindfeet on the ground too long.

Punishment usually cannot be used to establish a wanted behavior directly. No amount of spanking or scolding will, for instance, cause an immediate room-cleaning, arithmetic-solving, or piano-playing reaction. But punishment can immediately stop an ongoing behavior, resulting in suppression, avoidance, or escape. Our example of the dancing bear should not mislead us. The bear's avoidance reaction happens to be something that pleases the audience. Whether punishment causes an activity or an inactivity, it is always an avoidance, though to the observer it may appear otherwise. If we sit in the grandstand at a rodeo, we may believe that a Brahma bull is charging into the arena anxious to perform, while in reality he is escaping the electric shock of a prod applied before the stall door opens. Analogies on the human level can be found readily. A child runs home to the mother in order to escape a dilemma down the street or a new romance is desired because there is trouble in the present one. Goethe said, "One recognizes the motive and one becomes disappointed." Perhaps he was too pessimistic. Since humans have the capacity to discriminate and to compare, choices will always be relative.

Punishment techniques can be further separated into two classes: *power assertion* can be primary, as in physical punishment, or secondary punishment, as in the withholding of rewards and in verbal derision; *love-oriented* techniques include expressions of disappointment, ignoring, and withdrawal of love. Though the evidence in inconclusive, power-assertion tends to create aggression and hostility, while love-oriented techniques may create guilt and confession (Walters & Grusec, 1977).

What is difficult to define is pain itself—the primary element of punishment. Physiologically pain is caused by over-stimulating any sense organ and subjectively it is experienced in many different intensities and qualities. Dallenbach (1939) lists over 40 adjectives commonly used to describe pain. Among the list is biting, bright, burning, cutting, dull, itchy, piercing, tearing, sharp, and stinging. Hardy (1947) and his collaborators constructed a pain scale relating the intensity of the stimulus (radiant heat) to the perceived intensity. Their scale, measuring pain from its lowest perceivable point, is divided into units or *dols* (form the French doleur, pain). With the aid of the scale, they found that single individuals are fairly consistent in their reports of pain, but that different individuals report quite different sensations. The very same stimulus that causes considerable pain for some individuals may cause only mild pain in others or perhaps just a slight discomfort. If such large differences exist in controlled laboratory settings, we should not be surprised about the many diverse effects of punishment when applied in everyday life.

Variables in Punishment

Pain is nature's fastest and most efficient teacher. We touch a space heater only once and never again. We close a door by its knob because we have hurt our fingers once or twice holding on to its side. Why is there such a controversy about the effect of punishment when humans punish humans? We have already discussed the theoretical controversies. In practice there are just as many. With the infant, Albert, punishment worked well in the form of a loud noise. Only a few trials were needed to make Albert afraid of the rat. With adults, nausea and pain have been successfully used to inhibit smoking and drinking. But in many situations punishment does not work. Only 50 percent of the kindergarten mothers in Maccoby and Levin's survey who had punished their children believed that it did any good. Just as many, if not more, delinquents and aggressive children come from homes where they received physical punishment as from homes where other disciplinary methods were used (Walters & Grusec, 1978). Recidivism rates (repeater cases) for ex-convicts are around 70 percent, which shows that the punishing effect of imprisonment is highly ineffective. The number of murders committed is about equal in those countries that have and those that do not have capital punishment.

There are many other variables that influence the effect of punishment. Small differences in the time of its application, its severity, frequency, and type can be of utmost importance. Important also are the amounts of reward and punishment that an individual previously received, especially those amounts given by the punishing agent. Of all these factors, time seems to be the one most often mismanaged. It is clear that we learn very fast to avoid those actions that are punished soon and preferably during their occurence. While we are reaching out to touch a candle we feel pain; while Albert played with the rat he heard the loud noise; and while patients in some alcohol treatment centers drink alcohol they become nauseated to the point of vomiting (they are previously given a drug, Antabuse). In all these examples punishment was immediate and effective. The longer punishment is delayed the less effective it becomes. It is difficult to say after what lapse of time it will become ineffective. In Albert's case the loud noise may not have had any effect had it been given just a few minutes after Albert finished playing with the rat. For alcoholics, hangovers, headaches, and unpleasant social consequences generally have no effect because they are delayed until the "morning after." A sunburn this year is no assurance against a severe sunburn next year, because the pain in sunburn is delayed from the pleasure. Systematic experiments that examine the effects of delayed punishment while keeping all other variables constant apparently have not been conducted. Perhaps everyday observations about the ineffectiveness of delayed punishment are obvious enough.

Delay in punishment is common. In the household it may be hours until we discover a child's misdeed, in school it may be days before a test paper is returned with a bad grade; and prison sentences are often started months after the occurrence of the criminal act. It is not only time alone which makes delayed punishment ineffective. The longer the delay the greater the likelihood that the environment in which the misdeed occurred will have changed. For example, a mother may go into the garden and find her favorite flowers torn out. Angrily she runs back into the house to punish her child for it. In all likelihood this punishment will be ineffective because it is delayed and also because it is given in the wrong environment —an environment in which associations between garden and flowers and with not picking them can hardly be made. On such occasions some parents will call their children back into the garden and punish there, possibly in front of the flowers if some were left standing. But this method has a disadvantage. The child who responded to the parent's call will now be punished for having been obedient as well as for having picked the flowers.

What should we do to punish correctly in the above situation? Ideally we should go into the garden with the child and observe the child until it is about to reach for the flowers. At this very moment one light slap or one loud word will make the child withdraw from the picking. It is obvious that parents need to anticipate their child's behavior if they want to apply punishment correctly. This in turn requires the parents to be with their children a great deal of their time, especially in moments when forbidden or unwanted actions may occur. This requirement alone makes punishment somewhat ironic, because those parents who are with their children a great deal can guide them much more easily by rewarding the wanted actions than by punishing unwanted ones.

Many parents punish their children long after the child has done the misdeed. When these parents are told that such delayed punishment has little or no effect, they usually say that they tell their children very specifically why the punishment is given. This may be so, but how much attention will children pay to any words before or during punishment? Children may recognize by the way they are called that punishment is in store. Some will tremble, some will cry, some will struggle to get loose, but few will pay attention to the specific words, "I don't want you to pick my flowers!" or to the shouting, "Don't ever touch these flowers!"

Let us take another example, of a four-year-old boy in kindergarten who, while playing with wooden blocks, hits other children when they come too close to him. His punishment is likely to be much delayed. We generally instruct children in kindergarten not to hit back when they are hit. The teacher will be called, there will be some questions as to who hit whom, and the hitter may get a scolding, be asked to stand in the corner, or his mother may be informed later during the day. In all probability none of these methods will be effective because the punishment is not given in the same situation in which the misdeed occurred. It would be more effective if this child were watched and punished as soon as he lifts up his arm to strike another child. The punishment at that instant need not be severe. A firm grip of the arm or a loud "no" may be sufficient. We should not expect that hitting will cease if the child is verbally reprimanded or instructed not to hit. Some children act impulsively, meaning that their thoughts do not intervene between the stimulus they perceive (a child coming close) and the response they make (hitting with block). If these children were in the habit of thinking in these moments they would not hit others in the first place.

We cannot assume that delayed punishment works any

better with older children or adults because their language and their thought processes are advanced. Quite the contrary. Older children can use these very processes to rationalize. They may connect the punishment not to their own acts, but to those of siblings, parents, teachers, judges, jailers, or whoever else they may blame for their misdeeds. Let us look in detail at a case that occurred at an Oregon high school.

A 14-year-old student threw a tennis shoe and a burst of derogatory remarks at his gym teacher. Instead of being punished right away, nothing happened. The teacher, most likely, needed to get permission to punish. The punishment when given the next day or so will appear quite unnatural to the pupil who in the meantime may have reasoned as follows: "Will I get the punishment or not? If there needs to be a conference on it, my act could not have been so bad. If they decide to punish me, they are doing it only because they do not like me." After having gotten the punishment our pupil may continue to rationalize, being now quite *sure* that "they had it in for" him. After being punished a second or third time for other misdeeds in a delayed manner the culprit may become irrevocably convinced that the punishment was carried out as an act of vindictiveness and not as one of correction.

Laws intended to be humane and educational forbid teachers in certain states to punish their pupils physically during or after a punishable act. In some school systems the teacher must wait 24 hours; in other systems another teacher must be present. All such regulations that necessitate delay make punishment ineffective. Worse yet, they may even cause more delinquent behavior as the culprit may learn to hate the authorities rather than his own misdeeds.

Perhaps we could take a lesson from Neill (1960) who has reared and educated hundreds of pupils over a period of 40 years. In his book, *Summerhill,* he describes his unusual permissive methods and his great success. He never "planned" to punish a child. However, if a child kicked him, he kicked it right back, mildly enough not to injure the child. He found this procedure effective. It did not set up any animosity, rationalizations, or a hatred towards Neill on the child's part.

It will be apparent from the previous discussion that time and not severity is the important factor in the success of punishment. If the punishment is applied before an undesirable act, it merely needs to be strong enough to cause withdrawal. For the child who moves the finger towards the stove, the heat needs only be severe enough to halt the motion or to make the hand move back. Or, in general, a very slight tap on the hand while the child reaches for the forbidden object would be much more effective than a severe hitting after the child has terminated the muscular movement that leads up to the punishable act.

The effect of the severity of punishment given after a punishable act is much harder to assess. Severe punishment has often prevented successful training. It is quite possible that the severity destroys or prevents the formation of the associations between the verbal cue and the punished act. When a child is beaten very severely, the words that accompany the beating might make no impression on the child. The child will most likely fight the pain and pay little attention to the words spoken.

A number of studies investigating the effect of punishment in conjuction with verbal explanations (cognitive structuring) have shown that verbal information makes punishment of moderate intensity more effective than punishment of high or low intensity. In these experiments the children who received mild forms of various punishments such as loud noises, giving up candy, and verbal threats touched the "forbidden" objects less frequently, even in the absence of surveillance, than did those for whom the punishment had been severe (Cheyne et al., 1969).

Interesting results have been obtained in comparing the effects of loud and soft deterrents. Parke (1969) found that a loud buzzer was more effective with young boys than a soft one, but O'Leary et al. (1970) found that soft verbal reprimands in a classroom situation were more effective than loud ones. It is possible that the loud reprimands in a classroom heightened the

attention of the peers—an approval that may have offset any
negative effect of the loudness. Whatever the reasons, the differences in the two results show again that it is difficult to form
any general rules about the effect of punishment because slight
changes in the type of punishment and in the social situation
can produce very different results.

SIDE EFFECTS OF PUNISHMENT

We have already described various conditions under which
punishment is likely to be ineffective. Moreover, it can have
detrimental effects, causing aggression in some people and withdrawal in others. For obvious reasons the causes for these detrimental effects have not been investigated in the laboratory. Our
knowledge about these causes is derived mostly from animal
data and general learning principles and is therefore speculative. We suspect that punishment is most damaging when it is
applied inconsistently—when a child, for instance, is called not
knowing whether it will receive a cookie or a spanking or when
we put our arm around a lover not knowing whether we will
be accepted or rejected. In everyday life there are usually
enough cues present by which we can predict. It has been
speculated that parents with emotionally bland personalities
may not offer their children sufficient cues. Dogs seem to be
sensitive to the utmost to intonation cues. They can easily
differentiate a "come here" to get beaten from a "come here"
to be locked up in the house, or a "come here" to get food, etc.,
and they show quite different response patterns to these commands.

In his laboratory Pavlov tried to eliminate the differences
between cues for reward and punishment. First he rewarded
dogs for responding to a circle and punished them for responding to an ellipse. After the dogs had learned this discrimination,
Pavlov made the circle more elliptical and the ellipse more
circular. At a certain point the dogs' discrimination ability

broke down and they showed various abnormal behaviors. Some dogs became wild and aggressive, others showed a sleep-like immobility. Pavlov called these states *experimental neurosis*—experimental because he established it by an experiment. As yet it is not known why one dog will suffer one type of neurosis and another dog another type. Sargant (1961), a British Surgeon General in World War II, observed similar differences in soldiers with war neuroses.

The effects of punishment can also be detrimental because they can generalize to desired behavior. If a child is punished for many things, for touching dishes, books, flowers, etc., it may learn to touch all things with great hesitation, if at all, and in extreme cases this hesitation may even generalize to the child's own toys. This example is perhaps somewhat academic for the American scene as visitors to the United States are continuously surprised by how many things American children are allowed to touch, to say, and to investigate.

Punishment can also *concentrate* on a certain person. Generally, the same person, the parent, punishes the child for a diversity of misdeeds so that the parent will become the feared object rather than the misdeed for which the punishment was given (for going into the street, for hitting a sibling, etc.). This greatly hinders the child's socialization process. As already pointed out, new responses are best built up by rewards and any training will be difficult once the parent has lost his or her reward value.

To direct concentration away from a person, dog trainers suggest that dogs be hit with a newspaper. Parents and teachers have used belts and canes hoping that these objects will become feared rather than they themselves. In his memoirs, Louis Armstrong (1967) pictures a chinaball tree. Each time before his grandmother whipped him she sent him out to get a switch from that tree. In spite of this he had some fond memories of that tree. He writes: "With tears in my eyes I would go to the tree and return with the smallest branch I could find."

The overall effect of punishment and whether it will generalize or concentrate may depend a great deal on the nature of the punishing agent. Punishment from a parent who rewards frequently and punishes rarely will have a greater effect than a punishment given by a parent who punishes often and rewards rarely or not at all. Often we feel greatly hurt if a person who loves us, who has given us many rewards, gives us but the slightest reprimand. In the laboratory, Carlsmith et al. (1974) have found that children are more likely to comply with a request from a rewarding experimenter than from a punishing one. These results were only observed when the children were relaxed and not in a fearful state.

At times punishment increases the misdeed for which it was received. A boy may hit his younger brother and may be spanked for it by his parent. However, he may blame this punishment on his brother and may hit him even more forcefully the next time. Some drivers who get speeding tickets transfer their anger towards the officer—the ticket in these cases teaches them to dislike traffic cops, but not their own speeding. Other drivers will be more self-admonishing. They will blame themselves for having driven too fast, but still others will blame themselves for not having driven faster so that the police could not have caught up with them. The ticket will teach this latter group to go even faster the next time. Again we cannot explain why some people will react in an extrapunitve way, blaming others for their punishment, and why others are intrapunitive, blaming themselves. Many variables, which perhaps relate to punishment, have not been investigated. It would be interesting to know if there are genetic differences as to our sensitivity to pain and to which degree they influence the effect of punishment. There are also no data on the relationship of IQ and punishment. It is conceivable that a smart child will learn the discriminating effect of punishment faster than a less intelligent one who may be more prone to generalize.

Having reviewed over 300 studies relating to punishment, Walters & Grusec (1978) believe that it is a gross oversimplification to assert that punishment is bad and reinforcement is good. They also believe that in many situations punishment is more effective than reward and that, although it can be wrongly administered to cause more harm than good, it will always be a necessary tool of behavioral change. If punishment is here to stay it will be useful to summarize its optimal conditions. Punishment should be applied mildly, immediately, and consistently in a matter-of-fact manner without guilt feelings on the part of the punishing agent. It should be given as a logical consequence of a misdeed, possibly with a provision of an impersonal rationale. Severe and frequent mild punishment should be avoided at all times because it may cause physical damage and may generalize and suppress desirable behavior. It may also cause aggression and concentrate on the punishing agent. Severe as well as mild but inconsistent punishment can cause a breakdown of the capacity to discriminate between allowed and forbidden actions.

NEITHER REWARD NOR PUNISHMENT

Aristotle (384B.C.-322B.C.) thought that we remember two things or events because they are either similar, dissimilar, or because they occur at the same time. He believed that these three types of associations are basic to learning and memorizing and he did not consider reward and punishment as necessary conditions for learning. Few psychologists have explored this nonreinforcement type of learning because it is less obvious than learning by reward and/or punishment. For example, when we hear a song for the second time we are likely to remember the singer, the restaurant, or any other circumstance that was present when we first heard it. It makes little difference if we liked the song or disliked it or whether we want to remember the particular circumstance or not. Such mere association learning confounds our notion of reward and punishment and of motivation in general.

One learning theorist, Edwin Guthrie (1886–1959) believed that rewards and punishment are artifacts and that is why they sometimes work in the same direction. He tried to point out that both reward and punishment have an interruption effect that prevents us from unlearning. In his seminars he used to give the following example: Suppose we were called out of class for a rewarding event (having won in the lottery) 15 minutes after the class started. Suppose at another time we are also called out 15 minutes after the class had started, but this time for an unpleasant event (a death in the family). In both instances we are likely to remember what was said in class just before we left. The pleasant as well as the unpleasant surprise interrupted our listening activity and both made us remember the foregoing event. It is doubtful that we would have remembered what was said 15 minutes after the hour had started had we remained in class for the full hour.

Guthrie's theory fits those situations in which punishment works in the same direction as reward as, for instance, in Elizabeth Hurlock's (1925) classic experiment on the effect of reward, punishment, and neglect. She found that a group of arithmetic students that was praised after weekly quizzes showed improvement. But she also found improvement, though not as much, in a group that was reproved after the quizzes. A third group that received the same instructions but was neither praised nor scolded improved the least. The fact that Hurlock's praised or verbally-rewarded group improved more than her reproved or verbally-punished group fits into many learning theories. But the fact that a "punished" group should learn more than a group which was neglected with respect to punishment and reward fits only into Guthrie's "noninterference" theory. His theory, to repeat, says that behavior, whether good or bad, is best forgotten if it is not interrupted by either punishment or reward.

Feldman (1961) has found results similar to those of Hurlock. He tested the effect of shock on learning with 60 male undergraduates at McGill University. He found that these students learned the solution of a finger maze faster when shocked for the correct response than when shocked for the wrong response. We see again that there are situations where punishment can further the repetition of a response more than a reward can.

As this chapter has shown, both the physiology and the psychology of reward and punishment are poorly understood. That is why each "rule" or theory has so many exceptions, and that is why Skinner suggests that psychologists should as yet not theorize because too few facts fit into any one theory. He therefore advocates that all reward and punishment be given on an "experimental" basis and with frequent checks to see whether the desirable behavior is brought out or whether the undesirable behavior diminishes.

Chapter 5

PARENTAL MILIEU

In our society the role of the family is important for both children and parents. Our cultural beliefs and our economy recognize the family as the primary socialization unit, giving communal childrearing such as day care, kindergarten, and preschool only peripheral and secondary responsibilities. We still consider the family environment, the milieu, as ideal for the development of character and morals, even in those cases where the children spend most of their waking hours in day care centers where we entrust day care personnel with the child's physical well-being. Psychologists have long emphasized the influence that parents have in shaping their children's behavior. To study the parent/child interaction they have examined the more subtle influences of modeling and learning and the finer degrees of reward and punishment by which family members react to each other. In this chapter we shall describe various styles of parental control such as warmth, permissiveness, authority, and hostility, emphasizing their effect on the child's socialization.

100

Parent-Child Interaction

Babies differ in temperament; so do mothers, fathers, and other caretakers. Parents expect different things from their babies, and they have different patterns of interaction with their babies as well. Some parents talk quite naturally to the baby right from birth. Each interaction is accompanied by cooing and loving sounds as well as by "real conversation." Some infants are handled a lot; others are handled only when they are diapered, fed, and bathed. Some infants are given much visual stimulation, such as mobiles over the crib and varied and colorful objects to play with. Other babies are given fewer such stimulating things. Some mothers like babies; some do not. Nor do some mothers feel confident or comfortable about taking care of their infants. The research findings on differences in mothering suggest that generally, better educated mothers talk to their infants more than do mothers with less education and that mothers talk to first babies more than to later ones.

Such differences in maternal style of interaction with the infant have an impact on the child's behavior during infancy and in some instances over a longer period of time. For example, there is evidence that babies who are talked to a lot during their early months vocalize more themselves. They make more cooing and babbling sounds than babies who have had less vocal stimulation. Such children may also begin talking at an earlier age. In one study (Korner, 1971) it was found that a baby who is held at her mother's shoulder rather than being cradled in her arms, is more visually alert. These findings suggest that some specific aspects of early handling may have equally specific effects on child development.

Other researchers (Yarrow, Rubenstein, Pederson & Jankowski, 1972) have found that infants who receive a high amount of social stimulation (including being held, being talked to, being looked at, and being played with) are more likely to be advanced in some aspects of early cognitive development. Even the richness and variety of inanimate stimulation such as number and variety of toys, textures to feel, and things to look at make a difference in the child's early cognitive development. Babies of five months who had received a rich variety of stimulation showed somewhat faster motor and perceptual development, more reaching and grasping, and more exploration of the environment.

Another facet of the mother's behavior, other than the pattern of stimulation she provides for the baby, is her own feeling of competence or emotional well-being. Broussard and Hartner (1971) have done one of the most comprehensive studies of the effects of mother's emotional state on her interaction with her infant. They have found that mothers who are depressed and irritable after the birth of the baby are more likely to think that their baby is below average in development. They are also more likely to be bothered by the infant and by the demands that caring for the infant makes on them. But which way does the causation run? It may be that these mothers are realistically depressed; they may have babies who are *noncuddlers:* fussier, harder to soothe, more colicky, and generally difficult (Schaffer & Emerson, 1964). But it could also be that the mother's own personality characteristics—her inclination to depression and irritability—make her see a perfectly ordinary, normally fussy baby as a great burden and strain.

Broussard and Hortner also found that the babies who, at one month of age, were considered by their mothers to be below average in development and functioning turned out to have more problems when they were four years old, when they were more likely to require some kind of therapy. Again, it may be that the mothers were simply good judges of their babies at one month. More likely, if a mother were depressed and overwhelmed by the demands made on her by an apparently normally difficult baby, there would develop between the two of them a pattern that resulted in later emotional difficulties for the child. In any case these findings are intriguing and need further study.

So far we have only mentioned the interaction between

mother and infant. But what of father—what is father's role? How available are fathers to their children during their infancy? Pederson and Robson (1969) studied fathers' activities with their infants, until recently a neglected area of investigation. Unfortunately, they interviewed mothers instead of fathers to gather the information. They discovered that 6 out of 45 fathers of eight- and nine-month-old infants engaged in two or more caretaking tasks on a daily basis and that these fathers spent an average of eight hours per week playing with the child. The range of time spent was from 45 minutes to 26 hours. Nine of the 45 fathers were extremely patient and tolerant with fussy or irritable babies, but ten habitually became angry or irritated with their infants. Of those ten irritated fathers, eight were fathers of girls. Fathers also tended to be more apprehensive about the well being of female infants. Seven fathers were very authoritarian in their conduct with the child, restrictive and ready to slap or spank in order to enforce their will. On the other hand, eleven were very permissive and tolerant of the baby's getting into things. The fathers tended to roughhouse with their boys but some criticized their wives for being too rough with the baby. Fathers were in the home while the baby was awake on the average of 26 hours per week. Pederson and Robson ascertained the babies' attachment to their fathers by their smiles, vocalization, and excitement upon seeing the father after separation. At around eight months of age, approximately three-fourths of the babies showed intense attachment to their fathers while only two babies began to show distress or protest when their father held them.

When more precise measuring instruments were used by Rebelsky and Hanks (1971) a gloomier picture of father/infant interaction emerged. Beginning in the second week of a baby's life, 24-hour tape recordings were made approximately every two weeks for a three-month period. A microphone was attached to the infant's shirt and the researchers told the parents that they were studying how infants live and what they do, and that they did not want to interfere in any way with the normal household schedule. It was found that these fathers spent very little time talking with their infants. The average number of vocal interactions per day was 2.7 and the average number of seconds per day that the fathers vocalized to the baby was 37. Even the father who interacted the most averaged only ten and one-half minutes per day vocalizing to his infant. Unlike the mothers who vocalized to the baby an increasing amount during the first three months of its life (Moss, 1967; Rebelsky, 1967), most of the fathers spent less time vocalizing during the later months of the study. This decrease in vocalization was especially true of fathers of girls.

Though at present put to little practice, Bower (1977) has reported that communication between father and infant is an important factor in personality development for girls as well as boys. It seems that substitute mothering, in which someone else, such as the father, looks after the baby, has no adverse effects either on social or cognitive development. Due to economic and cultural conditions the fathering of infants is still rare (see "Sex Roles").

Parent-child interaction is a two-way street. Children do play an active role in determining the form and direction of parental behavior. For instance, Michael Lewis (1977) finds that even young infants undertake to control their mother's actions. As an example, the infant and the mother may be looking at one another. Should the baby look away and upon turning back find that it has lost its mother's gaze it will start fussing. When the mother again gazes at the infant, it stops the commotion. Lewis points out that infants quickly learn elaborate means for securing and maintaining their caretaker's attention.

Researchers also note that the child's sex may play a part in influencing parental behavior. Brown and her associates (1975) found in a sample of urban black mothers that the mothers rubbed, patted, touched, kissed, rocked, and talked more to male than to female newborns. Similar findings concerning white mothers were reported by Moss (1967). It has also been found that mothers of firstborn infants spent more time feeding their infants than did mothers of later-born infants (Bakeman & Brown, 1977). Mothers most often hold babies to perform caretaking functions while fathers most often hold babies to play with them (Lamb, 1977) and Biller (1974, 1976) notes that mothers are more likely to inhibit their children's exploration of the environment while fathers encourage curiosity and challenge their children to attempt new cognitive and motor activities.

CHILDREARING PATTERNS AND PRACTICES

Social and behavioral scientists have long been interested in the effects that different childrearing practices have in shaping a child's personality and behavior. It is assumed that all parental actions, intentional or not, play a part in fashioning a child's potentialities. Researchers have attempted to identify the aspects of parental behavior that have especially strong influence. Three major dimensions repeatedly emerge in this research: (1) The warmth or hostility of the parent-child relationship (acceptance-rejection), (2) the control or autonomy of the disciplinary approach (restrictiveness-permissiveness), and (3) the consistency or inconsistency that parents show in using discipline.

Much research suggests that one of the most significant aspects of the family climate or home environment is the warmth of the relationship between parent and child (Sears, Maccoby, & Levin, 1957). Parents show warmth toward their children through affectionate accepting, approving, understanding, and child-centered behaviors. When disciplining their children, warm parents use words of encouragement and praise, tend to employ frequent explanations, and only infrequently resort to physical punishment. In contrast, hostility is shown through cold, rejecting, disapproving, self-centered, and highly punitive behaviors. Reviewing the research on parenting,

Becker (1964) found that love-oriented techniques tend to promote children's acceptance of self-responsibility and to foster self-control through inner mechanisms of guilt. In contrast, parental hostility interferes with conscience development and aggravates aggressiveness and resistance to authority.

Becker suggests that the effectiveness of love-oriented techniques comes from a number of factors. First, love tends to beget love. Accordingly, the parents become important to the child and the child wants to please the parents by complying to their wishes. This eliminates the need for severe punishment. Second, children reared by love-oriented techniques are not subjected to physical punishment and aggression in the home. Consequently, the parents serve as immediate and continual models of self-control and self-restraint. Third, love-oriented parents reason with their children and explain the reasons for various requests and rules. This facilitates communication of parental expectations and helps children anticipate the consequences of misbehavior.

The *control-autonomy* dimension concerns parental restriction of the child's behavior in such areas as sex play, modesty, table manners, toilet training, neatness, orderliness, care of household furniture, noise, obedience, and aggression toward others (Sears, Maccoby, & Levin, 1957; Becker, 1964). The research suggests that highly restrictive parenting fosters dependency and interferes with independence training (Maccoby & Masters, 1970). However, Becker mentions in his research review that it is difficult to come up with a "perfect" all-purpose set of parental guidelines because both permissiveness and restrictiveness entail certain risks. Restrictiveness fosters well-controlled, socialized behavior, but it also tends to lead to fearful, dependent, and submissive behaviors, and to a dulling of intellectual striving. Permissiveness, on the other hand, fosters outgoing, sociable, assertive behaviors and intellectual striving, but tends to inhibit persistence and to increase aggressiveness.

Some researchers believe that the control-autonomy dimension is made up of two related but distinguishable factors: first, a *psychological control* versus *psychological autonomy* dimension, and second, a *firm control* versus *lax control* dimension. Psychological control refers to "covert, psychological methods of controlling the child's activities and behaviors that would not permit the child to develop as an individual apart from the parent" (Schaefer, 1965, p. 555). Firmness of control indicates "the degree to which the parent makes rules and regulations, sets limits to the child's activities, and enforces these rules and limits." Armentrout and Burger (1972) asked 635 children to fill out a questionnaire reporting the childrearing behaviors used by their parents. The children attended the fourth through eighth grades at five working-class Catholic schools. Their responses were appraised in terms of the psychological control and firm-control dimensions. For the most part, the children perceived the psychological control exercised by their parents as decreasing from the fourth to sixth grades. At the same time, they felt that the firmness with which their parents enforced rules increased. In contrast, seventh and eighth graders reported a lessening in both psychological control and firmness of control. It seems that as parents relinquished some of the psychological control, they compensated at first by an increase in overt rule-making and limit-setting. Later, however, they progressively relinquished both types of control.

Diand Baumrind (1966; 1971a), a developmental psychologist, provides another scheme for examining and analyzing patterns of parental authority. She distinguishes among the terms authoritarian, authoritative, and permissive in defining parental control. The *authoritarian* parent tries to shape, control, and evaluate the child's behavior in accordance with traditional and absolute values and standards of conduct. Obedience is stressed, verbal give and take discouraged, and punitive forceful measures are used to curb the child's self-will when it conflicts with what the parent considers correct conduct. The parent attempts to inculcate respect for authority. The *author-*

itative parent, in comparison, provides firm direction for a child's overall activities but gives the child considerable freedom within reasonable limits. In other words, the parent attempts to direct the child's activities in a rational issue-oriented way. Parental control is not rigid, punitive, intrusive, or unnecessarily restrictive. The parent encourages verbal give and take and provides reasons for given policies, meanwhile responding to the child's wishes and needs. In contrast, the *permissive* parent avoids the responsibility of control by diverting or indulging the children in a nonpunitive accepting and affirmative environment. The children regulate their own behavior as much as possible. They are consulted about family policies and decisions and parents make few demands upon the children for household responsibility or orderly behavior. The permissive parent does not encourage children to adhere to external standards.

In a number of studies of white middle-class preschool children, Baumrind (1971) found that different types of parenting tend to be related to quite different behaviors in children. The offspring of authoritarian parents tended to be discontented, withdrawn, and distrustful. In contrast, authoritative parenting is often associated with self-reliant, self-controlled, explorative, and contented children. The least self-reliant, explorative, and self-controlled children were those with permissive parents who are warm but noncontrolling and nondemanding.

Based upon her research, Baumrind (1972) believes the types of behaviors most parents want to see in their children may be grouped under her label *instrumental competence.* These behaviors include friendliness, cooperation, achievement orientation, dominance (as opposed to submissiveness), and purposiveness. In short, the behaviors that characterize instrumental competence may be described as *socially responsible* and *independent.* These two dimensions of competence are of obvious value in an achievement-oriented society. In order to achieve instrumental competence it is helpful when the parents themselves are socially responsible and self-assertive and can serve as daily models of these behaviors. Parents should also be consistent in rewarding socially responsible and independent behavior and in punishing deviant behavior through operant conditioning techniques discussed in previous chapters. Non-rejecting parents are more attractive models than rejecting ones, though they should not be overprotective since they may inhibit the development of independence, shielding children from stress and providing easy alternative to self-mastery. Baumrind also suggests that parents encourage individuality, self-expression, initiative, divergent thinking, and socially appropriate aggressiveness, values which can be realized as parents make demands upon their children and assign them responsibilities. These practices are most successful if the children perceive their parents as being fair and when parents give reasons for their directives.

Baumrind's suggestions describe an ideal parental milieu and are, of course, easier said than followed. Given her guidelines, the parent still has to be the ultimate judge of whether a specific action is permissive or restrictive. Are we permissive if we let our youngster shout an insult to a neighbor or are we stifling self-expression if we forbid it? Are we overprotective if we do not allow our teenager to ride a bicycle with improper brakes or are we inhibiting self-mastery? It is obvious that psychologists can only give general guidelines and that the parent has to decide which specific action is to be encouraged or discouraged.

COMBINATIONS OF PARENTING DIMENSIONS

Two parents may both be highly permissive and deal with their children in a calm manner, yet they may still differ in other dimensions of parenting, affecting their children's personalities in different ways. One parent could be permissive, calm, and democratic; the other permissive, calm, and neglecting. Schaefer (1959) and Becker (1964) have explored the effects of various combinations of warmth-rejection and restrictiveness-permissiveness parenting. As the following table indicates, the parent in the warmth-restrictiveness category is likely to be indulgent and overindulgent, protective and overprotective, and also possessive. The child being reared in this milieu will tend to be submissive, dependent, polite, neat, obedient, minimally aggressive, and noncreative. Several experimenters have reported similar relationships. Eleanor Maccoby (1961) found that twelve-year-old boys who had been reared in warm and restrictive homes were strict rule enforcers with their peers. Compared with other children these boys also displayed less overt aggression, less misbehavior, and greater motivation toward school work. Another study by Kagan and Moss (1962) also showed that restrictiveness had an inhibiting effect on children from ages one to three. It had little effect between the ages three and six and an almost opposite effect from the ages six to ten. At that age children reacted to restrictiveness with hostility rather than submissiveness.

Children whose homes combine warmth with permissiveness tend to develop into socially competent, resourceful, friendly, active, and appropriately aggressive individuals (Kagan & Moss, 1962; Becker, 1964; Lavoie & Looft, 1973). Where parents encourage self-confidence, independence, and mastery in social and academic situations, the children are likely to show self-reliant, creative, goal-oriented, and responsible behavior. When parents fail to encourage independence, permissiveness often produces self-indulgent children with little impulse control and low academic standards.

Although permissiveness is a polar opposite of restrictiveness, it does not necessarily produce independent children. The way that permissiveness interacts with other dimensions is of crucial importance. Permissiveness in a climate of warmth seems to produce fairly positive characteristics (active, outgoing, creative, etc.). But when it is accompanied by high hostility, permissiveness is more likely to result in noncompliance

Table 5-1   Parental Environment and Its Consequences[a]

Milieu: warmth-restrictiveness		Milieu: warmth-permissiveness	
Parent	Child	Parent	Child
Indulgent	Submissive	Accepting	Active
Protective	Dependent	Cooperative	Outgoing
Possessive	Polite	Democratic	Friendly
	Neat	Liberal	Independent
	Obedient		Creative
	Nonaggressive		Normally
	Noncreative		aggressive
			Mature

Milieu: rejection-restrictiveness		Milieu: rejection-permissiveness	
Parent	Child	Parent	Child
Dictatorial	Neurotic	Detached	Impulsive
Antagonistic	Withdrawn	Indifferent	Maximally
	Shy	Neglecting	aggressive
	Quarrelsome		Delinquent
	Boys: self-		Disobedient
	aggressive		Goalless

[a]Modified after Becker (1964).

and aggressiveness. Many early studies of juvenile delinquents show that the delinquents' home evironments had exactly this combination of hostility and permissiveness (Bandura & Walters, 1959; McCord & Zola, 1959; Becker, 1964).

Rejection and restrictive parenting tend to interfere with children's developing self-identities and a sense of personal adequacy and competence. It fosters resentment and inner rage. Some of the anger is turned against the self or experienced as internalized turmoil and conflict which often results in "neurotic problems," self-punishing and suicidal tendencies, and inadequacy in adult role-playing (Becker, 1964).

The dimensions and their respective variables just discussed may be to some readers too abstract and too general to define the subtleties of parent-child interaction. Parents and children differ, both within the same family and between families so that in many respects each parent-child relation is unique (Elkind, 1979). The family climate is of course not the only factor influencing the socialization process. There are age, sex, and inborn temperament and health factors which partially determine a child's characteristics. Childrearing practices are also affected by social class, the number of children in the family, whether one, both, or neither parent works, and whether or not the parents are divorced or otherwise separated.

Social Class Differences

Both sociologists and psychologists have pointed out that different social classes experience the world in different ways. In 1958 Urie Bronfenbrenner surveyed studies of childrearing practices in various social classes during the previous twenty-five years. He concluded that class patterns in feeding, weaning, and toilet training reveal a clear and consistent trend. From about 1930 until the end of World War II, working-class mothers were uniformly more permissive than those of the middle class. After World War II the situation reversed itself: middle-class mothers became the more permissive. Even today Kagan (1978) reports that working-class American parents punish and restrict their children much more than middle-class parents, but the differences are not large enough to be of much practical significance.

The sociologist Kohn (1969), who studied middle-class and working-class parents, found that white-collar parents stress the development of internal standards of conduct in their children. In other words, they are more likely to discipline their children on the basis of their interpretation of the child's *intent* or motive for a particular act. In contrast, blue-collar parents place greater emphasis on conformity and tend to react to the consequences of the childrens' behavior. According to Kohn, middle-class mothers are more likely to use physical punishment when children "lose their temper" than when children engage in "wild play." "Loss of temper" is perceived as a loss of self-control, which is contrary to their expectations that children learn self-restraint. Working-class mothers use physical punishment in both situations. They are concerned with the disruptive consequences of both kinds of behavior—loss of temper and wild play. In 1974 Gecas and Nye, using another sample, confirmed Kohn's findings, but again they conclude that the difference between classes are not significantly large.

SIBLINGS — BIRTH ORDER

The number, sex, and spacing of siblings have been studied extensively for their effects on the child's development and socialization. An only child, an oldest child, a middle child, and a youngest child all seem to experience a different world of roles and relationships. Even though parents may facetiously say "never have a first baby," fortune seems to favor the first-born child. Research through the years has shown that first-borns are overrepresented in college populations (Altus, 1965), at the higher IQ levels (Zajonc, 1976), among National Merit and Rhodes scholars, in *Who's Who in America*, and among American presidents (52 percent). However, these birth-order advantages of first-borns do not seem to hold true for persons of lower socioeconomic class backgrounds (Glass, Neulinger, & Brim, 1974).

A cross-cultural study of thirty-nine societies reveals that first-borns are more likely than later-borns to receive elaborate birth ceremonies, to have authority over siblings, and to receive respect from siblings. When comparing sons, first-born sons have more control of property, more power in society, and higher social positions (Rosenblatt & Skooberg, 1974). What are the explanations to account for differences between first-born and later-born children? First, research suggests that parents attach greater importance to their first child (Sears, Maccoby & Levin, 1957; Clausen, 1966). There are more social, affectionate, and caretaking interactions between parents and their first-borns (Jacobs & Moss, 1976). It seems that first-borns spend more time with adult models and are thus exposed to more adult expectations and pressures. Also, parents generally have higher expectations for first-borns than for later-borns (Sutton-Smith & Rosenberg, 1970). This could certainly account for the fact that first-born children are more achievement-oriented than later-born children (Adams & Phillips, 1972).

A second explanation of the differences between first-born and second-born children may come from the interaction that takes place between siblings. Many times the first-born acts as a surrogate parent in dealing with later-born siblings and may become an adversary of the later-born children in dealing with the parents (Breland, 1974). This "helper" role appears to be instrumental in the development of verbal and cognitive skills (Cicirelli, 1973). Zajonc (1975) has further shown that the oldest sibling has a much richer intellectual environment than the later-born since the number of adult-mind interactions decrease as the number of interactions with child-sized minds increases. Zajonc suggests that we think in terms of the average developmental level of the people the infant contacts. The lower the average developmental level in the family, the slower the child's cognitive development will be. The first-born in a family encounters a very high average developmental level, since only the parents are involved. But the second child has the parents plus the older sibling. Suppose, for example, that an infant has a three-year old sibling who is still rather immature, so the maturity level of her surrounding is less than mature. With each succeeding child the average level drops and so does the IQ of the child.

If we follow Zajonc's suggestion further, we would expect that a child born after a large gap in the family should do better intellectually, since the older siblings are now quite a lot older and can provide higher levels of intellectual stimulation. In fact, such later-born children can have higher IQs on the average than we would expect from their family position. Zajonc's rather simplified conception of the influence of the environment must be viewed with caution but we cannot ignore the influence of older siblings. More recent research suggests that the decreasing performance for later-born children in large families can be reversed as older children mature and provide them with a richer environment (Davis, Cahan, & Bashi, 1977).

It was Alfred Adler (1870-1937), Freud's contemporary, who had still another explanation for the "superiority" of the first-born. He believed that a crucial event in the development of the first child was the "dethroning." With the birth of a sibling, the first-born suddenly loses the personal monopoly on parental attention. This loss, Adler said, arouses a strong lifelong need for recognition, attention, and approval which the child and later the adult seeks to acquire through high achievement. And Adler believed that the competitive race for achievement with older, more accomplished siblings is an equally critical factor in the development of personality in the later-born child.

Even a child's sex role identification may be influenced by the sex of his or her siblings. Helen Koch (1956), in one of the classic studies in the area, showed that children imitate their older siblings' behavior. Few children who grew up with brothers or sisters can deny that sibling relationships deeply influence the way children learn both to think of themselves and to relate to others. In families where parents are too busy to give attention to the children, siblings may even be the main socializing agents. Older siblings often act as models, and research suggests that children with older siblings of the same sex tend to show stronger sex-typed behavior than children whose older siblings are of a different sex (Koch, 1956; Sutton-Smith & Rosenberg, 1970). However, a study done by Gerald S. Leventhal (1970) reveals that men with older sisters often display more masculine behavior as traditionally defined in the United States than do men with older brothers. In a family of two male children, the younger boy may adopt behavior patterns opposite to those of his older brother to avoid unfavorable comparison with a more accomplished brother. But another study made by Karen Vroegh (1971) shows that neither the sex of all a child's siblings nor the sex of a child's older siblings has any consistent effect on sex role identity. Once more we must be cautious. The relationship between sex of a child's older siblings and sex role identity is considerably more complex than was once suggested by Koch's earlier research.

SINGLE PARENTING

The American family is in transition. According to the 1977 census and labor statistics, more adults are remaining single or postponing first marriages; the number of households composed entirely of unrelated persons is rising; divorces are rising; greater numbers of families are being maintained by persons without spouses; the number of youths living with one parent is increasing while the population of youths decreases and most mothers work. Only about one family in four now conforms to the stereotypical nuclear family—breadwinning Dad, homemaking Mom, and dependent children. Now more than half of all married women with school-age children hold some kind of job outside the home. At the end of the 1970s, couples with no children under 18 made up 47 percent of all families, which reflects both the longevity of American couples and the increasing number of those who are delaying or forgoing having children. At the same time, increases in divorce and children born to nonmarried parents have created millions of single-parent families while the rising rate of remarriage has produced the "blended" family. Family structures are shaky. About 38 percent of all first marriages fail and as many as four children out of ten born in the 1970s will spend part of their childhood in a single parent family, usually with the mother as head of the household; 17 percent of all children under 18 lived in single parent families in 1978 (Newsweek, May 15, 1978).

A decade ago the single-parent family was defined as a defective, lamentable arrangement. Many professionals referred to it as "broken," "disorganized," or "disintegrated". But recently the single-parent home has become increasingly recognized as a viable family form (Brandwein et al., 1974). The sociologist Rossi pointed out that what was defined a decade ago as "deviant" is today labeled "variant" in order to suggest that there is a healthy, experimental quality to current social explorations beyond monogamy or beyond the nuclear family. Single families are more likely to have economic problems, and are more dependent on welfare. In 1974, 51 percent of American children under the age of 18 who were living in homes with a female head also had an income that fell below the poverty level (U.S. Bureau of Census, 1975).

There are a number of reasons why mothers without husbands find themselves economically deprived: the greater prevalence of divorce, separation, and death among families at the lower socioeconomic levels; low and irregular payments for alimony, child support, and public assistance; fewer adult earners; fewer opportunities for female heads of families to work; and job discrimination against women, especially women with young children (Bane, 1976).

In the United States, the major cause of single-parent families is divorce. The most frequent family arrangement in the period immediately following a divorce is one in which children are living with their mothers and having only intermittent contact with their fathers. Mavis Hetherington and her coworkers (1976; 1977) made a two-year longitudinal study in which they matched one preschoold child in a divorced family with a child in an intact family on the basis of age, sex, birth-order position, and the age and education of the parents. Forty-eight divorced couples were paired with forty-eight intact families. It was found that the first year after the divorce was the most stressful for both parents because the divorced mother frequently felt helpless, physically unattractive, and of having lost the identity associated with her husband's status. Fathers complained of not knowing who they were, of being rootless, of having no structure or home in their lives. The separation induced profound feelings of loss, previously unrecognized dependency needs, guilt, anxiety, and depression in both parents. They often felt that they had failed as parents and spouses and doubted their ability to adjust well in any future marriages. They also felt they were socially inadequate and sexually incompetent.

The stresses and changes in life style following divorce are reflected in the parents' relationships with their children. Researchers found that the interaction patterns between divorced parents and their children differed significantly from those experienced in the intact families. Divorced parents made fewer demands, were less affectionate, and communicated less well. They were also less consistent in their discipline during the first year after their divorce. These deficiencies disappeared two years after divorce when positive relations return again.

With this information at hand, can we say that divorce is necessarily disastrous for the children? Most authorities do not believe that it is. Burchinal (1964) found small or nonexistent differences between children from one-parent and two-parent homes of comparable social status in respect to school achievement, social adjustment, and delinquent behavior. Moreover, adolescents from single parent homes show less delinquent behavior, less psychosomatic illness, and better adjustment to their parents than those from unhappy intact homes (Nye, 1957).

How do we then attempt to explain why children of divorced parents seem to have severe behavior problems if these problems seem not to be directly related to the disruption of the family bonds? Rutter (1974) has pointed out that behavior problems may derive from the difficulties in interpersonal relations with which the divorce is associated. Other researchers point to the part that parental conflict, tension, and discord play in feeding negative self-conceptions and identities and in jeopardizing a child's sense of well-being and security (Despert, 1953).

Psychiatrists and clinical psychologists report many cases in which divorce actually serves to reduce the amount of friction and unhappiness that a child experiences; consequently, divorce leads to better behavioral adjustments. Most divorced mothers believe that their children are living better lives in a divorced family than in a family disrupted by marital conflict (Goode, 1956). All in all, research strongly suggests that it is the *quality* of children's relationships with their parents that matters much more than the fact of the divorce (Rutter, 1974).

In the United States an estimated 800,000 men are raising minor children in homes without a mother. The number of single fathers has grown since more men are awarded custody of children in divorce proceedings and as a growing number of women are abandoning their families in search of new life styles and working opportunities. Only ten years ago a father was awarded custody of his children only if he could demonstrate in court that the mother was "unfit" for parenthood.

A number of studies have shown that even though single fathers are confronted with some unique adjustment requirements, most of them are successful in raising their children (Mendes, 1976, Gasser & Taylor, 1976; Orthner, et al. 1976). Single fathers with preschool children especially have difficulty in adjusting work and child care schedules. Many fathers try at first to have someone come into their homes and care for the children while they are at work. However, the vast majority soon find this to be an unsatisfactory arrangement. Fathers generally report that their children are inadequately supervised and cared for by hired baby sitters. In addition, this kind of arrangement tends to be unstable with a high turnover rate among the caretakers. As a consequence, fathers tend to make use of nurseries and child-care centers where there is a professional staff.

As has been pointed out earlier, *father absence* has a different effect on boys than on girls and it also makes a difference how old the child was when the father left and whether it was divorce or death that caused the separation. Boys seem to be more affected by father absence than girls. The absence of a positive father-son relationship seems to impair a boy's overall school and academic achievement and his IQ test performance (Biller, 1971; Epstein & Radin, 1975). The extent of the impairment is greater the younger the child was when he lost his father and the longer the father has been absent (Blanchard & Biller, 1971).

Since fathers are somewhat more preoccupied with urging their daughters to be feminine than with promoting their education, perhaps their absence influences the thoughts of their daughters more than those of their sons. A study by Santrock (1972) seems to support this assumption. There also seems to be a definite relation between the daughter's personality and the cause of her father's absence. Hetherington (1972) examined the personality of a group of girls who lost their fathers through death and compared it to a group whose fathers' absence was caused by divorce. One of the main differences observed was in the ways the girls interacted with males. The daughters of the divorcees sought more attention and physical contact from men, while the daughters of widows avoided males, preferring the company of females. While sitting in front of a male experimenter, Hetherington found that the daughters of divorcees tended to sprawl in the chair with an open-arm and -leg posture, often leaning slightly forward with one or both arms hooked over the back of the chair. In contrast, the daughters of widows sat more stiffly, often with their hands folded, with less eye contact and fewer smiles.

REMARRIAGE AND STEPPARENTING

But what of the single parent who remarries? Studies have shown that the mother's remarriage, especially if it occurs early in the child's life, appears to be associated with an improvement in intellectual performance on the part of the boy (Lessing et al., 1970; Santrock, 1972). What happens when the single mother with her children merge into a marital relationship with a single father and his children? The experts call this arrangement a "blended" or "reconstituted" family which can be complicated by extraordinary feelings of sibling rivalry and parental jealousy. Each adult member has to deal with his or her former spouse as well as with the former spouse of the current partner. Then there are stepparent-stepchildren relationships—one's own childrens' reactions to the current spouse, one's reactions to the current spouse's children, and the children's reactions to one another. Approximately 40 million Americans today have made the decision to deal with the jealousies, mixed loyalties, and changed life styles that come with marrying an entire family. According to parents who have experienced this situation, there is no easy role to assume when one becomes a stepparent.

As mentioned in their book *Stepparenting*, Jean and Veryl Rosenbaum believe that loyalty is one of the hardest problems for both children and stepparents to cope with. The children may feel that the stepparents are trying to replace the real parent, or else they may feel guilty if they begin to like the new parent. Children may have been hurt when the natural parent left and they may worry that this could happen again with the new stepparent. As one six-year old said, "I'm going to love my real mother the most until I am eight and then I'm going to love my new mother the most." This is the kind of problem that certainly challenges a stepparent. Being a stepparent means focusing on the children, but the stability of the stepparent relationship is the key to success in fulfilling that role. They must be a couple first; the children then have to be integrated into that relationship.

Most "blended" couples find that disciplining someone else's children is a big problem. The natural parent also may feel some antagonism when his or her child is disciplined by someone else. Therefore, there may be the tendency for the disciplining parent to be more authoritarian with natural children and more lenient with the stepchildren. Because of this approach some stepparents report that they consider their stepchildren more as friends than just stepchildren.

WORKING MOTHERS

Bronfenbrenner (1978) has voiced his concern that a mother who cannot be at home when her children are home, no matter how excellent she may be in other respects, cannot fulfill her role as a mother. Many modern mothers also share this concern and feel uneasy about placing the responsibility of childrearing with someone else. But need they worry about the consequences of day care? Cherry and Eaton (1977) studied 200 lower-income families in order to determine possible harmful outcomes due to maternal employment during a child's first three years of life. When the children were seven and eight years old, they were all compared with respect to physical growth and scholastic performance. It was found that those whose mothers had worked were no different in physical and mental development from those whose mothers had not worked.

The results of several other recent comparisons between day-care and home-reared children likewise reveal no important differences. In a study done by Kagan et al. (1978), the psychological development of 33 infants who attended a specially run day-care center from three and one-half months through 29 months of age was compared with infants of similar ethnicity and social class who were being raised at home. The subjects were assessed on eight separate occasions with a battery of procedures designed to evaluate attentiveness, sensitivity to discrepancy, fearfulness, language, memory, social behavior, and attachment to mother. There were no important differences between the day-care and home-reared children. But good quality day care is important. The ideal ratio of staff to children should be low—about three infants to one staff member during the first two years of life and seven to ten children to one caretaker during the years from two through five. The caretaking staff should be reasonably knowledgeable about child development and be sensitive to the values of the families in their charges. Finally, the children should have the opportunity to practice the linguistic, inferential, and social skills valued by their society. If these conditions are met, children raised in day-care centers and those brought up entirely at home seem to be equally mature, socially competent, and attached to their mothers.

Chapter 6

SEX ROLES

In its existence mankind has never experienced such distinct and rapid sociobiological changes as those which occurred in the 1960s and 1970s with respect to the woman's life cycle, to the number of children born, and to the age composition of the population. Medical advances of the last century have caused the infant mortality rate to decrease in the developed countries from 250 to about 15 deaths per 1,000 live births and women live now almost twice as long as they did a hundred years ago. Since a woman, on the average, needs to bear only 2.1 children to maintain the present population figures, only about one-fifth or so of her adult life will be taken up by childrearing tasks. Further changes which evolved through technological advances have made physical strength economically unimportant and females are now able to perform as well as males on all jobs. Economically and perhaps psychologically, there seems to be no reason for the sex roles which have been in our culture since biblical times to be maintained. Yet sex-role changes leading towards equalization of the sexes are difficult to accomplish:

our roles are taught to us throughout our entire socialization process, by many facets of our culture, often in redundant and overlapping ways. In this chapter we shall examine the various parental, educational, and economic factors which condition our sex roles. We shall also discuss certain equalization approaches, their suggested modes, and their psychological feasibilities.

ORIGINS

Sex roles have a long past but a short history. They existed for millions of years, but it is only recently that we have questioned them, wondering whether they are fair, useful, or necessary. With this questioning began an interest in their origin. Are they biological and have they always existed? Are they conditioned and, if so, when and by whom? Anthropological accounts indicate that in almost all cultures men were more dominant and aggressive than women. Stephen Goldberg (1974), in his book *The Inevitability of Patriarchy,* points out that male dominance existed for thousands of years in many isolated cultures and he suggests therefore that patriarchy is genetically determined and is not a cultural coincidence. The anthropologists Kay Martin and Barbara Voorhies (1975) describe some cultures in which women had certain powers through the manufacture and distribution of goods. Though in general they agree with Goldberg on the ubiquity of male rule, they believe that sex roles—whether or not they are of biological origin—should be abandoned if they become a hinderance for one or both sexes.

The industrial revolution, which freed the males from heavy work to which they are biologically better fitted than women, did not free women of their biological task—childbearing. Moreover, the sex roles became more pronounced with the separation of the workplaces into home and factory. In spite of this crystallization of sex roles, they were generally accepted because they were a biological, an economic, and consequently a psychological necessity. What is a necessity is often capitalized into a virtue and both sexes took pride in their roles without questioning. Only until very recently were the sex roles questioned and suggestions for their equalization made.

How much of our sex-role behavior is inherited and how much is culturally conditioned? This issue is of concern to many who advocate sex-role changes or abolishment because of the strong belief in America that the inhibition of any natural desire is detrimental to a person's normal development. Though seemingly unnecessary, those who advocate sex-role changes are inclined to maintain that all sex-role behavior is solely a matter of social conditioning. The evidence, however, is unclear one way or the other. There are a number of distinct anatomical, hormonal, and other physiological differences between the sexes, some of which have already been pointed out in the chapter on maturation. But in general it is not known if and to what degree these differences influence the behavior, attitudes, and feelings of females and males.

To mention a few inherited sex differences aside from the obvious (or not so obvious) anatomical ones, males in comparison to females are aborted more often in the fetal stages, develop slower after birth, are more colicky, more active, sleep less during infancy, and have about five times more difficulties with such problems as bedwetting, stuttering, autism, dyslexia, and hyperactivity. Yet adulthood males weigh on the average 20% more and are 6% taller, but die seven years earlier. Their pulse rate is slower, their red blood count higher. Females, in comparison, are more mature in their skeletal development, being two months ahead at birth and two years ahead at puberty. Between the ages of six and nine they are slightly taller. In early infancy girls sleep longer than boys, babble and vocalize more. Throughout their lives the sexes produce different hormones in different amounts. At adolescence the male's testosterone level increases tenfold. At around age 60 it begins to diminish to almost zero unless the male keeps sexually active or resumes sexual activity whereby he can maintain the hormone level of his younger years (Elias et al., 1977). In contrast, the estrogen level of the female does not seem to depend on her sexual activities. It diminishes after menopause whether intercourse is practiced or not.

Many studies have tried to examine whether the male hormone, testosterone, forms a biological basis for male aggression. This connection has been well established on the animal level. When animals are injected with male hormones they become more aggressive and more active sexually. This was observed as early as 1849 by Arnold Berthold who discovered the action of testosterone by transplanting testes into the abdominal cavity of a castrated rooster whereafter the rooster's characteristic masculine activities, such as crowing and mating, reappeared. There seems to be a dynamic relationship between testosterone and aggression. While the hormone can cause aggressive behavior, the behavior can also affect the hormone level. For example, when a male rhesus monkey is put into a cage with dominant male monkeys and subjected to defeat, his testosterone level will diminish, but it will be rapidly restored to normal if he is exposed to female companions (McEwen, 1976). There are fewer hormone experiments with humans. Testosterone injections administered to male homosexuals increased their sexual desires but did not change the objects of their affection from male to female as the investigators had hoped (Glass and Johnson, 1944). The findings that older men can increase their hormone level by engaging in intercourse after a period of abstinence show again the reciprocal effect of biology and environment.

While the evidence for the biological nature of male aggression is inconclusive there is also no evidence for its cultural origin. One could also hypothesize that our present culture inhibits male aggression and that without our cultural influence boys would be even more aggressive, perhaps as described in Golding's *The Lord of the Flies*. As mentioned before, it is not necessarily detrimental to inhibit a biologically caused behavior. Whether or not hunting, for example, is biologically or culturally conditioned, it must be inhibited among city dwellers as it is counterproductive to their survival.

There are other aspects of sex-role behavior where interaction between heredity and environment has been postulated. It has been observed by Moss (1967) that mothers cuddle and hold their newly-born boys for longer periods than their newly-born girls. Moss believes that mothers react to the more restless behaviors of their boys by trying to calm them. After the infants are several months old the mothers change their behavior. Taking care of three-month-old infants, mothers spend more time vocalizing with their girls than with their boys. Again, this extra vocalization may be a reaction to the girls who begin to babble sooner than boys. It should be pointed out that certain biological sex differences are minimal in their initial stages but can become more pronounced if they are reinforced by the environment—mostly by the mother. Mistakenly, heredity and environment are often seen as opposing each other. In many instances, however, they go hand in hand. Children who babble more stimulate their parents to babble and vocalize back to them and are thereby given more reinforcement for further babbling. This type of *interaction* between heredity and environment occurs throughout our entire lives. It is the adolescent who is by nature big and strong whom the coach selects to play football and who receives the extra environmental training that makes him still stronger. The weak adolescent who needs most to be strong is not selected.

Another type of interaction between heredity and environment exists when two individuals receive the same environmental treatment which has, however, a differential effect because the two individuals are biologically different. For example, when Heinstein (1963) examined the effects of bottle- and breast-feeding he found that bottle-fed boys, in comparison to bottle-fed girls, are more frequent bedwetters, but have fewer fears and better appetites. When both sexes are being breast-fed these effects reverse themselves with the girls being the more frequent bedwetters, having fewer fears and better appetites.

This example shows the intricate and often confounded relationship between heredity and environment which will again be mentioned in the discussion on intelligence in a following chapter.

A number of studies of sex roles are concerned with their onset. In the course of human development sex-roles manifest themselves earliest in the play behavior of young children. In a very detailed experiment, McCall (1974) investigated manipulative play behaviors of infants between 8 and 11 months old. He presented toys varying in configuration, plasticity, sound quality, and familiarity to both infants and mothers, and he observed the infant's selection preferences, length of playtime, and attention. He found no consistent sex differences in the nature of the play behavior, nor in the preference for any toy. However, at the 13–15 month level, McCall found that males played more vigorously with mechanical and manipulative toys and girls more often with stuffed animals and cuddly toys. These differences, however, were small and dependent on specific toys. These minimal differences seem to increase slowly until they crystallize by the end of the second year. The activities of two-year-olds were studied in several experiments and it was generally found that girls were more likely to paint, help the teacher, look at books, and listen to stories. Boys preferred to hammer and to play with transportation toys. At this age boys were observed to have a larger range of selection, spending more time than girls in opposite-sex activities (Etaugh, et al., 1975; Fein, et al., 1975). This trend, as already mentioned, reverses itself in middle childhood when girls play quite often with boys' toys, but boys rarely with girls' toys (Rosenberg & Sutton-Smith, 1960).

CONDITIONING

How does the parent teach sex roles? This is easy to answer for those families in which the children are only given "sex-appropriate" toys. But sex roles have also been observed in families who made special efforts to eliminate them by giving their children both sex "appropriate" and "inappropriate" toys. Fagot (1974) interviewed parents of two-year-olds as to their sex-role attitudes. She found some parents who were very conservative and others who were very egalitarian who tried to raise their children without sex stereotypes. However, when Fagot observed the children of both groups in a nursery situation whe found no differences among them. The children of the egalitarian parents showed the same sex-role stereotypes, as measured by a toy preference test, as those of the conservative parents.

It is possible that even those parents who try not to teach role behavior do so unintentionally. An experiment by Will et al. (1976) describes such a differential treatment of which the parent was quite unaware. As already mentioned in our discussion on learning, a six-month-old boy was presented to some mothers with blue pants under the name of "Adam" and to others with a pink dress and the name of "Beth." The mothers were asked to hold the infant and to play with him or her for several minutes. All mothers had small children of both sexes of their own and most of them reported that they perceived no differences in the action of their male and female infants and that they encouraged roughhouse play with their own daughters and doll play with their sons. Yet in the experimental situation they handed a doll, which was in the experimental room, more often to "Beth," and a train, which was also present, more often to "Adam." The mothers also smiled more often when they believed they were holding a female, but none were aware of this differential treatment. Other differential interaction patterns such as mother-son and father-daughter relationships have already been discussed in the chapter on parental milieu.

The type of learning which results from situations such as the above may be called "habit formation." By being given the sex-appropriate toys the children become accustomed to playing with them and at the same time they do not become familiar with the sex-inappropriate toys. In this type of learning the choice is made by the parent and the toy itself, its color, form, or manuverability constitutes the reward. There is also "instrumental" learning by which sex roles become established at a very early age. As previously described (see "Learning"), the behavior in this type of conditioning is "emitted," meaning that the choice of a certain toy is made by the child and after that choice has been made it is rewarded, ignored, or perhaps punished by the parent. If children have both dolls and trucks, for instance they may initially touch both of these toys equally often. But if a girl touches the doll the parents may nod somewhat more approvingly, smile, and talk in a more pleasant voice than they would if the girl touches the truck. The parental rewards or approvals and disapprovals may be reversed when a boy touches or plays with the respective toys. Margolin and Patterson (1975) have tried to analyze the parents' actions by which they reinforce or inhibit their children's actions. As positive rewards or reinforcers they list approval, attention, compliance, laugh, play, talk, and touch; those actions listed that inhibit behavior are negative command, disapproval, humiliate, ignore, noncompliance, tease, and yell. Any such actions, whether approving or disapproving, are also called "contingencies" because the parent's action is contingent upon (comes after) the child's action. The above listings, to which nonverbal responses such as facial expressions and body motions may be added, show that parental contingencies can be expressed in a variety of ways and that it is not surprising that parents are not always aware when and how they approve or disapprove a certain toy selection or any other behavior of their children. Perhaps this explains Fagot's findings that children of "egalitarian" parents learned the sex-role stereotypes to the same degree as children of "conservative" parents.

Few studies have as yet been designed to tell us which specific sex-role behaviors are conditioned by which specific parental contingencies, although some general aspects of these contingencies are known. Fagot (1974) observed, for instance, that both parents gave girls more praise as well as more criticism and that they joined boys' play more actively than girls' play. In another study it was shown that fathers gave twice as many positive responses to their sons as to their daughters, whereas mothers gave almost the same number of positive responses to boys and girls. Therefore, boys received more total positive rewards from both parents together than girls, since the parents did not differ in the total number of rewards they gave (Margolin & Patterson, 1975).

MODELING

At the three-year level, toy preferences are quite distinct. McCandless and Evans (1973), who observed three-year-olds in a nursery, found that girls play about 90% of the time at "girlish" activities, and boys at "boyish" activities 90% of the time, in spite of the fact that both sexes are much more often rewarded for girlish than for boyish activities. A count showed that out of 230 rewards given to boys, 198 were for such "feminine" activities as painting and art work and only 32 for such "masculine" tasks as block building and playing with transportation toys. It is not surprising that both female and male nursery teachers are more anxious to reward female activities since hammering, riding a tricycle, or fighting are annoying in the usually restricted space of a nursery school. More surprising is the observation that the boys were not influenced by the frequent rewards. After a year's observation period McCandless and Evans found that the boys had not changed. They still engaged in "boyish" activities about 90% of the time.

If instrumental conditioning is effective on the two-year-level, we may ask why it is ineffective with three- and four-year-old boys who do not seem to respond to the frequent reinforcement they receive for their feminine activities. We may postulate that they have been too thoroughly conditioned by their parents when they were two years old. However, it is more likely that children begin to model sex roles around the age of three, at a time when the, are first able to form a "self-awareness" about their own sex. There is much evidence that children model other children, adolescents, and adults of their own sex more than members of the opposite sex. Bandura (1965), in a much popularized experiment, investigated the modeling of aggression and found distinct sex differences in the performance of aggression. His subjects, boys and girls between the ages of three and five, watched a five-minute television program in which a man model pushed, beat up, and scolded an adult-sized, plastic doll called "Bobo." After the film the children were taken into a playroom containing a Bobo doll, balls, mallets, dart guns, as well as some nonaggressive toys such as farm animals and miniature furniture. In this active play situation the boys modeled aggression about twice as often as the girls, attacking "Bobo" on the average about four times in a ten-minute period.

It is very difficult to teach children sex-role equality, or to teach them that sex roles exist but ought not to, when they live in a culture where certain behaviors are only modeled by one sex or the other. In the U.S. pipes and cigars are smoked almost exclusively by males, skirts are worn by women, and children rarely see a couple in which the man is smaller than the woman. No wonder that a child forms categories and a strong belief that what the sexes do has to be that way. Even mere sex-role labels become strong motivators. Montemayor (1974) presented children between six and eight years with a neutral toy figure into which marbles could be inserted. He found that boys inserted more marbles into the toy when it was labeled as a toy for boys and that girls played more often with it when labeled a toy for girls. Another experiment by Wolf (1973) showed the influence of an actual person playing with a sex-inappropriate toy. This experiment was conducted in a summer camp and involved eight- and nine-year-old boys and girls. Some boys watched another boy, the model, play with a toy oven and kettle—the sex inappropriate toy. After a few minutes the model left and the boy who had watched was left alone with the toy. Other boys watched a girl-model play with the oven and kettle whereafter they were likewise left alone. The experimenter who was hidden in a nearby Jeep observed that the boys who had watched the girl-model did not play with the oven and kettle when alone, while those boys who had watched the boy-model did. "Same-sex" modeling was also effective for girls who saw another girl play with a truck and tire. Wolf's data show the strong influence of "same-sex" modeling. The appropriate sex won out over the inappropriate toy.

As has been shown, the cultural conditioning of sex roles, like the socialization process in general, occurs through various methods and agents. Mothers, fathers, siblings, peers, relatives, teachers, and TV at times all supply differential rewards to the actions of boys and girls and they also serve as models for the formation of sex roles. Because of this overabundance of causes the omission of any single one does not seem to alter the development of sex roles. Children in day-care centers show as much sex-role behavior as children reared at home and boys who grow up in fatherless homes develop similar sex roles as those who grow up with fathers. This causal redundancy makes it difficult for the experimental psychologist to pinpoint any specific causes and it also makes the task of equalizing any sex-role differences rather complicated.

EDUCATION

Our educational system is an additional source for the development of sex roles and it has received much criticism for propagating them. For decades the reading material used in the primary grades presented the sexes in the usual "stereotyped" manner—the males as heros and inventors, the females as mothers and housewives. In the 1970s, however, many textbook firms have published new primer series portraying females and males in equal numbers and in equally "important" occupations. In education it has always been a question whether children should be taught "what is" or "what ought to be." In other words, should our education reflect the existing social trend or should it pioneer in new social orders, and if so, how much effort should be expended toward the new? It is conceivable that our primers are unconvincing if the pupils read in them that Jane is a firefighter and Dick a nurse when on the outside almost all firemen are males and almost all (98%) nurses are females. The sex-role equalization in the schools is similar to the busing issue: the implementation of the integration is left to the children while the adults are unable or unwilling to model it by moving into each others' neighborhoods.

Whether and to what degree our educational system reinforces the sex roles that exist outside of school is difficult to judge, but many surveys show that there is a difference in the average school performance between the sexes. Most notable are the differences between the performances in science and literature. A "National Assessment of Educational Progress" study (Sauls & Larson, 1975) showed that the sexes' performances are equal in all subjects up to the age of nine. By the age of 13, however, females have fallen back in arithmetic and geometry and remain behind in their adult years. On the other hand, females are ahead in their reading ability and in their literary knowledge. The causes of these differences, which had also been observed in previous decades (Binet, 1908; Book, 1932; Tyler, 1965), are difficult to discern. It has been found that female infants babble more than male infants (Moss, 1967) and that girls are significantly more advanced in language acquisition at the toddler age. Schachter et al. (1978) report, for instance, that the longest utterances of toddler girls consisted on the average of 4.6 words and those of boys of 3.5 words. It has been postulated by Moss that the girls' earlier maturation, which in turn elicits environmentally more linguistic stimulation, is responsible for their early language acquisition. Females maintain their linguistic advantage throughout their lives. In early childhood they engage in more verbal play activities and in the first grades they are better readers and have superior word recognition. Maccoby and Jacklin (1974) point out that female superiority increases through high school and possibly beyond. More specifically, girls are superior in such tasks as understanding and producing language, verbal analogies, creative writing, word fluency, and spelling.

Unlike the girls' liguistic advances, which already manifest themselves in infancy, the boys' numerical and spatial abilities do not become apparent until the third or fourth grade. The boys maintain this lead throughout high school and college, although women do better in computations and counting. This perhaps contributes to the fact that girls receive better arithmetic grades than boys while in grammar school. It should also be mentioned that grades reflect the amount of work done, attentiveness, and cooperation (areas in which girls excel) rather than capacity or how fast and how well something is learned. The abilities and interests between the sexes with respect to literature and science do not become equalized during a decade or more of schooling. To the contrary, the differences widen during high school and again during the college years as more and more women select the pursuit of humanistic subjects rather than of the sciences. The proportion of women graduating from college in some of the more verbal disciplines are 75% in education, 75% in foreign languages, and 65% in English, but only 10% in physics and 2% in engineering (Yearbook of Higher Education, 1977/78).

Whether by nature or by environment or by both, girls are advanced in liguistic skills by the time they enter high school. Here they have a choice whether or not to take science subjects. Except for a year or two of mathematics, science courses (especially chemistry and physics) are electives in most American high schools, while several years of English are required. This tends to give the (false?) impression that the humanities are more important for one's education than the sciences. In addition to this glorification females feel more competent in the literary subjects and it is not surprising that they choose them in preference to the sciences. Even a very slight preference will tip the scale if there is a choice. Their choice is reinforced further by modeling. In coeducational high schools about three-fourths of the pupils attending physics classes are males and it is easy for an entering freshman girl to get the impression that physics is for boys. Ormerod (1975) found that females in British coeducational colleges harbor more prejudice against physics, chemistry, and mathematics than females in all-women institutions.

The elective system in the American high schools favors the males because they are required to take several years of English and thus "forced" (if they want to graduate) to get more practice in the linguistic area in which they are deficient. Girls, on the other hand, need not take any courses in the area in which they are less competent. In spirit, the educational policies of "electives" and coeducation may have been designed to further the educational and social equality of the sexes. In practice, however, they seem to allow the reinforcement of the literary preferences the females obtained before entering high school. In most other countries sciences are not electives. In order to graduate from high school every student—male or female—has to have four years of chemistry, biology, mathematics, and physics. This gives every high school graduate the prerequisite for studying medicine, dentistry, or any other science. If they choose not to enter these areas it is not because they lack the skills to pursue them. In some Western countries, for instance, up to 25% of dentists are women; in eastern European countries, 50 to 80%. In the U.S. only about 2% of dentists are women. If we are free to choose upon high school entrance we may be less free to choose after graduation. Sometimes the freedom of choice plays peculiar tricks.

INEQUALITIES

Women have become more dependent on work in order to satisfy basic needs, economic independence, or vocational interests. From 1955 to 1975, 17 million women joined the U.S.

work force in comparison to 15 million men (U.S. News & World Report, 1975). In all Western countries 30 to 50% of all women work; in Eastern European countries, 60 to 90%. In the West women earn from 30 to 40% less than men. In comparison to men, the proportion of women is higher in lower-paying occupations. There is also an inequality in the home. The Hungarian sociologist Alexander Szalai (1972) investigated how people in twelve different countries use their time. He found that single males spend, on the average, 25 minutes per day on housework; single women spend about 2.5 hours. When married, working, and without children, the male will increase his daily housework to 35 minutes, the female to 4 hours. Couples with children keep about the same hours as those without. Szalai also found that the full-time housewife in Jackson, Michigan, who has all the modern household appliances spends as much time (7 hours per day) doing housework as her equivalent in Kragujevac, Yugoslavia, who has none of the modern conveniences, no running water, and only a wood stove to cook on.

While the necessity of some of the housework can be argued, childcare is a continuous must for many years. In most single as well as two-parent families, it is almost entirely done by women. As already mentioned, one study found that fathers interact vocally with their newly borns only 37 seconds per day. In the U.S. alone, about 12 million women who work have children of preschool age.

There are also many social and political inequalities in sex roles. Even though the law guarantees equality there are still social barriers for women taking the initiative in dating, going to bars alone, etc. There have been very few women in political positions on the upper echelon. In the 1970s only one woman was elected to the U.S. Senate, none appointed to the U. S. Supreme Court, and only two were among the fifty state governors. Not all sex-role inequalities are to the woman's detriment. About five times as many men as women are arrested for crimes and thirty times more men than women are in prisons. Women commit less severe crimes than men, and they are also less likely to receive prisons terms for crimes of equal severity.

Psychologically both men and women see themselves quite differently in many respects. Even very young children believe that they should only play with certain sex-appropriate toys and by the time they enter school the sexes wish for themselves different professions—most of the boys want to be policemen, most of the girls nurses. (They apparently want to make the world safe and healthy.) Girls engage more in boyish activities than vice versa, a "tomboy" being socially more acceptable than a "sissy." In spite of or on account of these additional choices, girls wish more often than boys to be of the other sex. Several surveys show that adults of both sexes believe it is better to be male. In China (Snow, 1971) as well as in the U.S. (Peterson, 1973), about 90% of both males and females wish that they would have a boy if they would have only one child. Several surveys have shown that adults characterize males with more favorable attitudes than females. Williams and Bennett (1975) used a psychological scale, the "Adjective Checklist," on which they had their subjects indicate whether an adjective better described males or females. Among the 300 adjectives on this list, 33 were associated with men and 30 with women by more than 90% of both female and male raters. Among those considered as typically masculine were: adventurous, aggressive, coarse, confident, forceful, independent, stern, strong, tough, and unemotional. Among those judged as typically female were: affectionate, emotional, fickle, flirtatious, fussy, nagging, prudish, sentimental, submissive, and whiny. It is readily apparent that there are many more "positive" or "favorable" adjectives among those ascribed to males than to females. Many more studies could be cited to attest to the attitudes and the stereotypes people hold toward each sex. These beliefs can be found at all age levels, in almost all countries, and are held by males as well as females, though females hold these beliefs to a lesser degree.

APPROACHES TO EQUALIZATION

Since man is seen in a more favorable position it is understandable that the major emancipation efforts are directed towards the "masculinization" of women. The suffragists at the turn of the century demanded voting rights and access to jobs which males had preserved for themselves. However, after the voting rights were obtained women did not use them in their favor as they voted in the same porportions as the men did for candidates and issues. The present concern about sex roles was first aroused by the French writer Simone de Beauvoir in the 1950s. In her book, *The Second Sex,* she maintains that motherhood is not an instinctual nor a social must and that females will only be equal if they no longer bear children and do housework. Influenced by de Beauvoir's writing, Betty Friedan wrote *The Feminine Mystique* (1963) in the U.S., in which she advocates the education of women so that they will be able to compete with men in the business world. The sociologist Jo Freeman (1973) considers Betty Friedan's book and the addition of the word "sex" to Title VII of the 1964 U.S. Civil Rights Act the two most important events in the women's liberation movement.

The masculinization efforts have only been partially successful. Women do have fewer children and in the U.S. they graduate from college in almost the same numbers as men. But this increased education did not narrow the pay gap between the sexes as envisioned by Betty Friedan. To the contrary, the pay gap widened as the difference in pay increased from 37% in 1956 to 43% in 1974 (U.S. News & World Report, 1975).

Another approach to equalization is the "feminization" of males. This means that men should be less aggressive and less driving in the business world and should spend more time at childcare and housework. Fathering has not been too popular. In spite of such books as *Father Power* (Biller & Meredith, 1974) and *What's a Father For?* (Gilbert, 1975) it was estimated that only about 10,000 children from 6 million born annually receive solo fathering (Time, 1975). In Sweden, one of the first countries to legislate equal rights, either parent can obtain a year's leave with pay from any type of job (the baby-year) after a child is born, but only 7% of the fathers make use of this "privilege." One of the legislators in Germany, where similar benefits are planned, proposed that a full year can only be granted if each parent takes six months leave from work.

An amalgamation of masculinization and feminization is the "androgyny" approach (andr=man, gyne=woman). It means that each sex acquires the sex-role characteristics of the other sex in addition to its own. The psychologist Sandra Bem (1975), who designed an androgny scale, the "Bem Sex Role Inventory," envisions the androgynous individual as being less restrained by conventional sex roles, and as being more flexible and freer to choose from both feminine and masculine response repertoires according to the appropriateness of the situation. Bem (1976) has called these characteristics a "psychological bisexuality."

Though androgyny is often recommended, details about its mode and its consequences have not been worked out. It may be relatively simple to train a person to have both masculine and feminine traits which do not interfere with each other as, for instance, being "intellectual" and being "gentle." The acquisition of such opposing traits as "aggression" and "submission," however, may be much more problematical. It may lead to frustration and perhaps to inactivity unless additional guidelines are given which tell the individual when to be aggressive and when to be submissive. In an adrogynous society both sexes would have to be taught to accept the same values so that they would react alike in like situations. The question remains whether people would be freer reacting to the dictates of the situation than to the dictates of their respective sex role. Would it still be possible for some girls to play only with dolls and for some boys to play only with trains? If psychologists succeed in making all people alike with respect to their male-female characteristics and perhaps also with respect to their IQs, they may soon make Huxley's "brave new world" braver.

Equalization approaches, whether based on masculinization, feminization, or androgyny, have largely been unsuccessful because habits and beliefs cannot be changed as fast as laws can. One of the greatest hinderances to equalization is the pay gap between the sexes. In spite of the fact that the number of women college graduates has doubled during the last decade, that the Equal Rights Act demands equal pay for equal work, and that 14,000 women, including the wives of three presidents, attended the "National Women's Conference" in Houson, Texas, in 1977, there has been a small but constant decrease in the earnings of women in comparison to those of males. Even women who in general are not sympathetic to the liberation movement find the females' lesser earnings disturbing and unfair.

Several factors may be responsible for this comparative decrease. In what has been called the "life cycle squeeze," many women in their forties enter employment for the first time to offset the effects of inflation and to supplement the family income needed to support their teenage children. Most of these women must accept low-paying jobs because they are unskilled and lack seniority. Another factor is that of "crowding." Fuchs (1975) has pointed out that about two-thirds of all employed women work in only seven occupations: secretarial, retail sales, household, teaching, bookkeeping, waitress, and nursing, and more than 50% of all professional women "crowd" into two professions—teaching and nursing. When crowding occurs women compete against each other and some economists believe that this lowers their income.

As mentioned previously, women scarcely participate in any of technological and engineering work. Of over 1 million engineers in the U.S. only 1% are women. Florman (1978) believes that the females' aversion towards engineering is class-related. He found that male engineering students came mostly from lower class families and that some decades ago few daughters of lower class families went to college. Children of upper class families—sons and daughters—rarely studied engineering. Whatever the reasons, the dearth of women in the mechanical and engineering fields deprives them of a good portion of their earning potential. Labor in our society becomes less and less important as mechanization progresses. Due to mechanization, only 4% of Americans work in agriculture and are capable of producing twice as much food as the country needs. Our future and that of many third-world countries will depend more and more on technological accomplishments, especially in the areas of transportation and energy consumption. It is unlikely that women will reach financial equality in a free-market economy unless they participate in equal numbers in technological planning and production. Perhaps equally important as their financial gains would be their full partnership in the development of our future society.

While we can describe some of the final solutions necessary for economic equalization such as "equal participation in technology," there is still much guesswork as to how to accomplish such aims. Should we, for instance, motivate young girls to play with transportation toys, introduce mechanical courses in grammar school, and require physics in high school? The sexes could become equal without becoming psychologically, educationally, and vocationally alike. We may wonder if inequalities would still be felt if there were equal respect and equal remuneration for all types of work, for office management as well as for secretarial work, for housework as well as for mechanical work, and so on—if our economic equality would not be related to the length and the type of education we receive or choose for ourselves. None of these questions can be answered unless some of these changes are implemented and their results examined a decade or so later.

Chapter 7

SOCIALIZATION ISSUES

Children can be well nourished without eating spinach. Youngsters can masturbate without becoming crazy and it does not hurt adolescents to know all about sex. Changes in values and in psychological and physiological information have made certain childrearing and educational practices questionable. In this chapter we shall discuss some socialization practices such as birth, contact-love, toilet training, and sexual practices—about which psychologists, as well as the public, have different opinions.

Birth: Linked to the advances in medical technology, the birth process has undergone drastic changes during the last century—from births attended by midwives at home to modern hospital settings. As already mentioned, the death rate has drastically decreased from about 200 to 15 deaths per 1,000 live births. In spite of this tremendous advancement further improvements are frequently suggested—especially on the psychological level. During the 1940s pediatricians and psychologists became concerned about the sedatives given to mothers to alleviate labor and birth pains. These sedatives enter the bloodstream of the baby and it was feared that they retarded the onset of breathing. The brain can be without oxygen only a few minutes and a delay in breathing may permanently damage it. In order to prevent this delay, anesthesia techniques through a spinal block were more frequently applied. This method anesthetizes the spinal cord directly without first permeating the mother's bloodstream.

To obviate all anesthesia and to further the most favorable mother-child interaction certain modern hospital methods have been challenged by those who advocate "natural" childbirth. There is perhaps nothing more natural than birth, but in any event, *natural childbirth* refers to a variety of approaches that stress the preparation of the mother and father for childbirth and their active involvement in the process. The English obstetrician Read (1944) began popularizing the view that pain in childbirth could be greatly reduced if women understood the birth process and learned to relax properly. He argued that childbirth is essentially a normal and natural process. Anxiety and tension, however, prevent the rhythmic cooperation of the muscles in contraction and interfere with relaxation, all of which contribute to the tearing of tissue and the intensification of pain. He suggested that cultural attitudes and practices in western societies serve to instill fear and anxiety in the mother. One of the authors' mother described childbirth as the "time when the woman goes through the valley of the shadow of death." In a tradition compounded of biblical legends, misconceptions, rumors, and old wives' tales, childbirth is commonly depicted as a barbaric experience that produces agonizing pain.

Read trained prospective mothers to relax, to breathe correctly, and to develop muscular control of their labor through special exercises. He emphasized that calm and supportive attendants be present throughout labor. Read believed that anesthesia should be available to women, but that it should not be imposed upon them or routinely administered. It was his purpose to make childbirth a less fearsome and a more emotionally satisfying experience.

About the same time—during the 1930s and 1940s—

Soviet doctors began applying Pavlov's theories of the conditioned reflex to childbirth. Like Read, they operated on the premise that society conditioned women to be tense and fearful during labor, emotional states that increase pain. They suggested that if pain was a response largely conditioned by society it could, therefore, be substituted by a different more positive response. Accordingly, they developed the *psychoprophylactic method* that encourages expectant mothers to substitute tension and fear with special breathing techniques.

After a visit to the Soviet Union, Fernand Lamaze (1958) introduced the principle of psychoprophylaxis in a French maternity hospital. Even more than Read, he emphasized the active participation of the mother in every phase of labor. He developed a precise and controlled breathing drill in which women in labor respond to a series of verbal cues by panting, pushing, and blowing. The Lamaze method has proved popular among some American physicians and prospective parents who prefer natural childbirth. Organizations such as the Association for Childbirth Education and the Prepared Childbirth Association prepare prospective parents—both mothers and fathers—for the Lamaze method.

Natural childbirth offers a number of advantages. One is that childbirth classes can relieve the mother's anxiety and fear. Secondly, the mother takes no medication or is given it sparingly in the final phase of delivery. A wide variety of techniques are available to the modern practitioner, most of which are safe if used with care and with due precaution for minimizing shortcomings. Some studies report that infants whose mothers received medication tend to perform less well when a year old (Scanlon & Alper, 1974; Goldstein, Caputo & Taub, 1976). Other studies show no discernible long-term effects of drugs administered to the mother during the birth process (Muller et al, 1971; Yang et al, 1976). The reliability of all of the above studies should be questioned since children's behavior at the one-year level fluctuates. We also do not know what additional benefits the natural-born children receive from their mothers.

The third advantage is that many couples find their joint participation in labor and delivery a joyous, rewarding occasion, describing it as a "peak" experience.

Natural childbirth, however, is not suitable for all women. In some cases the pain becomes so severe that medication becomes necessary. Breech delivery and other complications may likewise call for it.

FAMILY-CENTERED HOSPITAL CARE

A growing number of American hospitals are introducing family-centered hospital care in which childbirth is made a family experience. Home-like "birthing rooms" for labor and delivery are provided as an alternative to the old procedure of the cold delivery ward. The birthing room looks like any bedroom in an attractive suburban home—complete with rocking chair, hanging plants, and stereo set. During labor the mother may walk around. When time for delivery comes the husband is urged to be present. Almost immediately afterward, he is handed the baby, cuts the umbilical cord, and gives the infant its first bath. Instead of rushing the infant to the hospital nursery the baby remains with its parents.

Rooming-in of this nature offers the advantage of allowing the mother to get acquainted with her child and of integrating the father into the child care process early. But as is true with natural childbirth, rooming-in is not suitable for all women. Some women prefer a more gradual introduction to parenthood, allowing them a few days to recover from fatigue and to adjust to the infant.

ATTACHMENT BEHAVIOR—EARLY MOTHERING EXPERIENCE

One of the most recent controversial issues is the effect various childbirth methods have on later development, such as the new method described by a French obstetrician in a book that has become a bestseller in the United States, *Birth Without Violence* (Leboyer, 1975). Leboyer, concerned with the emotional impact of childbirth, criticizes the traditional childbirth practices. Leboyer's method includes dimming delivery room lights so that the baby will not be startled by bright lights. Immediately after delivery, the newborn is placed on the mother's warm abdomen and allowed to retain the prenatal curved spinal position as long as possible. The mother is encouraged to cuddle and fondle the infant while they are in close contact. The baby's umbilical cord is not cut until the infant's respiratory system is well established. The baby continues, for up to six minutes after birth in some cases, to receive oxygen through its prenatal respiratory system. After the cord is cut the baby receives a warm, comfortable bath, often to soft music, and breast-feeding is encouraged minutes after birth.

Critics of the Leboyer method point out that these procedures may be dangerous in some cases. Bright light is necessary to see facial color. The cord should be cut immediately to prevent the risk of infection. The doctor needs to hear the cry of the baby to be sure of forceful breathing. Leboyer has answered that all these precautionary measures can be used with his method when necessary but are not needed routinely. His advocates point out that follow-up studies, at the Sorbonne, of French babies born by the Leboyer method seem to show that these children are spared the usual infancy psychopathologies and are noticeably active, exhibiting avid interest in the world about them (England, 1974).

BONDING

Several pediatricians and psychologists believe that there are important benefits in immediate "bonding" of mothers with their newborns. As far back as the turn of the century, Pierre C. Budin, author of one of the first texts on newborn disorders, observed that "mothers separated from their young soon lost all interest in those whom they were unable to nurse or cherish." Later investigators expressed similar concern about the possible psychological cost of interfering with the interaction between parent and newborn. Klaus and Kennell (1976) of Case Western Reserve Medical Center in Cleveland have been carrying out studies showing that there is a sensitive period in the first minutes and hours of life when a mother must have close contact with her infant if later development is to be optimal. As described in their book, *Maternal-infant Bonding,* these two pediatricians have found that when mothers are given their babies shortly after birth, they behave in special ways. They speak to them in high-pitched voices, as if they know instinctively that babies are more receptive to such tones. A linking seems to develop between mother and infant which can be observed on slow-motion films. The baby sees, hears, and moves to the rhythm of its mother's voice.

Comparing mother-child pairs who have spent hours together immediately after birth with pairs who had only brief contact, Klaus and Kennell found that the bonded babies gained more weight and had fewer infections during their first year. During the second year the long-contact mothers spoke to their children more frequently and gave them fewer commands than the mothers who had no bonding experience. At five years, the long-contact children had higher IQs and superior scores on language tests. If the birth was normal and not premature, one can assume that mothers who are willing to bond earlier are also more willing to support their children all along their developmental years—a variable which may also explain the higher IQ of the long-contact group.

CHILDBIRTH AT HOME

It is estimated that less than 20 percent of the babies born in the world today are delivered by physicians. Outside the U.S.

the vast majority of births are handled by midwives—experienced lay practitioners who attend women during birth. Even in such technologically advanced nations as Sweden, Germany, the Netherlands, and England, professional midwives handle the majority of normal births. As recently as 1905 midwives delivered about half of the babies born in New York City, and in the United States today, "granny" midwives deliver babies in Appalachia, Mississippi, and the Rio Grande area of Texas (Sousa, 1976).

In the past decade the rising cost of hospital care, as well as the dissatisfaction among some couples with impersonal hospital procedures, has led to a renewed interest in home births attended by midwives. Paralleling this movement, a number of programs have been established that allow a registered nurse with a baccalaureate degree to earn a master's degree and certification in nurse-midwifery. However, in contrast with the independent practice found among European midwives, the American nurse-midwife usually works under the supervision of a physician.

Although it is not illegal in the United States to have a baby at home, through the years most states have enacted legislation which regulates those persons who may attend a birth. An increasing number of states are currently broadening their laws to permit licensed midwives to deliver infants in both hospital and home settings. However, couples who are interested in childbirth at home should find out which laws pertain in their particular state. The parents' legal liability in the event of either the mother's or the baby's death during a home birth is not entirely clear. There is also the more obvious danger that in a home birth immediate and skilled attention is not as readily available as in the hospital and if complications develop, the infant is further away from medical attention. Couples need to weigh this risk with its associated tragedy against the advantages of a home delivery (Sousa, 1976).

It is hard to prove that natural childbirth methods or infant bonding cause any permanent psychological advantages with respect to the character development of an individual. Studies cited in the following section on breast- or bottle-feeding have shown zero correlation between a person's psychological make-up and the birth and feeding practices he or she experienced.

BREAST OR BOTTLE?

There is also a return to the natural in the breast-bottle issue. For the last decades, mothers, especially American mothers, have generally bottle-fed their babies. Bottle-feeding does not tie down the mother physically and formulas for bottle-feeding guarantee well-fed babies. In spite of these conveniences there has been a return to breast-feeding during the 1960s and 1970s. The *La Leche League International* is greatly responsible for this back-to-the-breast movement. Its members believe that breast-feeding is physically and psychologically healthier for both mother and child than bottle feeding. The La Leche League organizes neighborhood meetings for expectant and nursing mothers to discuss the details, the conveniences, and the pleasures of breast-feeding. However, as the following will show, not all aspects of socialization are favorably influenced by breast-feeding.

Freud (1949) thought that much sucking during nursing is necessary for a child's normal development. He postulated that sucking satisfies a basic or innate drive which he called "oral gratification." Conversely, Freud and his followers argued that a deprivation of sucking during infancy would lead to an "oral character." An oral character or an "oral personality" is described as a person who is suspicious, dissatisfied, yet demanding sympathy and protection. As a child such a character is said to suck his thumb and bite his nails. As an adult he or she is said to talk, eat, smoke, or drink to excess.

The Freudian assumptions have stimulated many experiments. Infants have been watched for the amount of thumbsucking. Children have been observed for their sociability during play, and college students have been tested with personality tests. Reports from their mothers were obtained as to the type and length of nursing they received. In their book *Child Development and Personality,* Mussen and Conger (1956, 1963) have described many of the studies that tried to investigate whether breast- or bottle-feeding and whether short or long sucking periods in infancy influence later personality. They found some studies which indicated that children with longer nursing periods showed less thumbsucking and were better adjusted in play situations. They also found other studies that reported the opposite, and still others that reported no personality differences between bottle- or breast-fed subjects. Mussen and Conger believe that the conflicting results are due to experimental errors. As one error, they suggest the memory of mothers on which these studies relied. Another error may have been that of causality. A mother who nursed her child longer may have also taken more patience in subsequent years to teach her child to be more sociable during play activities. Thus the better social adjustment reported in some studies may not have been directly related to the length of the infantile nursing periods.

In a longitudinal study, Heinstein (1963) avoided the above errors. He contributed one of the most extensive research projects available on the breast-bottle problem. His data were collected on 94 subjects, participants of the University of California Guidance Study Sample, on which mental and physical data had been collected from birth to maturity over a span of 17 years. These types of records made Heinstein's data independent of mothers' memories and facilitated the investigation of many variables that could not be assessed in previous studies. Data for each subject were independently recorded at the time of occurrence by nurses, physicians, mothers, psychiatric social workers, and psychologists, all showing fair agreement in assessing the following five points:

(1) Length of breast feeding,
(2) length of nursing (breast and/or bottle),
(3) "warmth" of mother (friendliness, affection, contact),
(4) nervous stability of mother, and
(5) marital adjustment of parents.

The influence which each of the above variables had on the possible maladjustment of the child was measured. Maladjustment was operationally well defined. Its measurement consisted of data on the frequencies of bedwetting, loss of appetite, thumbsucking, speech problems, overdependence, fears, tantrums, and other observable events.

After evaluating all the tested variables, Heinstein's results showed that there were no general behavioral differences favoring breast- rather than formula-feeding. Nor were there any indications that breast-feeding was physically more healthful. While there were no general differences, the combination of certain factors did result in several peculiar interactions or differential effects. For instance, formula-fed boys showed more bedwetting than breast-fed boys, but had fewer fears, a better appetite, fewer speech problems, and sucked their thumb less often. Much of this relationship was reversed in girls, where the breast-fed ones showed more incidents of wetting and thumbsucking, but had fewer fears and food problems. The most pronounced maladjustment was found in boys who were nursed for a long time by a "cold" mother. Boys breast-fed by "warm" mothers showed no particular maladjustment. Girls who were breast-fed by stable mothers with good marital adjustment showed the greatest amount of thumbsucking and more jealousy, but had a better appetite and fewer tantrums. When combined with breast-feeding, few of the abovementioned parental and environmental variables had behavioral advantages. Most had disadvantages.

When breast-feeding was compared with bottle-feeding, while all other things were kept constant, it was found that food problems, thumbsucking, and speech problems were positively related to breast-feeding, which means the more breast-feeding, the more such problems. The Freudians included these problems in their definition of the "oral syndrome" or "oral personality." They thought that the breast-fed child must have more satisfying nursing periods and therefore fewer problems later on. Heinstein's experimental results suggest just the opposite. He found that the "oral syndrome" was increased through breast-feeding and that it was the bottle-fed child who had fewer troubles.

Newton (1968) reported a relationship between mothers' attitudes towards breast-feeding and actual success in it. Those mothers who, previous to the birth, expressed a desire and determination to breast feed needed fewer supplemental formulas than mothers who were less determined about breast-feeding. Newton and her collaborators also compared maternal behavior of breast-feeding mothers with that of nonbreast-feeding mothers. Only one difference was found. Breast-feeding mothers shared their bed more often with their babies. In other respects the two groups were very much the same. About 90% of the breast-feeding mothers reported that they never spanked their babies. So did 90% of the bottle-feeding mothers. Again, about 90% of the mothers in both groups reported that they spent less than three hours per day away from their babies. There were also 60% of the mothers in both groups who held their babies one-half hour or more per day.

The authors surveyed the opinions of mothers who had both bottle- and breast-feeding experiences. About 50% of these mothers reported that they found no differences in either the physical or the psychological health between their breast- and bottle-fed children. The remaining 50% were of divided opinions. A slight majority of them thought that their breast-fed children were healthier, mentioning fewer colds and fewer allergies as the main reasons. With respect to the mothers' own health there was an almost equal number of pro and con judgments. A small majority reported better health during bottle-feeding, giving "less tired" as the main reason. Mothers who thought that they felt psychologically better during breast-feeding listed feelings of satisfaction and accomplishment as the main factors. Mothers who thought that they felt psychologically better during bottle-feeding said that they worried less about being able to give the baby enough milk. Though the breast-fed child fared slightly better in the mothers' judgments, it is interesting to note that the same mothers who gave this judgment decreased breast feeding from child to child. On the average the first-born child is breast-fed for 4 months, the second child for 3 months, the third for 2.5 months, and the fourth child for only 2 months. In a sample of 50 mothers there were only 5 who breast fed a later-born child longer than one born earlier.

Breast-feeding has certain medical advantages. Smith (1969) recommends breast-feeding when there is a family history of allergies. Breast-feeding can also be combined with bottle-feeding to assure that the baby is getting enough milk. Negatively, on the medical side there has been the suspicion that some carcinogenic agents may be transferred through the mother's milk to the baby. Caplan (1978), of the Princeton Center for Infancy, lists nutrition, digestibility, and simplicity as the major advantages for breast-feeding, but he also suggests that mothers should not breast-feed unless they have a strong desire to do so. He mentions that nervous and embarrassed mothers may not produce enough milk and may also convey negative feelings to their infants. Thurston and Mussen (1951) collected feeding data on male college students and found no recognizable differences in personalities between those who were breast-fed and those who were bottle-fed in infancy, nor between those who were weaned early or late. Smith (1969) reassures mothers who have chosen not to breast-feed for medical or psychological reasons. He states that bottle-feeding does not cause blight or adult neuroses and that warmth, security, and affection can be given to a child in many ways besides breast-feeding.

THUMBSUCKING

The majority of children suck their thumbs. Yarrow (1954) analysed longitudinal data on a group of 66 children at the Child Research Council, University of Colorado School of Medicine. He found the following relationships between thumbsucking and age,

64%	55%	46%	32%	16%	9%
birth	6 months	1 year	4 years	6 years	7 years

Percentagewise the thumbsucker is in good company. There seems to be no evidence that thumbsucking is physically harmful. There is also very little evidence that it will dislocate teeth, unless a bad bite exists to begin with and unless the thumbsucking is still practiced when the second set of teeth appears (Longstreth, 1968). In spite of the consoling data given above, thumbsucking arouses strong anxieties in many American parents. Somehow they wish that their children would not suck their thumbs too long. If parents consult psychologists about alleviating thumbsucking they may receive quite contradictory advice. Freudian psychologists would tell them to allow as much sucking as possible, because they believe that this will satisfy the innate sucking urge. They further believe that once this innate urge is satisfied future sucking will not occur. Behavioral psychologists would recommend the opposite. They would allow as little sucking as possible, because they believe that thumbsucking is a habit which becomes more firmly established the longer it takes place.

The controversy about the innateness of thumbsucking and whether or not it needs to be satisfied has been one of the earliest and longest arguments between Freudians and behaviorists. We shall discuss it in some detail, because it will illuminate not only the sucking issue, but the viewpoints of the two major psychological schools in general. Freud believed that the sucking urge is innate and that it must be satisfied in early infancy for the person to have a normal adult life. Should infantile urges or desires not be satisfied they then would increase during the ensuing years. Freud further postulated that the increased urges or desires may lie dormant or "unconscious" for years. After decades they may manifest themselves directly or indirectly through behavior that is a substitute for the original inhibited urge. Thus, a frustration of sucking in infancy may create an increased urge for overeating, smoking, excessive talking in the adult years. In other words it will create the "oral personality" discussed in the previous problem.

Freud's rationale on sucking follows the framework of his general theory. He believed that all neuroses consist of certain substitute behaviors that have gotten out of hand and grown to socially unacceptable limits. The desires, in other words, have increased over the years because they were thwarted in childhood. Freud thought that all this occurs without an individual's awareness. Psychoanalysis, his prescribed cure, is supposed to lead the patient's memory back to her childhood in order to make her aware which urge was repressed or inhibited at that time. This realization on the patient's part is said to cure the neurosis.

In contrast to Freud the behaviorists relate sucking to conditioning, pointing out that it occurs so often under the pleasant and satisfying circumstance of obtaining food. Due to such frequent pairings, sucking will take on all the pleasant features of food-getting. After sufficient pairing, sucking in itself will create a pleasure. It will be desired and practiced even if it is not accompanied by food intake. This type of sucking, such as thumbsucking, sucking on toes, blankets, and other objects, is called "nonnutritional" sucking. From the rules of conditioning, behaviorists would predict that the longer a child is allowed to suck under any pleasant circumstances such as nourishing, resting, or cuddling, the greater will be the desire to suck the thumb or other nonnutritional objects. The habit, in other words, will become more firmly established. Conversely, if nonsucking is the objective, behaviorists would suggest little or no sucking in infancy. They would not be concerned about the frustrating effects of this inhibition. They would argue if an organism has to be frustrated, it would take the least amount of frustration if it were frustrated early when the habit was not too firmly established. Also, if the habit were never established in the first place, frustrations connected with getting rid of it would never occur. Thus, if an infant were cup-fed from birth, the weaning process would be eliminated since the sucking habit would never have been established.

In 1934 Levy conducted an experiment that was supposed to end the argument between the Freudians and the behaviorists. He found that puppies fed with large nipple holes showed more nonnutrituonal sucking that those fed with small nipple holes. From this the Freudians reasoned that larger holes necessitated less sucking time, not allowing for sufficient sucking exercise. This lack of sucking opportunity, they maintained, increased the innate urge, which found its outlet through more nonnutritional sucking, such as sucking on paws and blankets. The behaviorists interpreted the same results to support their learning theory. The large-nipple group (the short-time feeders), they maintained, showed more nonnutritional sucking because their sucking activity was rewarded more thoroughly. The reward per unit of sucking time was greater for this group, hence the more nonnutritional sucking. The small-nipple group, on the other hand, may have had a very strenuous sucking time, the reward not outweighing the effort. McCandless, in his book *Children: Behavior and Development* (1967), states that Levy's six dogs "may well have influenced the handling of more babies than any other six dogs in history" (p. 114).

The experiments conducted with humans likewise did not settle the argument. Levy (1928) interviewed 122 mothers about the sucking habits of their children. He found that the severity of the thumbsucking habit is in proportion to the insufficiency of the sucking time during feeding. Roberts (1944) examined the sucking habits of 15 infants who were thumbsuckers and of 15 who were not. She also found that the amount of time spent in sucking determines the amount of thumb- or fingersucking. While these two studies support the "instinct hypothesis," there are also the following well-controlled studies supporting the "learning hypothesis."

H. Davis, Sears, Miller, and Brodbeck (1948) found that babies who were cup-fed for ten days did not develop a sucking reflex as strong as those who were fed by means of a large nipple for ten days. A third breast-fed group showed the strongest sucking reflex. A subsequent experiment conducted by Sears and Wise (1950) involved 80 infants. They were divided into three groups: those weaned before two weeks, those weaned between two and three weeks, and those weaned after four months. It was found that the later-weaned groups showed increasingly more thumbsucking as well as increased frustration reactions at weaning time, such as refusing food, crying, irritability, and thumbsucking. Brodbeck (1950) fed 36 infants by bottle for the first four days of their lives and by cup for the next four days. He had a control group fed by bottle for the entire eight-day period. All of his cup-fed babies showed less nonnutritional sucking. Another well-controlled study was conducted by Bernstein (1955) at a well-baby clinic in New York. He gathered his data on 50 infants from direct observations, interviews with mothers, and medical records. Summarizing his data he states, "The hypothesis that thumbsucking is related to sucking deprivation during infancy was not verified, but, on the contrary, the evidence tended to support a reinforcement explanation more strongly" (p. 31).

The four studies reported above support the learning hypothesis. Yarrow's study (1954), previously mentioned, offers an additional support. He reports no differences in duration or severity of thumbsucking between children who had no breast-feeding and those who were breast-fed beyond the average breast-feeding time of three months. However, some components of Yarrow's data support the instinct hypothesis. He found, for instance, 18 thumbsuckers among a group of 21 children who were breast-fed for only two months, but no thumbsuckers among six babies who were breast-fed longer than six months. Weaning periods of a year or so were again associated with prolonged thumbsucking. Yarrow postulated a "phase specificity," suggesting that the strength of the oral activity may be large (instinctively) at birth, may diminish later, but may again become strengthened (by learned habit) through late weaning.

The heredity-environment issue becomes less controversial as more detailed data become available. It is perhaps useful to distinguish the innate capacity to suck—the reflex which occurs as soon as mouth or lips are touched—from the self-initiated thumbsucking which lasts for hours on end. Both hereditary and environmental aspects may influence thumbsucking. Kessen, et al. (1967) gave pacifiers connected to a polygraph to 30 newborn infants. This was done immediately after birth before they had their first feeding. This nonnutritional sucking had a tendency to quiet the babies and reduce their movements. Since the sucking of these babies had never been rewarded by food, the calming effect of the nonnutritional sucking must be regarded as congenital in origin. But sucking can also be easily influenced by environmental conditions. Lipsitt, et al., (1966) tested infants within two to five days after birth and found that sucking on a tube increased when it was rewarded with a dextrose solution, but decreased when not rewarded.

There are also enormous individual differences in the sucking rates of newborns. Levin and Kaye (1964) measured nonnutritional sucking in 48 infants three days after birth. A pacifier was connected to a polygraph that registers each individual sucking motion. In a nine-minute test period 16 infants made only 0 to 60 total sucks, while seven others, for instance, sucked from 361 to 420 times in the same interval, and one sucked over 600 times.

If thumbsucking is to be avoided, early cup-feeding may be helpful. It can be started immediately after birth. Though somewhat cumbersome in the beginning, it makes later weaning unnecessary. Fredeen (1948) cup-fed 71 premature babies and reported more daily weight gain in comparison to a noncup-fed group. He also reported that cup-fed babies suffer from fewer ear disorders, which are apparently aggravated by prolonged sucking. The use of a pacifier will also lessen the chances of thumbsucking. We should again emphasize that there is no evidence that adolescents or adults who have not sucked their thumb in infancy are any different from those who have.

SLEEP

As humans develop they sleep less and less. What is the right amount of sleep for the various ages? Investigators have tried to establish norms or averages. Kleitman (1939), for instance, lists 22 hours as the average for a newborn infant, Parmelee, et al., (1961) list 16 hours. Most three-year-olds will sleep 12 hours, but as L. H. Smith (1969) reports, there are some very healthy three-year-olds who will only sleep 9 hours per day, going to bed at 9 P.M. and waking up at 6 A.M.

All investigators agree that there is a wide range of individual differences which decreases with age. The graph representing "sleep norms" is therefore drawn in a wedgelike form. This emphasizes that all amounts of sleep within the upper and lower borders of this wedge are normal.

Not only does the amount of sleep change drastically during the first six months, but also its pattern. Kleitman (1963) found that the newborn child sleeps in seven periods distributed over the day and night. At six months 75% of sleep occurs at night, and by the age of one all sleep except a short afternoon nap is done at night. There is a fair amount of agreement that the morning nap should be gradually shortened beginning at the age of one and be eliminated by age two. Some experts say that the afternoon nap should last one hour during the ages two to five, others suggest two or three hours, and still others say that the afternoon nap is not necessary after age three.

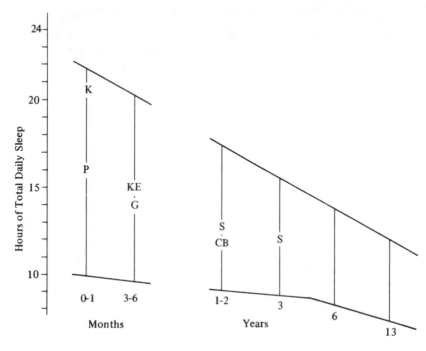

Sleep Norms
Hours of Daily Sleep. Ranges of individual differences at various ages and
reported averages. Averages reported from: CB = Charlotte Bühler (1930);
G = Gesell (1925); K = Kleitman (1939); KE = Kleitman & Engelmann (1953);
P = Parmelee (1961); S = Smith (1969).

Research on sleep has markedly increased during the last
decades. Investigators find various, more or less distinct, stages
and cycles of sleep during which different amounts and types
of bodily movements, rapid eye movement (REM), brain
waves, dreams, and so forth occur. Children have been found,
for instance, to do most of their sleeptalking during nondream
stages. Sleepwalking is likewise not associated with dreaming.
In general the research on sleep tells us which events occur in
the various stages. As yet we neither know the causes nor the
purpose of dreams, talk, or movement during sleep, periods of

"light" and "deep" sleep, and so on (Kleitman, 1963; Murray 1965; Foulkes, 1966; Berger, 1970).

The physiology of sleep is poorly understood, as are the cultural or sociological factors that influence it. How much of our "normal" pattern of sleep is a physiological necessity and how much of it is learned? Newborn infants, for instance, sleep in scattered intervals throughout the 24-hour day. Gradually they begin to sleep more during the night and less during the day until a *circadian* (day-night) rhythm is established. Many investigators believe that the formation of such rhythms is guided by inborn mechanisms. Campbell (1968), however, suggests that mothers are likely to pay much less attention to an infant's wakefulness during the night than during the daytime —thus shaping the circadian rhythm. Murray (1965) discusses several possible reasons for excessive sleep. A child may sleep to avoid chores and anxiety. Sleep may be learned by imitation or it may be more actively taught by the parent who is especially quiet, provides a darkened room, or responds slowly to signs of awakening.

Some books on childrearing suggest that infants and young children should not sleep in the parents' bedroom. They state that the parents' intercourse may frighten the child and may disturb his sexual development. To the knowledge of this author there has been no experimental evidence to support such an assumption. The noises and movements made during intercourse may not bother the child any more than a barking dog or a television program. There are millions of European families who have several children and who live in one- or two-bedroom apartments. In such circumstances it is customary that one or two of the youngest children sleep in the parents' bedroom. Ames and Randeri (1965) report that in India the child sleeps often in the same bed with an adult. Children, adolescents and adults in these countries are sexually no less and no more maladjusted than their equals in the United States where separate bedrooms are more often available and in vogue.

Toilet Training

Toilet training is an important step in the socialization process. Its success has much practical value for the parents, saving them the washing of diapers and bedding. Its nonsuccess has often embarrassing social implications: self-blame on the parents' side and a reluctance to let the youngster spend a night out. The learning process in toilet training is complicated. A child must first learn to feel when the bladder is full. Then it must learn *not* to urinate and to hold the urine until an appropriate place can be reached. All this is quite contrary to our natural urges. Finally the child must learn to start urination with a full or partially filled bladder.

The neurological and muscular mechanisms involved in urinating are complicated and not yet fully understood. Some of the muscles that eventuate urination are involuntary muscles. This means they cannot be directly controlled as can the arm or leg muscles. They can only be activated through other muscles or physiological processes. The indirect way in which urination works can perhaps best be pointed out by the work of the urologist Muellner (1960), who examined the urination process fluoroscopically in about 1,000 people. He found that adults do not start urination by contracting the muscle around the bladder or by opening the sphincter muscles around the urethra. These muscles are started off by a gentle contraction of the diaphragm and by contracting parts of the anal muscle. These two actions lower the neck of the bladder. This squeezes urine into the neck of the bladder, which is the cue for final bladder contraction and urethra opening. Muellner observed that an improperly directed starting effort, and especially an overstraining in some young children, will result in the suppression of the bladder neck, the cue needed to start the chain of reflexes. Muellner emphasizes that bladder control cannot be taught, because the skills that are required for it are so complex they cannot be communicated to another person. The reader will appreciate this view and will now understand why we cannot expect much help from our knowledge of the internal mechanism. As with learning in general, we will have to be satisfied with the arrangement and manipulation of outside or environmental factors. From the above paragraph we have not gained any practical knowledge about toilet training, perhaps only a more patient attitude.

The actual toilet training can be facilitated by setting the stage for imitation and modeling. Parents should adopt a matter-of-fact attitude about toilet matters and children should be able to observe their parents bathing, showering, and toiletting. Loud noises, rash movements, slappings, and scoldings should never be used in connection with toiletting since they automatically inhibit elimination. The parent, the potty chair, or the toilet must all be free from negative associations. In general the actual toilet training should be started when the child is 20 months old (Mussen, et al., 1969; McCandless, 1967). However, Sears, et al. (1957) have found the period of 6 to 12 months equally successful. In his 1961 edition of *Baby and Child Care,* Dr. Spock recommended the onset of training within 12 to 15 months. In his 1967 edition he gives equal emphasis to the 20 to 24 month starting period. It is understandable why training at this early period can also be successful. There is much physiological regularity at this age and parents can more readily pick up such anticipatory cues as scratching the genital area, changes in breathing, reddening, and the like. Defecation is much easier to train than urination because it is preceded by much more obvious anticipatory cues: a flushed-face, straining, etc. The observation of urinary anticipatory cues, however, requires much individual attention, perhaps more than the average parent is willing or able to give. Hence starting periods before 20 months are generally not recommended.

The main task in toilet training is to put the child on the potty chair the minute it is ready to urinate. Most of the time this very moment is missed by the parent and toilet training therefore takes sometimes years rather than weeks. In most instances the child is put on the potty chair after it has urinated into the diapers—at a time when it is impossible to urinate again. Azrin and Foxx (1977) have demonstrated that it takes only a few associations between the act of relieving and the potty chair. As described in their book *Toilet Training in Less Than a Day*, they allow a child to drink as much as possible. Then they engage the child in play and observe it. One play consists of giving a toy doll liquids and of putting it on a toy potty chair to observe its urination and of praising the doll for it. Every few minutes the child is told not to urinate into the pants but to use the nearby potty chair. They check the child's pants every few minutes and reward the child (with an M & M candy) for not having urinated. It is almost a continuous monitoring until urination occurs when the child goes to the potty chair or is placed on it. Once urination into the potty chair has occurred the child is rewarded with bigger toys and more drinks for a second or third training session. The toilet training which is started this way is usually maintained even though toys will not be forthcoming after the initial training periods. However, it is likely that secondary rewards, praise, and parental smiles will continue to reinforce this behavior. Note that while many parents punish after inappropriate urination, Azrin and Foxx reward for staying dry.

Punishment in connection with toilet training should be avoided at all times. Bostook and Shackleton (1951) and Sears, Maccaby, and Levin (1957), and several other studies have shown that children who are punished by their parents are much more likely to become bedwetters than those who are treated permissively. Punishment does not seem to prevent or to alleviate bedwetting. Such findings should not surprise the reader. We have seen in our discussion on learning how easily punishment can spread to the punishing agent, the parent. We have also seen in our discussion of punishment how many things can go wrong with it. Finally, there is Muellner's account which pointed out that children who strain or try too hard (something they are likely to do so while under the threat of punishment) depress the diaphragm too much and prevent urination.

For the record it should be mentioned that Sears et al., found that mild types of punishment have been successfuly used in toilet training. They reported that parents who are both permissive and firm are usually most successful in toilet training. More specifically, they found that mothers who rate high in anxiety about sexual matters, but who treat their children warmly and affectionately, do train them most proficiently.

There has been much speculation about the influence of toilet training on the person's later personality. Most of this speculation comes to us from Freud's pychoanalytic theories. Freud (1940) thought of toilet training as one of the most influential periods in a child's development. He termed this period the "anal" stage, in which, among other things, the child is supposedly preoccupied with the manipulation of its feces. In this stage urination and defecation are said to be especially pleasing acts. (This is similar to Freud's "oral" stage, where the child is said to gain all satisfaction from the stimulation of the mouth.) During toilet training, the child is often rewarded for retaining urine or feces. Hence, he is rewarded for inflicting a more or less painful action upon himself. The more strict the toilet training, the more punishment will the child receive for giving in to the immediate pleasure—for not waiting till the toilet could be reached. Pain is rewarded and, conversely, pleasure is punished.

Following his analytic framework, Freud thought that this pain-seeking, learned during toilet training, can accompany an individual for the rest of his life and can spread to many other if not to all other activities. Character traits such as self-punishment, masochism martyrdom, pedantism, and compulsiveness are all ascribed to strict toilet training. They form what Freud and his followers call the "anal personality." On the other hand, Freudians believe that pleasure-seeking personalities were formed during lenient and permissive toilet training.

The behaviorists who emphasize learning would basically agree with the Freudian theorizing. They can also predict from the conditioning model that rewarded pains will become rewarding in themselves (secondary reward). The behaviorists, however, would not consider toilet training as the most important factor in personality development. The behaviorist would also want to investigate the pleasures received or denied from other childrearing situations such as eating, sleeping, nose picking, and scribbling on walls. Data collected by Sears, et al. (1957) indicate that about half of all children with harsh toilet training are not properly trained, not even after several years of training. This suggests the influence of nontoilet-training variables, because the same type of training did not have the same effect. In general, psychologists have had limited success in measuring and assessing personalities and they have had hardly any success in signaling out specific causes for specific personality traits.

BEDWETTING

About 20% of all three- to five-year old children wet their beds at night. Between the ages of five and seven there are 10% bedwetters. This percentage decreases further to about only 2% among ten-year-olds. These data, collected by Long (1941) and again verified by Bransby, Blomfield, and Douglas (1955), show that except for a few cases, bedwetting (enuresis) disappears eventually. In spite of this fact, cures are desired as bedwetting causes many practical inconveniences and brings about certain social disadvantages over prolonged periods.

Psychologists and psychiatrists have done a great deal of experimentation as well as speculation about the cure of bedwetting. Their various theories about the causes of enuresis can again be divided into two major camps. The reader may guess that there are the Freudians on one side, who believe that enuresis is one of the symptoms of a more general and "deep-scated" emotional disturbance, and the behaviorists on the other hand, who postulate that the bedwetter has neglected to learn or has unlearned a specific habit necessary for bladder control.

One of the cures for bedwetting was discovered in a rather roundabout way by the German pediatrician Pfaundler in 1904. He invented a pad consisting of linen and metal strips wired to a battery and a bell. The pad was put under the child's bed sheet. When moistened by urine, a circuit would be completed and the bell would ring. Pfaundler built this apparatus to inform the nurse that a certain child had wetted and needed changing. He found to his surprise that many children discontinued wetting their beds after several weeks. He also found that the mere explanation of the apparatus prevented some children from continuing their bedwetting. Pfaundler's pad was used again by Uteau and Richardot in 1916 who tried to investigate malingering of soldiers in France. They connected the pad to a clock that stopped when urination occurred. They reasoned that a soldier who wetted his bed at night was sick, but that one who wetted just before getting up was malingering (Mowrer and Mowrer, 1938).

Mowrer and Mowrer improved Pfaundler's apparatus and used it in more controlled situations. They found it equally successful. If the bell is loud enough, it will stop the flow of the urine and wake the child. Then the child can go to the toilet by himself or be assisted by the parent. The pad works on a conditioning principle, whereby the bell acts on the nervous system, which inhibits micturation. In this case the bell works as the "unconditioned" stimulus, the one that works naturally —in a reflex way without previous learning. It is not clear which stimulus is the "conditioned" stimulus in the pad procedure. We need a stimulus accompanying the bell, which later inhibits the urination by taking on the function of the bell. It is likely that the internal sensation of a filled or distended bladder functions as such.

For an ideal conditioning experiment it would be best if the bell would ring before urination starts while the bladder is distended. As it is, the muscles that stop urination are activated a short time after urination has begun, but apparently soon enough so that the bladder is still distended. Lovibond (1964) has measured the urine spot on the pad and found its diameter to decrease from about 10 to 2 inches in the first two weeks of training. This indicates that the body learns to react faster and faster to the bell until eventually the urination is halted after only a few drops of urine have passed. In the third week of training with the pad the closing reflex seems to occur right after the opening reflex, soon enough to prevent an actual out-flow. The pad is usually removed after seven consecutive dry nights.

Lovibond has very thoroughly surveyed the results of ex-periments which tried to eliminate bedwetting through various conditioning procedures. Tabulating only noncommercial data (obtained by academic investigators), he reports on nine inde-pendent experiments which used the Mowrer pad and involved a total of 488 subjects. Bedwetting was arrested in 90% of the tabulated cases after an average treatment period of eight weeks. Lovibond lists four more separate experiments with a total of 116 subjects which used a similar method and reported an average cure of 80% (Lovibond, 1964, p. 75, Table 15).

Unfortunately, the high percentages of initial arrests are offset by a high relapse rate. The longer the follow-up periods used in the various studies, the higher the reported number of relapse cases. A number of studies show an average of 14% relapses but Lovibond estimates that this percentage might increase to 30% if all studies had used at least a two-year follow-up period. Half of the relapse subjects respond well to a second treatment. Baker (1969) tested the pad in the New Haven, Connecticut, area and demonstrated convincingly an overall cure of 75% of children who were chronic bedwetters.

In spite of the high success rate of the pad and in spite of their availability in mail order houses under "patient supplies" or "bedpads," Baker found few pediatricians recommending it. McClelland (1978) points out that most pediatricians and many parents falsely believe that the bedwetter is not loved enough by his (about 80% of all bedwetters are boys) parents and that he takes it out on them by wetting the bed. Having made this false premise they further believe that a cure of bedwetting would prevent the release of anger, which may then manifest itself in worse character disturbances and in worse asocial behaviors.

A number of research data have not supported the above assumptions. Lovibond (1964) tested the personalities of enuretic children (bedwetters) by comparing them with nonenuretics. He used six different types of personality tests and found that none of them could differentiate basic personality differences between bedwetters and nonbedwetters. Some differences that did occur can all be termed "reactive maladjustment," which means an adjustment or a maladjustment that arose as a result of the bedwetting but was not the cause of it. It is understandable that a child of 10 or 12 who is aware of his bedwetting might be shyer or more reticent in his social activities, being embarrassed to accept overnight invitations, and so on.

The personality and the training technique of parents with enuretic children were also assessed by Lovibond. No differences were found when comparisons were made to the training habits of parents with nonenuretic children. Baker (1969) reported that the pad did not only cure his patients of enuresis, but that they were also relieved of signs of unhappiness and maladjustment which the enuresis apparently had brought along.

Summarizing the results of his own tests and of those employed by other investigators, Lovibond states, "Considered as a whole, the test data constitute formidable evidence in favor of the specific habit deficiency theory" (p. 83). This means that enuresis is not a symptom of a more general and "deep-seated" personality disturbance. Thus, when establishing or re-establishing proper toilet habits, one need not worry that one neglects thereby the cure of an overall emotional disturbance. In spite of the high relapse rate the conditioning therapy seems highly successful with all ages from 6 to 14 and over. All methods are absolutely harmless, physiologically and psychologically. However, the method using bells is easier to apply than the method using shocks since the latter is more threatening to child and/or parent.

DATING AND MATING

The development of our sex roles has already been discussed. In childhood and preadolescence we learn from our culture the aesthetics in partner selection, the rules of dating, sexual mores, and notions about romance and marriage. At puberty, increased hormone production and other physiological changes stimulate sexual urges which are usually satisfied by modeling the cultural norms. These norms have changed considerably with regards to marriage, children, monogamy, and divorce and the adolescents of the 1970s have more choices than they had a decade ago.

Depending on country and social class, about 20 to 40% of adolescents from 16 to 18 years engage in sexual intercourse. Two-thirds of all adolescent girls have their initial intercourse with males older than they, including one-third who are introduced to sex by male adults. But only 2% of the boys were introduced to sex by female adults and as Schofield (1965) remarks, "the proselytizing older woman in search of virgin boys is either a myth or very unsuccessful." There are also many differences between the sexes regarding their motives and feelings for engaging in their first intercourse. The boys indicated a "sexual desire," while the girls' predominant response is "being in love" (Schmidt & Sigusch, 1972). Sexually experienced teenagers seem to have different life styles than those who are sexually inexperienced. They leave school earlier, change jobs more frequently, and spend less time at home. In 1965 Schofield reported from England that sexually experienced girls as compared to inexperienced ones were more inclined to dislike their mothers, earned more money, and practically all of them smoked more than 20 cigarettes a day.

Not all of the dating and mating rules learned during childhood stay with us. Schlaegel et al. (1975) found, for instance, that nearly all 11-year-old boys and girls want to wait for sex until marriage, but by the ages 14–16 almost all rejected this type of abstinence. Their physiology perhaps got the better of them. Schlaegel and his coworkers used a rather unique method of questionning the younger teenagers. They encapsulated their questions into the discourse of cartoon figures in order to avoid direct question.

In spite of these changes, many attitudes which the sexes have or acquire during adolescence stay with them during their adult years. When asked to name the most desirable attributes for a partner, women mention as the first five most important criteria: achievement, leadership, occupational ability, economic ability, and entertainment ability. The males' criteria are predominantly physically and erotically oriented. They mention: physical attractivencess, erotic ability, affectional ability, social ability, and domestic ability (Centers, 1972).

A man is more inclinded to perceive his sexual relations as something separate from himself, as something anatomical or functional, while a woman's sexual satisfaction depends more on psychological factors, on her inner feeling, and her love (or loves), something which Matussek (1971) has called "inner preparedness." Men are more sensation-seeking than women. About 50% of men have extramarital relations at some times in their lives as compared to 25% of women. Participants at swinger parties are 72% males and 28% females (Smith & Smith, 1970). Kinsey believed that the human male would be promiscuous if there were no social restrictions. While the lack of opportunity seems to be the major deterrent for males, social pressure and moral compunctions discourage the women. In monogamous relationships there is a dramatic fall off in sexual interest for both partners during the first year. This drop off, or boredom, occurs faster for males than for females and after a certain time, with the love bond having been established, the female may have a greater desire for intercourse than the male whose interests are likely to wander to other women. As Wilson and Nias (1976) remark: "Women want a lot of sex with the man they love, men want a lot of women."

The male's diversified sexual interests make him appear to have greater sexual prowess. Physiological data, however, speak against it. Females, for instance, can have multiple orgasms while males in general cannot. Those males who are able to have sequential orgasms report that the first one is the most satisfying, while women who experience them report that the second or third is the most satisfying one. Furthermore, the frequency with which males can have orgasms decreases with age, while the female's capacity for orgasms is much less age-dependent (Kinsey, et al. 1953). The male's wishes, interests, and desires for sex, his "libido," are only somewhat congruent with his actual sexual performance until age 25 to 35. From then on until his sixties and later, his libido increases constantly even though his sexual performance may fall to once a fortnight or to a zero rate. The female's libido is more congruent with her sexual performance. She is more attuned to reality with respect to her sexual desire, talks, and fantasies.

Some individual differences, perhaps inborn, are stronger determinants of sexual behaviors and feelings than gender differences. Both male and females with extroverted personalities have sex more often and in more diversified ways than introverts. However, as Eysenck (1976) has shown, neither the frequency nor the diversity of sex is necessarily linked to the feeling of being satisfied about one's sex. Eysenck found that stable introverts, females or males, with low sex drives gain considerable satisfaction from their sex lives. They are generally content in monogamous relationships. Equally content is the "happy philanderer" who devotes much energy to sexual frequency and diversification. Two groups of males and females are generally not satisfied. Those with low sex drives who are unstable introverts with inhibitions and guilt feelings and those with high sex drives who combine hostility, aggression, and impersonal attitudes with their sexual desires.

Eysenck's findings show that there are no rational grounds for following one life style rather than another. Either chastity or promiscuity or anything in between can lead to satisfaction if the individual is biologically and psychologically attuned to it.

PLAY

Creative play, dramatic play, formal play, sex-role play, skill play, therapeutic play—you name it, if the psychologists have not beaten you to it. Hundreds of play situations have been described in the developmental literature, but references to "work" are conspicuously absent. A child's play may have a purpose or it may not. A judgment about the purpose will depend entirely on the observer's interests. When a child knocks over the same building blocks for the tenth time, we may say that this action serves no purpose for the development of a skill. Yet, we may say that it does have a purpose if we consider this action as a physical exercise.

In spite of the many studies investigating amounts and types of play, there seems to be no agreement on its definition nor on its effect. It would require many long-term studies to find out which type of play and how much of it had which effect on a person's adolescence and adulthood.

It has been speculated that creativity is furthered by play-fulness (Bishop & Chase, 1971), especially by a type of solitary play where the child has an opportunity to fantasize (Singer, 1973). Hopefully, of course, that the child fantasizes about that which society considers beneficial and unique. The history of science does not indicate that play and fantasy are more condu-cive to creativity than work and reality. There have been many imaginative and creative persons who worked much and played little in their childhood.

While some psychologists advocate solitary play, others suggest group play. "Getting along with peers" got first billing when American mothers were asked to list the traits they desire most for their younger children. In a cross-cultural study, Wesley and Karr (1968) found that German mothers rated this trait in seventh place. They think that obedience, honesty, cleanliness,and good school work are all more important than sociability. It is perhaps an American preoccupation with being "social" that casts a stigma on the child who prefers to play alone. There is much psychological advice telling mothers and kindergarten teachers how to intergrate the "lonely child" into group activity in spite of lacking evidence that children who play in groups will be better adjusted to the demands of later life. It may be superfluous to train for sociability in childhood when we know that certain nonsocial traits will be at a premium during adolescence. Eysenck (1965) has pointed out that traits that are sociable, active, optimistic, impulsive, changeable, and excitable go together; and that traits like unsociable, quiet, careful, and thoughtful also occur together. There may be no need to stress sociability unless we are willing to take all the traits which are linked with it in the bargain.

Our discussion and evaluation about play has been from an adult's view. How about the child's feelings? There is no evidence that it is more satisfying for a child to play in a group than alone. Group play can be fun, but it can also be annoying through noise, pushings, sand throwing, and having things taken away. Martha Wolfenstein (1955) has described the play of French children, pointing out that French parents are perfectly content when their child plays alone. Small children are often forbidden and rarely encouraged to play together or to use each other's toys.

Children often manipulate their own sex organs, show a curiosity for the sex organs of others, peep into bathrooms, undress in front of company, etc. Such activities, called *sexual play,* have received much attention in the psychological literature, especially from Freudian writers. We should, however, question if any of these activities are "sexual" from the child's point of view or if they are merely interpreted as such by the adult? In a controlled experiment we might find that children manipulate their toes, lips, thumbs, and ears as much as their penises and clitorises. One might also find that children would show anxiety or curiosity to see us reading the paper in the living room if we always left the bathroom door open, but locked the door to the living room every time we entered it.

Play has been described as following various socialization stages like *solitary* play, playing alone; *parallel* play, when children play side by side with different toys or games; *associative* play, when children play together without interaction, building their own sand castles, for instance; and finally as *cooperative* play, where they interact, taking turns playing ball at hop scotch, etc. (Stone & Church, 1963). It should again be emphasized that the above types of play are arbitrary categorizations and do not give us any information about short- and long-term effects. As yet, psychologists have no information about which type and amount of play benefits mental growth and socialization.

Chapter 8

MENTAL DEVELOPMENT

The definition of the mind has always plagued psychologists. Some study the mind by investigating the process of thinking or problem solving, others by investigating the accumulation of knowledge and memory, and still others by looking at the nature of ideas, be they simple, complex, or novel. Detailed approaches may be needed before the mechanism of the mind will be understood. Without knowing all the details some psychologists have formed theories hoping to get ahead understanding and predicting the human mind—and hoping to fill in the missing pieces as the theories develop. The three major psychological systems, those of Waston, Freud, and Piaget, will be discussed in this chapter.

WATSON—BEHAVIORISM

In the previous chapters we have discussed the various detailed ways of learning on which behaviorism is based. In this discussion we shall breifly review some of behaviorism's historical antecedents and its recent development in the area of behavior modification. Behaviorism assumes that a child's mind is mainly formed through teaching and training, and that the more complex mental acts are composed of sequences of simpler ones. Such reasoning forms the basis of *associationism*, first formulated by Aristotle over 2,000 years ago. As previously mentioned, Aristotle believed that we think of an object or event experienced in the past because we associate it with something we experience in the present. He postulated further that associations are more likely to occur when the past and present events or objects are very similar, very dissimilar, or appeared closely related in time or space when first experienced. These Aristotelian principles of association have respectively become known as the laws of similarity, contrast, and contiguity after having been revived by the British empirical philosophers Hobbes, Locke, Hume, Hartley, the Millses, Bain, and others. Locke thought that the mind was blank at birth (tabula rasa) and that knowledge could only be absorbed via the senses. Hartley proposed a neurophysiological model for the laws of association in 1749, and Alexander Bain (1818–1903) pointed out that thoughts or actions associated with pleasure will reoccur, and those associated with pain will not.

In general, associationistic principles have been supported by philosophers who emphasized environmental and *mechanistic views*. They have been opposed by scholastic, religious, and *mentalistic* philosophers who thought that knowledge, ideas, values, and such are "god-given" and neither determined nor influenced through environmental learning. The Russian physiologist, Sechenov (1829–1905), for instance, demonstrated that a spinal frog (head neurologically severed) will activate the left leg to scratch off a drop of acid put on the right leg and vice versa. This showed that certain "purposive" acts can be carried out by reflexes alone or by neuronal associations within the spinal cord—not involving the head. The church at that time believed, as many people still do, that purposive or willful actions can only be carried out by the mind, which is ruled by the soul, and that its function does not depend on any physical or material substrata, for instance on the nerves or the spinal cord. When in 1863 Sechenov wanted to publish his findings in a book entitled *An Attempt to Establish Physiological Bases of Psychical Processes* the church censors of St. Petersburg (later Leningrad) forbade it because they thought that such knowledge would corrupt the morals of society. He was finally allowed to publish his results when he changed his title to *Reflexes of the Brain,* omitting the liaison between the physical and the psychical.

Sechenov's work became known as *reflexology.* Though Pavlov did not know Sechenov in person he considered him his mentor and considered Sechenov's work on the reflexes the basis of his work on the conditioned reflex. John B. Watson (1878–1958) was the first to apply Pavlovian conditioning methods to infants and children at his laboratory at Johns Hopkins University. His work, and that of his students Rosalie Rayner and Mary Cover Jones, has already been discussed. They demonstrated that many infant fears and desires can be established by Pavlovian conditioning or association. Watson called his theories of associationism *behaviorism* because he was primarily interested in the associations between observable action or reactions—behavior.

Watson's behaviorism was readily accepted during the 1920s and the early 1930s. Watson became president of the American Psychological Association in 1915 and his books on child care were widely publicized. In the 1940s his views were largely displaced by Freud's psychoanalytic views on child development. In recent decades, however, behaviorism has flourished again. Mainly through the work of Skinner in the United States and Eysenck in Great Britain, methods were developed to deal with children's temper tantrums, enuresis, fighting, etc., and with adult's smoking, drinking, obesity, and sexual dysfunction. In the 1970s behavior modification broadened into more encompassing social approaches. More success was reported if individuals are punished, for instance, for drinking and also rewarded for not drinking or for drinking only limited amounts in various social settings (Hersen, et al., 1975–1977). Skinner envisioned in *Walden Two* that behavioral programming can be used for the betterment of society. Many behavior modifiers are now actually tested in areas of social significance such as racial integration, environmental pollution control, mass transit, medicine and psychopathology, school problems, penal reform, industry, and employment. There is hardly an area of human conduct which remains untouched by behavior modification. While this may be disconcerting we should realize that there has never been a time in history when parents, teachers, generals, philosophers, or kings did not try to influence, modify, or dictate the behavior of their charges. Behavior modification can be used for the detriment as well as for the benefit of society.

THE FREUDIAN MIND

Behaviorism puts its major emphasis on learning and environment while Freud's system emphasizes many innate urges, instincts, and desires only partially controllable by the environment. Freud has influenced Western thought in many respects. His belief and that of his followers with regard to punishment and various socialization issues such as sucking, breast-feeding, and toiletting have already been pointed out. In the following we shall give a more global view of his system.

Freud developed his model of the mind from working with neurotic adults. He came, however, to the conclusion that all neuroses stem from sexual frustrations experienced in early childhood. He therefore postulated many forces, stages, and periods within the child's mind which have, for better or for worse, become the trading stock of many American psychiatrists, psychologists, and educators for describing and explaining the mind of abnormal as well as normal children.

It is difficult to give a precise overview of the Freudian system because Freud defines many of his terms very broadly and changed some of his definitions during his 50 years of productivity. There are also individual and national differences in interpretation and emphasis given to various parts of Freud's writings. The following account shall therefore present only a very general sketch of Freud's postulations and shall lean heavily on Freud's own summarization work, on his booklet entitled *An Outline of Psychoanalysis* (1940), published a year after his death in 1939.

Freud thought that there are three *psychosexual stages* that characterize the pleasure-seeking desires in a child's mental development. He called the first stage the *oral* stage (usually up to two years). During this stage a child's actions and satisfactions occur mostly through the activities of the mouth by sucking, swallowing, or biting. The second stage is the *anal* stage (usually three to four years), when the child is preoccupied with his bowel movement and derives a certain pleasure by its expulsion (see "Toilet Training"). During the third stage, the *phallic* stage (usually five to six years), the child is said to receive his gratifications by manipulating his genitals.

The child's actions or behaviors described in the above stages are obvious and need no further elaboration. But why does Freud call these stages "psychosexual?" What is sexual about thumbsucking, biting, or eliminating? Most of Freud's definitions, and especially his definition of sex, are very general and all inclusive. Freud pictured the purpose of life as the propagation of the species. This requires sex, but it also requires growing up, living, sensing, and surviving. Hence anything pertaining to life such as eating, sleeping, eliminating, or almost any activity or desire can be defined as "sexual." Freud's treatment of human sexuality is quite different from that of *Playboy* magazine and lacks pictures!

Another postulate typical of the Freudian rationale is the notion that the desires which occur during the psychosexual stages are innate. In this respect Freud differs from Watson's behavioristic view. Examples of the controversy have been discussed more specifically under the topics of thumbsucking and bedwetting. It should be mentioned that in spite of this heredity-environment controversy both Freud and Watson agree in their mechanistic veiwpoint. Neither invoked the soul or any other god-given powers. Freud believed that the origins of thoughts are physical, coming primarily from an internal biology. Watson also thought that the origins of knowledge or thoughts are physical, but that they come primarily from the outside environment.

Most typical of Freudian reasoning and that of psychoanalysis is the assumption that behavior or desires that are thwarted in any of the psychosexual stages will become not less, but more pronounced in adulthood. A child, for instance, who did not get enough sucking in the oral stage will show increased sucking desires or an oral personality in adulthood. Since the child also learns that sucking or thumbsucking is not socially accepted, it's sucking desire will not manifest itself in adulthood by sucking, but rather in other activities of the mouth, in excessive eating, drinking, smoking, kissing, talking, in becoming a preacher or perhaps a teacher.

Frustrations during the phallic stage will also have their future consequences. They may increase fear of sexual matters or they may increase desires for vanity, exhibitionism, and other sexual forms of self-stimulation. Whether the behavior is sucking, biting, hitting, sex, or aggression, it is postulated that a certain amount of every type of behavior or desire is in every person and must "come out" in one way or another.

This assumption has had far-reaching theoretical and practical implications on American childrearing. In the last decades there has been a reluctance to simply punish or prevent undesirable behaviors. "Letting off steam," "ventilating," "acting out one's aggressions" in group or play therapy, and sensitivity training sessions have become very popular.

Haim Ginott in his best seller *Between Parent and Child* (1969) suggests that a jealous older child who hits the baby be given a doll and be rewarded for hitting the doll. In another instance he advised the parent to say the following, "If you want to, you can throw stones at the tree and pretend it's your sister. If you want to, you can even draw her face on paper, stick it on the tree, and then throw stones; but she is not to be hurt" (p. 119). Such bits of advice follow precisely the Freudian rationale. It is assumed that a certain amount of aggression (for example, hitting or stone throwing) is in every child, that this aggression must come out, and that the desire for it will end after it has come out.

From a behaviorist's point of view the above advice would be considered dangerous. If aggression is predominantly a matter of learning, then we would actually teach the children to be aggressive by rewarding them for hitting and throwing stones. This aggression may generalize back to the baby, to the sister, to other children, or to animals. A behaviorist could only be sure that aggression will not generalize if he performs a discrimination experiment. This would, for instance, require the repeated presence of baby and doll, with punishment when the baby is hit and with reward when the doll is hit. Such an experiment would, of course, be quite unfair to the baby, and at best may produce a child who hits dolls and throws stones at trees.

The psychosexual stages are followed by a *latency period* in which the child supposedly manifests no sexual activities, interests, or desires. It is said to begin around the age of seven lasting until the onset of puberty. While it is likely that children show less sexual curiosity or genital manipulation during this period, we should perhaps consider that they may have learned not to do so by the time they approach the age of seven. They may also have learned to perform their sexual play in more secret places—in the school's rest room, or at home under their bed covers hidden from parents or psychiatrists. In any event, Freud believed that humans are the only species who have this sexual rest or latency period in their development. He called the human sexual development *biphasic*, indicating that it develops in two phases. First, during the psychosexual stage (up to six years) and, second, during the *genital* stage that begins after the latency period with the onset of puberty.

At the beginning of this genital stage sexual interests are first directed toward oneself (narcism or narcissism), then toward others of the same sex (homosexuality), and finally toward others of the opposite sex (heterosexuality). This is described as the normal course of development. Sex is again broadly defined. A girl may be judged as narcissistic when she combs her hair for prolonged periods, or a boy, for instance, can go through his homosexual period by seeking out the company of other boys. Sexual relations need not take place. Similar to the psychosexual stage, the desires in the genital stage must also find satisfaction lest there be trouble later on. If an adolescent has gone through the homosexual stage, but not through his heterosexual relations he is said to be a *fixated homosexual*. If a person has had an inadequate homosexual development, he will have troubles in his heterosexual relations, and may practice or desire homosexuality after heterosexual relations. Such a person is said to be a *regressed homosexual.* In the Freudian system one always seems to have more than one chance.

In early childhood certain desires or fears are said to develop partially through inborn desires and partially through environmental conditions. They are called *complexes* and are supposed to linger on to influence thoughts in childhood and adulthood. There are two complexes for the boy. The boy loves his mother, considers the father as his rival, and hates him. This is called the *Oedipus complex.* The boy also fears that the father will detect his desires and will castrate him. To prevent this he turns around and loves his father. This is called the *castration complex.* The girl likewise has two complexes. She loves the father, the *Electra complex.* The more she loves him, the more she wants to have his penis, and the more she blames and hates the father for not having given her a penis. This is the *penis envy complex.* In his later writings Freud proposed only two major instincts. He thought individuals were torn between the **life** instinct, *eros,* and the death instinct, *thanatos.* The energy for the life instinct comes from the *libido,* the all-inclusive, sexual life force. Freud did not speculate on the energy source of the death instinct.

There is much interplay, often called *dynamic* relations, between the complexes and the conscious and unconscious wishes. Before we can understand these relationships, we have to look at another important Freudian classification of the processes of the mind. According to Freud, all basic urges stem from the *id.* The id, which in English means "it," is the most basic structure of the mind and its biological and sexual (in the broad sense) wishes are unconscious. The *ego* (the "I") is that part of the mind that is known to us. Most of the ego is conscious but some of it is said to be preconscious. Freud considers this preconscious a sort of twilight zone between unconsciousness and consciousness. Freud's third mental force is the *superego,* which represents a person's conscience or mores taught to him by parents and society. We are conscious of certain functions of the superego and unconscious of others.

The ego is often considered the middleman between that which the id wants and that which the superego does not want. The id may send wishes to the ego that are unacceptable to the ego or the superego. The ego can reject or modify these wishes in certain ways. This occurs through the ego's *censor* which screens the id's wishes. The censor can reject a wish. The censor can also let a wish pass into the ego temporarily and the ego can later send it back into its preconscious. This action is called *repression.* Repressed desires may be brought back into full consciousness with the help of a psychoanalyst. The censor has other alternatives. It can accept an "unacceptable" wish in modified form. This gives rise to symbolism. Much of the id's work is done during sleep, when the censor is allegedly off guard. When a woman reports that she has dreamed of walking in the woods, that is what is conscious in her ego. Her id, a psychoanalyst may say, was wishing that she could look at penises, for instance. The censor found the idea of a penis unacceptable and modified it to trees, or to other elongated objects. The investigation of the unconsicous depends on such symbolism. Many students after having read Freud will never again believe that a cigar is merely a cigar.

The interplay between the id, ego, and superego with such characteristics as unconsciousness, preconsciousness, and consciousness gives the Freudian system an unlimited possibility of describing and of hypothesizing causes for human thought and actions. This very flexibility has frustrated experimental psychologists who feel it necessary to investigate operationally defined or observable units of behavior. Experimentalists feel very uncomfortable with such broad categorization as, for instance, "oral personality." It may not be difficult to label a person an "oral personality" if he eats too much, smokes too much, and talks too much. But how are people labeled who excel in only one of these acts—people who eat much, but smoke and talk little, or those who talk much, eat little, and do not smoke at all?

The Freudian emphasis on the unconscious broadens once more the possibilities of labeling or interpreting. A person could go on a hunger strike. But if we invoke unconscious motives, we could lable even him as an oral personality. We could say that his unconscious (id) wants so much oral activity that he consciously (ego) fights against it by not eating. Such mechanisms have been termed *reaction formations.*

Freud's system is inexhaustible in possibilities, ideas, and hypotheses. In his early medical career he wrote on the subjects of aphasia and cerebral palsies. He was the first to investigate the anesthetic properties of cocaine after having read that Indians in Peru chew coca leaves to increase their energy. Freud took small amounts of it (1/20 gr.) internally and described the effects of it as "exhilarating," giving a "normal feeling of well being," producing "vitality," and an increased "capacity to work" (Jones, E., 1953, p. 81). Freud recommended cocaine to a colleague who was a morphine addict. Cocaine cured the morphine addiction, but his colleague became severely addicted to cocaine instead. Freud himself never became addicted to the drug and he began to search for the causes of this differential effect. A careful reading of Freud's articles on cocaine addiction and cocaine fear (see Jones, E., 1953, pp. 409–410) would settle many present arguments about the effects and dangers of drugs. It would show that other physiological and psychological factors, many of which are still unknown, interact as yet unpredictably with the drugs and their dosages.

Freud also pioneered with the local applications of cocaine and found it to have a pain-killing action on the mucous membranes of mouth, throat, and eyes. He described and demonstrated this local anesthetic property of cocaine to some of his colleagues in ophthalmology and urged them to use it in eye operations. One of these colleagues, Carl Koller, took Freud's suggestion, found it successful, and revolutionized eye surgery by the use of cocaine. But when Koller reported his findings in the medical journals, he gave Freud little credit for the discovery. Bailey (1964) suggests that Freud's contributions on this as well as on many other scientific matters was speculative and without confirmatory data and that it was Koller who did the experimental work, testing cocaine on the eyes of animals to establish its effect and dosage. In any event, to this day the *Encyclopedia Britannica* lists Koller as the sole discoverer of cocaine.

After this incident, which his biographer Jones calls "the cocaine episode," Freud wrote a letter to his fiancée saying that the next thing he would invent nobody would be able to take away from him. He accomplished this purpose. Many of his abstract and logic-tight statements and definitions have not been proven, but neither have they been disproven.

There has been some dissent within Freud's psychoanalytic school. One of Freud's colleagues, Carl Gustav Jung (1875–1961), severed his affiliation with Freud in 1914 (Watson, R. I., 1968). Jung thought that sexual urges are important, but he also thought that instinctive, religious impulses were equally, if not more, important energy sources for human action. Alfred Adler (1870–1937), another one of Freud's collaborators, considered organismic and social inferiority as the main human driving force. He postulated the *inferiority complex* and stressed such terms as *compensation* and *overcompensation* to describe the activities necessary to overcome the inferiority. There was also Otto Rank (1884–1939) who believed that neuroses were caused by a birth trauma and that man has an unconscious desire to return to his mother's womb.

There were other modifications of Freud's system by the neoFreudians, notably by Karen Horney (1885–1952). She accepted Freud's unconscious motivation and his biological determinism, but rejected the idea of the libido, Freud's concept of life, sexual energy, or the basis of the id forces. Horney also thought that the *Oedipus complex* was not a biological necessity. A contemporary neoFreudian, Erich Fromm, believes that the desire to get away from instinctual impulses is one of the main driving forces. There have been other psychoanalysts who differed with Freud in more or less important details. In the main, however, they have all stressed the mechanism of the unconscious.

In a special supplement of *The Atlantic* entitled "Psychiatry in American Life" (Mowrer, 1961), it is pointed out that Freud and his psychoanalytic system have found practically no acceptance in Catholic countries, but his system is practiced predominantly in Protestant nations, especially in England and America. Mowrer suggests that the Freudian system replaces a certain authority that was lost in the Reformation. Whatever the reasons, Freud's theories have dominated American psychiatry and clinical and child psychology for several decades.

In recent years, however, the emphasis in our society has been on fast and practical solutions, and Skinnerian behavior modification and drug-therapy techniques have gained acceptance. These methods do not dig too deeply into the child's mind or past and concern themselves little with theories and systems. In spite of the success and the practicality of behaviorism, Americans did not accept criticism against Freud's theories until it was voiced by activists in the women's liberation movement. Not only were Freud's assumptions about the major differences of the sexes wrong, but they were also degrading and insulting to women. Freud, for instance, assumed that the fetus is initially male and develops later into a female—a sort of "Eve-out-of-Adam" view. This, as already mentioned in the discussion on maturation, is opposite to the facts. Freud further assumed that the female clitoris is a stunted penis and that therefore females feel inferior. He wrote (*Imago,* 1940) that girls around the age of two either see a male penis or know "phylogenetically" (innately) that males have a penis. This makes them hate their mother whom they blame for their inferior physique. Hence, girls have to switch their love object— away from the mother towards the father. This leads to conflicts and feelings of insecurity which stay with the female for the rest of her life. But loving the father also has disadvantages because, as already mentioned, the female envies him for his penis which leads to further frustrations.

Freud considered a clitoral-vaginal shift as a necessary condition for normal, female sexuality. He stated that a girl, unlike a boy, should not manually stimulate her genitals too often during her phallic period (4 to 7 years) because she should not accustom herself to receive pleasure from her stunted penis, her clitoris. If she does receive this "masculine" pleasure in her childhood it may lead to homosexuality, inferiority, or to frigidity because her clitoris may refuse to give up its pleasure during puberty when the clitoral sensitivity is to be replaced in favor of vaginal sensitivity. Freud had no empirical evidence for his assumptions. Surveys involving hundreds of women have shown that clitoral stimulation is as pleasurable, if not more so, as vaginal (Fisher, 1973; Kinsey et al., 1953). Surveys have also shown that neurotic women experience not fewer but more orgasms than non–neurotic women (Sigusch, 1971). In summary, Freud believed that females as compared to males have a number of disadvantages: a psychic inferiority involving body parts, a faulty conscience (super-ego), a psychic love-hate ambivalence towards the opposite sex, and guilt feelings because they have to change their love from mother to father. All this, according the Freud, makes the female predisposed to envy and to an inadequate sense of justice (Freud: Collected Papers, 1892–1939). It is not to the credit of American psychologists and psychiatrists that they did not challenge the Freudian view for decades until its deficiency was pointed out by various female activists and female psychiatrists in the late 1960s.

Piaget's Developing Superstructures

In a dualistic fashion similar to that of Freud, Piaget postulates two major factors, the individual and the environment, which interact dynamically to form the basis of all intellectual functions. Piaget (Pia as in *pia*no, get as in *ja*de) believes that children learn through a continual interplay between their acting upon the environment and being transformed or modified by it in return. Their actions, directed upon the environment, occur through manipulative contact and in a feedback fashion these actions become internalized as thoughts. Thus our thoughts become transformed and modified by our own actions. Piaget views all of the child's cognitive behavior (thought processes) as assisting the *adaptation* to the environment and as being based on an underlying organization varying in quality and quantity with the child's age. In spite of these organizational changes there is a movement towards balance, an *equilibrium,* between child and environment which is the essence of Piaget's *adaptation.* Because neither child nor environment is static a permanent state of equilibrium is impossible; rather, it is an ideal state for which most human beings strive.

Piaget sees this quest for the equilibrium between child and the environment as composed of two major mental forces or functions which he calls *assimilation* and *accommodation.* Assimilation describes the organism's need to incorporate or fit the outside world into its previous experience and into its present needs. It is the child's attempt to make external reality fit his or her point of view. Calling the milkman "daddy" may be an example of assimilation since the child "adjusts" by perceiving something unfamiliar as something familiar. Hunt (1961) has pointed out that Piaget's concept of assimilation is similar to the Pavlovian concept of "stimulus generalization" found in conditioning experiments. Piaget points to play behaviors as a frequent example of assimilation. A stick, for instance, may be called a rifle. (The authors wonder if calling a rifle a stick would not be a better example.)

Every encounter with an object, whether it is familiar or novel, involves some amount of assimilation. But one product of the child's interactions with the world is that he or she discovers that certain existing categories are not appropriate for certain stimuli, so that these stimuli cannot be easily assimilated. Thus, assimilation is balanced by accommodation when the child changes his or her behavior to adapt to reality and the milkman will then be called "milkman." Imitating the walk or dress of an older sister is given as an example of accommodation.

Accommodation and assimilation interplay. They are independent of a person's age level and are present throughout life. Although the content of our thought processes change they are always the product of the interaction between the two antagonistic (dualistic) processes—assimilation and accommodation. Assimilation gets ahead of accommodation and then accommodation catches up to form, temporarily, the "ideal" equilibrium. This process is continuously repeated and gives rise to certain behavior patterns which Piaget calls *schemata*. Through the activity of certain schemata, new schemata arise. These schemata form the various developmental stages. Each stage has new behavior, but it arises from the previous stage. This successive formation of superstructures, one growing out of the other, is called "epigenetic" development by Piaget.

Piaget divides mental development into two major periods.

The first one is called "sensorimotor intelligence." It characterizes the development during the first two years of life and is divided into six substages enumerated below with their respective behaviorial patterns.

1   *Use of Reflex Schemata (up to 1 month)*. Neonatal reflexes such as sucking, vocalizing, grasping.

2   *Primary Circular Reactions (1 to 5 months)*. Some interaction with environment. Looking around, attending to sound and voices. Some coordinated movements.

3   *Secondary Circular Reaction (5 to 8 months)*. Reaction to feedback from environment. Shaking crib and doll will move. Soon shaking crib again. (In Skinnerian terms, able to increase operant level of crib shaking). Beginning of intentionality.

4   *Coordination of Secondary Schemata (8 to 12 months)*. Some problem-solving, goal-directed behavior. Looking or reaching around a barrier for hidden object. First intelligent behavior appears.

5   *Tertiary Circular Reaction (12 to 18 months)*. Curiosity for its own sake. Trial and error. Experimenting in order to see, or to discover. Inventive intelligence.

6   *Invention through Mental Combination (18 to 24 months)*. Appearance of conceptual and symbolic thought. Awareness of relationships. Conceptual intelligence begins.

The cognitive development of the sensorimotor period evolves as the child acts on the environment. The child becomes aware of the permanence of objects which makes symbolic thoughts possible. Piaget constructed the above substages during the 1930s while observing the development of his own children (Piaget, 1952; Hunt, 1961). His children must have been quite normal, because the behavior described by Piaget can frequently be observed. It is quite obvious that a child's behavior in the first two years of his life develops from simple reflexes to a capacity of some symbolic thought. Less obvious is Piaget's rationale for selecting six substages. Could we combine, for instance, stages 2 and 3? Can there be an interaction with environment without feedback from it? A three-month-old baby will cry when hungry. He will learn to anticipate food upon hearing his mother's footsteps and calm down. If the footsteps should lead to the telephone and not into the baby's room, the baby will soon start to cry again. This would show some feedback and intentionality, entities that Piaget did not postulate until the following stage which begins at five months.

We have just barely touched Piaget's notions on the interaction of stages. He postulates that they interact through hierarchization, integration, consolidation, structuring, and equilibrium. His explanations of these concepts are scattered throughout various books and articles and depend much on his own private vocabulary in "Piagenetic" language. Pinard and Laurendeau (1969) have summarized and interpreted Piaget's concept of "stage" and have made matters somewhat clearer.

Piaget calls the second major developmental period *mental operation.* It starts at the age of two and lasts until the beginning of adult intelligence. It has the following four substages.

1 *Preconceptual Thought (2 to 4 years).* Language, symbolic schemata, beginning of thought. Knowledge of difference between an object and an idea. Transductive reasoning.
2 *Intuitive Thought (4 to 7 years).* Thinking not yet logically based on immediate impressions. Prelogical schematization of perceptual data. No thinking about own thoughts. Centration.
3 *Concrete Operations (7 to 12 years).* Mental representation, object can be presented through senses, relations. Consideration of others views. Conservation— realization of constancy of certain concepts. Number concept.
4 *Formal Operations (from 12 years on).* Differentiation between real action and abstract hypotheses. Searching for alternatives. Solving problems in the abstract. Adult intelligence.

Piaget conducted a number of ingenious experiments that helped him form the above categories. Most significantly and most frequently mentioned is his water-pouring experiment on which much of the categorization and differentiation of stage 2, Intuitive thought (4 to 7 years), and stage 3, Concrete Operation (7 to 12 years), is based. Piaget poured the water contained in a low flat glass into a narrower, tall glass. Children under six will insist that there is more water in the taller glass. Children over seven will say that it contains the same amount of water because nothing has been added. They are able to detach quantity from a particular shape. Similar to this "transfer of liquid" problem is the coin problem in which children are shown two rows of coins having the same number of coins but different length, as for instance,

Row A: 0—0—0—0—0—0

Row B: 0-0-0-0-0-0

Children under six years will say that there are more coins in Row A, while the length of the rows will not influence the numerical judgment of children over seven.

Preoperational thought is somewhat "plodding," inflexible, irreversible, and is dominated by perception. But as the child moves into the concrete operations stage these characteristics gradually subside and logical thought begins to develop as is most clearly seen in what has been called the *conservation* problems. Conservation is the child's ability to realize that an object maintains certain aspects of its identity while changing others, like the amount of water and the number of coins which were conserved in the above experiments. As with all the other changes in cognitive structures (schemata) the change from pre-operational to operational is gradual and supposedly independent of learning and reinforcement.

Piaget did much experimental testing but even more theorizing. Superimposed or interwoven into his four stages of mental operations are his classifications of causes and logic. He differentiated between 17 distinct types of causal explanation (Piaget, 1929, 1930).

In the area of logic he distinguished between formal, quasi-logical, logicomathematical, and so on, functions. There are eight such subgroupings alone in his "concrete operation" stage. Interacting with all these concepts are Piaget's notions and still more classification of the interaction of children and their relation to objects and to society. He related "Egocentricity" to his many stages and substages. He speaks, for instance, of sensory motor egocentrism—the conquest of the object; of preoperational egocentrism—the conquest of the symbol; of concrete operational egocentrism—the lack of differentiation between assumptions and facts; and so on (Elkind, 1970).

Piaget and Inhelder (1968) and their coworkers have also done voluminous amounts of research on children's memory and intelligence. A specific section from their book *Memoire et Intelligence* will be described in some detail to give the reader an example of the literally thousands of variables that are being investigated by Piaget and his research group in Geneva. In a research section entitled "Memory of Configurations," different series of lines are presented to children of different ages. These lines are presented in equal length, | | | | | ; in alternating length, | ᵢ | ᵢ | ; in increasing length, ᵢ ᵢ | | | ; or decreasing length, | | | ᵢ ᵢ ; in M configuration, | | ᵢ | | ; and in many more different shapes and forms. Children of different ages are tested on their memory of these various figures. Five-year-olds, for instance, may remember lines of alternate length better than those of equal length, but may not remember the M configuration. Seven-year-olds will show a different memory pattern, nine-year-olds a still different one, and so on. From such differential findings Piaget attempts to form his theory on the development of memory.

The above examples of the memory of lines presents in itself almost unlimited, endless research possibilities. But Piaget and Inhelder's book goes on to investigate memory of differently arranged dots, matches arranged in dissimilar spaces, water levels in differently shaped containers, triangles presented in different sections. Each of these research units yields an enormous amount of data. There are eighteen such units in the book. The research reported in each unit or chapter is undertaken by various coworkers whose names appear in small print in a footnote at the beginning of each chapter. Alone, the titles of these chapters may indicate the large variety of approaches by which Piaget and his coworkers investigate memory. Some of these titles are as follows: "Memory of Sets of Numerical Equivalents Presented in Different Arrangements," "Memory of Similar Numbers Arranged in Dissimilar Spaces," "Memory of Intersection of Classes," "Memory of Causal Processes which the Subject Cannot Understand."

Piaget presents data and theories on many other subjects, notably on language formation and on the moral judgment of children, which are as voluminous as his work on memory described above. Since 1923 Piaget has written hundreds of books, monographs, and articles.

Piaget's books written in French are difficult to interpret, psychologically as well as linguistically, because he has used many subjective and abstract definitions. Moreover, his books are difficult to understand without having read his previous books and this again is difficult because he has written so many books— as many as six in one year! The diversity of his writings can be seen from the titles of some of his books: *The Moral Judgment of the Child* (1932), *The Origins of Intelligence in Children* (1936), *The Construction of Reality in the Child* (1937), *The Child's Concept of Time* (1946), *The Mechanism of Perception* (1961), *Insights and Illusions of Philosophy* (1965), *Biology and Knowledge* (1967), *Genetic Epistemology* (1971), *To Understand is to Invent* (1976), etc. In their review of Piaget's theory, Ginsburg and Opper (1978) cite over 30 books which Piaget has written. There are several other summaries of Piaget's work, notably those of Flavell (1963) and Cowan (1978).

Few psychologists are neutral regarding Piaget's system. Many accept it with awe, others reject it. Almost all psychologists, however, agree that Piaget's experiments and hypotheses have stimulated enormous amounts of research. From year to year an increasing number of articles are published that relate to Piaget's work. Those who favor Piaget welcome his "middle of the road" approach to child development. They consider his approach less rigid than behaviorism, but more objective than Freudianism. They also see in his system an individual approach to intelligence testing which explains children's mental development by their own developmental or biological stages and not by comparing them to others on a fixed intelligence scale.

The negative critics of Piaget's system could point out that his work is not entirely novel, and that Binet recognized the quantitative as well as the qualitative aspects of mental development decades before Piaget. Binet's test includes items dealing with objects, symbols, concepts, reversible concepts, conservation, abstract reasoning, and causal relations (see: "The Intellect"). There were others who investigated certain mental factors as extensively and in experimentally sounder fashion than Piaget. As early as 1923 Beckmann investigated the development of the number concept by presenting 30 different stimulus situations to 465 children ranging in ages from two to six years. He found that his experimental results depended on the intelligence of the subjects, the type of task involved, and the response criterion. Hull's (1920) early test of concept formation used sets of Chinese symbols with common elements. His subjects had to "abstract" to find these elements. They also had to "generalize" in order to classify the sets of symbols that had the same elements. Hull found that both abstraction and generalization occurred in a more or less trial and error fashion. There is also the work of Heidbreder (1928) who investigated problem solving and concept formation. She presented children and adults with plain and dotted boxes, hiding a doll under one of them. She wanted to know, for instance, when and how her subjects learned that the doll was hidden in the farthest box when the boxes were plain, and in the nearest one when they were dotted. Heidbreder found that ability increases with age while it changed from less to more adaptive and from more subjective to more objective behavior.

The novelty of a system, however, is far less important than the reliability of its data. Are Piaget's data correct? Several authorities state that his experiments have been replicated all over the world and that their results were found to be essentially correct (Elkind, 1970; Reese & Lipsitt, 1970). However, it is not Piaget's data, but the inferences that he draws from them which have often not been substantiated by subsequent experiments. An example of a series of water-level experiments shall serve to point out such a data-theory credibility gap.

Piaget and Inhelder (1956, 1968) and Inhelder (1969) report a series of experiments in which children were shown a transparent bottle partially filled with water. The bottle was shown in various positions: right-side up, lying down, upside down, and at a 45° angle. Children of various ages were asked to show or draw the water level while the bottle was in front of them in these various positions. Piaget and Inhelder called this task "perception." In another task they showed the bottle right-side up and asked the children to indicate or to draw the water level as it would be in various nonupright positions. This was the "prediction" task. Piaget and Inhelder found that five-year-olds respond quite incorrectly, that six-year-olds often draw the water line parallel to the bottom of the bottle, and that seven-year-olds have a tendency to draw curved surfaces (see drawings of jars below).

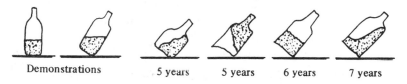

Demonstrations   5 years   5 years   6 years   7 years

Typical incorrect responses reported by
Piaget & Inhelder (1956)

From these and other findings, Piaget and Inhelder made the general conclusion that the notion of "horizontality" is acquired relatively late, around the age of nine. They concluded specifically that prediction of the water level, like its perception, develop together because their subjects performed equally on both tasks. They also believed that a child can neither be taught nor practice the water-level task because the "prediction" capacity depends on the innate "perception" capacity.

Ford (1970) repeated Piaget and Inhelder's experiment with 20 preschool children ranging from four to six years. He found that there was a significant difference between his subjects' perceptive and predictive capacities. His mean number of correct responses for eight different tilt positions was 2.5 for prediction and 4.4 for perception. Ford's results also cast doubt on Piaget and Inhelder's general conclusion about the onset of "horizontality." Ford found some understanding of it, although all of his subjects were below the age of six.

Essex, et al. (1971) and Wesley (1971) tested several hundred grammar school children from the ages of six to eight in the Sacramento, California, and Portland, Oregon areas. The children were asked to draw the correct level into a graph outlining the respective tilt of the bottle. It was found that correct levels could be predicted by about 30% of the six-year-olds, 70% of the seven-year-olds, and 90% of the eight-year-olds. Percentages on the perception task were still higher. Similar to Piaget and Inhelder studies, it was found that the subjects had most difficulties with the 45° tilt. But in no case were the levels drawn as grossly incorrect as some of Piaget and Inhelder's subjects who suspended the liquid in midair or placed it in the upper part of the bottle (see drawing).

Contrary to Piaget and Inhelder's results, the results of Essex, et al., Wesley, and Ford indicate that "horizontality" is generally mastered by the age of seven, that perception and prediction are not congruent, and that a good half of those children who drew initially incorrect levels can correct themselves within one or two practice trials. We can only guess why certain follow-up experiments yield different data than those found by Piaget and Inhelder. Thd 30 subjects used by Piaget and Inhelder ranged from ages three to eleven. There were, for instance, only nine subjects in the seven-year-old group and only two in the eight-year-old group. These small groups of subjects were again divided. Some were shown a rectangular bottle, others a spherical one. Furthermore, few subjects received uniform instructions as Piaget and Inhelder adjusted their comments to the subjects' responses. Thus, quite often Piaget bases a specific theoretical assumption on the performance of one or very few individuals.

Piaget's system assumes that his specific phases as well as their particular sequence are biologically determined. Thus it should not be possible to teach a child conservation tasks during his nonconservational stage. However, Halford and Fullerton (1970) among others were successful in teaching "conservation of number." They used a row of six dolls and a row of six doll beds. Children in the nonconservation stage (below seven) will usually say that there are more dolls when the dolls are spaced wider than the beds. In other words they will not conserve or maintain "numberness" when space is altered. Halford and Fullerton gave twelve of their subjects special practice and found that eight of them attained conservation as compared to one out of twelve control subjects.

Can the formation of concepts be dissected and categorized at all? W. H. King (1960) made an extensive experiment testing the development of such concepts as length, weight, time, direction, and volume. He tested approximately 2,000 children and found that the formation of certain concepts increased rather steadily during the developmental years. In his ball problems, for instance, children had to choose one of five given vertical directions in which to throw a ball as far as possible. The number of correct solutions increased steadily with age, from 16% at the six-year-old level to 50% at the nine-year-old level. An entirely different developmental picture was obtained when the same concept was presented with a jumping task rather than a ball-throwing task.

King found other concepts that increased steadily with age

and believes that in such instances Piaget's stages are unnecessary, if not misleading. King has also shown that the slightest change in the presentation of a task may show a different developmental pattern. This fact, which has been repeatedly demonstrated, makes any theorizing about the formation of concepts extremely difficult. King also found that certain concepts do not develop by growth, nor through normal experiences, but need to be explicitly taught. Concepts involving weight and volume fall into this category. Many adults have difficulty with them even after explanation. We also know that many adults are unable to consider "other views," a Piagetian requirement of the concrete operation period of the ages seven to twelve. When asked, for instance, in which way are day and night alike, some adults will answer, "They are not alike, they are opposites." Does this inability to see day and night as both measuring time classify these adults as "Preoperational?"

Many aspects of Piaget's theories have been proven, many have not. Piaget's experiments fascinate most children and are simple to conduct with such items as half-empty pop bottles, coins, buttons, or matches. Theories must be testable and it is to Piaget's credit that his theories lend themselves to experimental evaluations. One wonders, however, how many more theories should be advanced before follow-up experiments can catch up with their verification.

OTHER SYSTEMS

As already mentioned in the chapter on maturation, Gesell, like Piaget, has observed and classified child behavior for almost 50 years. His system has been widely accepted in America. It is based primarily on observations of physical growth and motor development. But since physical and mental growth are closely related, Gesell's work is also a scale for mental development. Gesell (1925, 1940) describes a child's motor characteristics (physical movements), language, adaptive behavior, and personal-social behavior at various age levels. Thus Gesell's system encompasses a range of behavior as broad as that covered by Piaget's work. Unlike Piaget, Gesell puts more emphasis on inheritance (Hunt, 1963). Piaget believes that the development of the mind depends on a constant interaction between biological and environmetal factors, while Gesell views the succession of environmental stages as being genetically determined. All investigators agree, of course, that care and nuturants are necessary for survival and health, but they do not agree on the amount of teaching and coaching necessary to develop the mind. This controversy between heredity and environment will flare up again in the discussion of the IQ in the following chapter.

There are several other "grandiose" developmental systems, which are perhaps more literary than observational in origin. As already mentioned there, is Erikson's (1960) system in the Freudian vein which postulates the following eight crises in the psychosocial development of man: "trust vs. mistrust" in infancy, "autonomy vs. shame" in early childhood, "initiative vs. guilt" in play age, industry vs. inferiority" in school age, "identity vs. identity diffusion" in adolescence, "intimacy vs. isolation" in young adulthood, "generality vs. self-absorption" in adulthood, and finally "integrity vs. disgust" in later age. In short, a crisis for every age.

Ilg and Ames (1955) in their book *Child Behavior* postulate quite different developmental periods. The one-, two-, and three-year-old periods are, respectively, designated as "self-confidence," "calm willingness," and "love to conform." The four-year-old stage is termed "out of bounds" followed by "good little five-year-old." Things become stormy again with the "tumultuous six," and so on, until the age of ten which is described as "very nicest age" where predictability and equilibrium dominate. So mothers and teachers really have something to look forward to.

More systems could be cited. But even those of Piaget and Gesell, which have been more carefully formulated, are criticized for the lack of scientific rigor and for their arbitrariness in categorizing (Alexander, 1969, p.345; Kimble & Garmezy,

1968, pp. 531–536). The non-system-building psychologists who investigated smaller units or special problems in mental development had it somewhat easier and received less criticism. But as we shall see in the following paragraphs much of their work has likewise been inconclusive.

Creativity is one of the mental functions that has received much recent attention. There is agreement in defining it as verbal flexibility, striving toward the less typical, open mindedness, sensitivity, artistic, but objective data obtained by Guilford (1962) show that creativity has a rather complex composition. The following are some of Guilford's major findings.

There may be two types of creativity. One type that requires *divergent* thinking, another *convergent* thinking. Divergent thinking is thought that fans out from one idea and can be measured by

1   *A fluency factor.* The examinee is asked, for instance, to name all things he can think of that are solid, flexible, and colored. (Possible answers: cloth, leaf, rose, hair, leather.)
2   *A flexibility factor.* For instance, the examinee must list all the uses of a brick. (Possible answers: build a home, throw it, paperweight, drive a nail.)
3   *An originality factor.* More difficult to define, and an *elaboration* factor, which requires the completion of a barely outlined plan.

Convergent thinking requires a novel or a typical solution from several given alternatives. A subject may be asked which of the following five objects, or their parts, could be used to start a fire: A fountain pen, an onion, a pocket watch, a light bulb, or a bowling ball? (Answer: cover of watch face for lens.)

Guilford isolates two other major abilities. The *cognitive* ability, which he relates to the discovery and recognition of information, and the memory ability related to the storage of this information. These two abilities seem to depend on each other. Good memory contributes to good thinking. Memory is not outmoded. We seem to need a good and detailed memory, but we also need to store it in organized or special ways.

Since creativity is composed of various factors it is not surprising that Guilford found it rare for one individual to be equally creative in science, arts, mathematics, administration, and musical composition. Fluency and flexibility in concrete material seem to be important for inventors, painters, and composers, while fluency and flexibility with verbal and abstract material are essential for writers and scientists. Personality-wise, creative art students are more of the "observer" type, and creative science students more of the "participant" type. In general the creative student as compared to the noncreative is more self-confident, bold, and finds ideas more important than people. He is not necessarily the teacher's pet. He may be compared to the *introvert* personality which Eysenck described as stimulus-rich and fast-learning. The creative person is generally more intelligent than the noncreative person. But many intelligent people are not creative. There are a great number of highly intelligent people who are not creative as measured by IQ and creativity tests.

Guilford believes that we can approximately identify potential creativity by the presence of certain or all of the above-mentioned character traits. Guilford also states that the correlation between certain personality traits and creativity does not help us in understanding the nature of creativity.

At the present stage of knowledge we cannot point to the factors that will make a child creative. Even the best-intended home or school environments may stifle creativity as often as they further it. Haimowitz and Haimowitz (1960) point out that the childhoods of such eminent, creative persons as Darwin, Schubert, Sarah Bernhardt, Brahms, Van Gogh, the Brontes, and Gauguin were not models of love and satisfaction, but of poverty, illegitimacy, and of one- or no-parent homes. Bernard Shaw's father was a drunkard who abused and left his wife before Bernard Shaw was born. Louis Armstrong did not learn to play the trumpet in his parental home. Many others should be added to the list of Haimowitz and Haimowitz, who suggest that creativity may emerge from dissatisfaction.

In general, creativity is studied or defined as that which creates something useful or wanted by society. Some Londoners were not jubilant about the first man on the moon. This creative venture began with Wernher Von Braun's V2 rockets and the destruction of some of their city blocks. Many basic value questions about creativity have neither been asked nor answered. As has been pointed out, our creativity score on the Guilford test will increase if we list "drive a nail" as one of the possible uses for a brick. But should we ever try, half of the brick is bound to land on our toe and we would wish we had never been creative.

The development of a child's mind has been frequently viewed as a process of concept learning. Psychologists have studied the formation of *concepts* usually in connection with "thinking" and "problem solving." There seem to be thousands of concepts, differing in quality, quantity, and complexity. In general a concept can be defined as a rule that requires constancy in the "mind" but nonconstancy in the physical environment. Some psychologists would consider that the following problem, for instance, does *not* require a concept for its solution, because X, the correct answer, can be chosen in each instance by its physical similarity. Select the odd one:

I.   O X O O O ....X .. X..

The mind is involved, but in a more simple memory or "pattern-matching" capacity, where the mental pattern (also called "memory," "symbol," or "representative factor") remains similar to the environmental pattern. All this becomes quite different if we consider the following problem:

II.   O X O O O ,,,,. * */* *

The above problem cannot be solved by the mere matching of a certain pattern. The "physical" aspect or the visual pattern of the correct solution changes from X to · to /. Such a problem can only be solved by a mental rule: "the odd one is it." It is truly a conceptual problem. The following is also a conceptual problem, perhaps a more difficult one, since the oddity concept changes from X to O.

III.   O O X O O   X O X X X

That which was incorrect (visually) on the first set becomes correct on the second set and vice versa. We may say that our mental rule must go against the visual image.

Nonconceptual problems of Type I can be taught to children of one or two years of age, while problems as shown above, under II and III, may require age levels of four to six years. Animal work shows similar differences. Nonconceptual problems can be taught in hours or days while such concepts as oddity, as shown in II and III, may take weeks or months.

The author has reviewed the literature on the formation of the number concept (Wesley, 1961). Numbers have been the most frequent media for the study of concepts. When, for instance, does a child have a concept of threeness? This depends again on the amount of physical likeness left in the choice situation. The following problem can be solved by one-or two-year-olds because physical size of threeness remains constant (larger in comparison to twoness.

Show which pile contains three. (Presenting two and three walnuts)

The problem becomes much more difficult when the size of the pile can no longer be used as an aid, as for instance,

Show which pile contains three. (Presenting two apples and three walnuts)

For a correct answer the concept of size would have to be temporarily disregarded while the concept of number is retained or in Piaget's term "conserved." A mixture of objects with a pile would make the task even more difficult, as for instance,

Show which pile contains three. (Presenting two apples and one apple and two walnuts)

Here the child would have to maintain or conserve the concept of number in spite of differences in size and in kind of objects.

Many other variables enter into the solutions of a number-concept problem. There is a difference whether the child is asked to point to the pile, or whether there is a large pile and the child is asked to take three away from it. We even obtain different results if we ask a child to take three away with one hand motion or with three different hand motions. The pattern in which threeness is presented is also important. There have been hundreds of investigations involving concept formation, thinking, and problem solving. The studies are also called "cognitive studies" or "cognition." The individual problem approaches have contributed a tremendous amount of individual facts or data. None, however, has given us as much general and detailed knowledge about the mind as the work on intelligence testing discussed in the following chapter.

Chapter 9

THE INTELLECT

When a French mother says that her child has a low intelligence, she is not fishing for a compliment. She really means it. This is a statement by Laurence Wylie (1957), an American teacher who taught school in France for several years. Wylie was frequently surprised by the objectivity with which French parents discussed their children's intellectual abilities. French parents seem to accept differences in intelligence as gracefully as Americans accept, for example, differences in their children's height. French parents are much less concerned whether or not their children's IQ can be increased. They have some confidence that their children will receive that type of schooling (and consequently the type of vocation) that best fits their intellectual capacity. This confidence is also shared by parents who have children with mental abilities below the average.

As the reader will know, Americans are somewhat "jumpy" when it comes to IQ issues. Teachers in American schools are often instructed not to reveal IQ scores since it is felt that the knowledge of a low IQ will discourage the child and anger the parent. Hence we often soft-pedal the issue. In merchandising we can sort Idaho potatoes into good, medium, and poor potatoes and call them U.S. No. 1, Premium, and Superior, respectively. Similarly, in education we can refer to an "un"-intelligent child as "not-so-highly" intelligent. We can call a slow learner a "slow-but-sure" learner, inferring that slow learning is linked to good memory, which is not the case. We are also inclined to attribute poor progress in learning to poor motivation, implying somehow that children could learn better if they wanted to do so and if somebody could teach them how to "want to."

Are Americans less realistic than the French in recognizing the intellect as an important socialization factor, or are they more realistic in taking intelligence testing with a grain of salt? An answer to this question is not simple. It involves cultural and economic values and requires some technical knowledge about mental tests which will be discussed in the following paragraphs.

BINET'S IQ

The IQ is the score of a test that is designed to measure intelligence. But what is intelligence? There are now many definitions of intelligence and hundreds of tests to measure it. Almost all of these tests are related to the intelligence test originally designed by the French psychologist Alfred Binet (1857–1911) at the turn of the century. Since this time there have been three major revisions of Binet's tests—the Stanford-Binet revision of 1916, and the Terman and Merrill revisions of 1937 and 1960. Thus, in one form or another Binet's test has been used over decades and has been administered to millions of people. For simplicity, and perhaps even for scientific accuracy, we shall center our discussion of the IQ around Binet's test.

The majority of school children had a tough time before

Binet. Mistakenly the Western educators believed in the classic motto *mens sana in corpore sano* meaning that there is a healthy mind within every healthy body. Thus every child who looked healthy was considered to be capable of top mental performance. Consequently all healthy children who performed poorly were thought to be lazy. As punishment for their laziness they were scolded and beaten. In many cases this did not help. Perhaps the teachers began to realize that children's mental capacity cannot be assessed by their looks. Perhaps they also began to realize that in spite of beatings, goadings, or special instructions, the poor performances of certain pupils remained poor. In any event, the French Minister of Public Instruction commissioned Binet to find out which children could benefit from public instruction and which could not. He also wanted Binet to find out whether some children did not learn because the instructions were poor or because they were unintelligent. Binet went about his task the following way.

Binet gathered hundreds of items representing several mental traits or abilities, such as rote memorization and abstract reasoning, with both verbal and numerical material. The items varied in difficulty and were ranked from easy to difficult. They were given to children from ages three to fifteen. Those questions which could be answered by 75% of the three-year-olds were considered the norm for a three-year-old child. Those which could not be answered were used on four-year-olds and maintained as their their norm, if answered correctly by 75% of four-year-olds. This gradation process was continued until age fifteen. The following items are some sample tasks that the majority of children in the respective age groups can execute correctly.

Three-year level
   *(1).   Point to nose, eyes, mouth
    (2).   Copy bridge made from three building blocks
   *(3).   Give family name

*Starred items from original Binet & Simon scale (1908).

*(4). Repeat a six-syllable sentence
*(5). Repeat two digits

Four-year level
*(1). Name own sex
*(2). Name common objects (keys, knife, pennies)
*(3). Compare two lines
*(4). Repeat three digits

Six-year level
(1). Distinguish between morning and afternoon
(2). Define words as to usage
*(3). Copy a diamond
*(4). Count 13 sous (pennies)
*(5). Repeat five digits

Eight-year level
*(1). Compare two objects from memory
(2). Note omissions from pictures
(3). Similarity and differences (baseball and orange)
*(4). Count from 20 to 0
(5). Memory for sentence (12 words)

Ten-year level
*(1). Name nine pieces of money
*(2). Name the months
(3). Criticize absurd statements
(4). Define abstract words (satisfaction, grief, pity)
(5). Repeat six digits

The original scale had six items for each age from two to fifteen. Many revisions and additional tests were subsequently designed to test intelligence from infancy to adulthood. An examiner guesses the intelligence level of the subject and then begins to test with items from levels one or two years lower, where the subject is likely to answer all questions correctly. Binet made this provision to assure that the subject understands and does not fear the experimenter and to test whether a child categorically answers "I don't know." Only after all the items of a lower year level have been correctly answered can an examiner continue to test higher year levels. The highest level reached (averaged out) on this age scale is considered the child's mental age, abbreviated MA.

Thus the testing procedure tells us the child's mental age, which is actually the chronological age of those children on whose level our examinee performs. It is the age group with which a child's mental performance is comparable. We also need to know the examinee's own age so we can get an idea if he or she is mentally ahead, even, or behind in comparison with other children of the same age. This gives us two figures for every child. It is customary to express these two figures by a quotient, dividing the child's mental age by his chronological age (CA). The resulting number is multiplied by 100 to avoid decimals. Hence we get the following formula for computing the IQ:

$$IQ = MA/CA \times 100$$

There is no magic about this formula. The MA is on top of the fraction because we want people who lag behind to have smaller quotients than those who are ahead of their age group. To demonstrate the working of this formula, we shall give an example of three boys, all eight years of age, who have performed or have reached different age levels on their IQ tests.

Name	Age (CA)	Highest age level reached on test (MA)	Intelligence quotient MA/CA × 100 = IQ
Carl	8	6	6/8 × 100 = 75
John	8	8	8/8 × 100 = 100
Paul	8	10	10/8 × 100 = 125

Most eight year olds will test like John. Their mental age will be the same as their own age. It has to be this way because Binet selected the items for the eight-year-olds by actually testing eight-year-olds and by finding out which items the majority of them could answer. Parents who have children who test 100 or slightly above or below 100 should consider their children's IQ as quite normal. Even those who have IQs below 100 should consider themselves in good company. Binet designed the IQ so that 100 is the average score. This means that 50% of all people must have IQ scores of 100 and below, as shown by the following distribution obtained by Terman and Merrill (1937), who tested 3,000 children from ages two to eighteen.

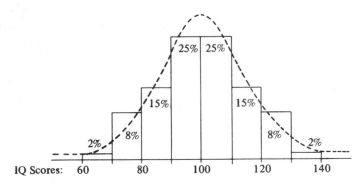

Percentage of population falling into respective intervals

For a final comparison we should point out that Binet's age scale is similar to the classification used by grade school teachers when they say, for example, that a certain third-grade student performs on a fifth-grade level. This is similar to saying that this student belongs in the third grade in regard to age, but in the fifth grade in regard to mental ability.

DEFINING INTELLIGENCE

We have just seen a typical sample of an IQ test. The reader can look at it again and make up his or her own definition of intelligence. This may be a backward, do-it-yourself approach, but this is how things happened historically. It took

Binet only one decade to construct and to perfect his scale. But seven subsequent decades have not been long enough for psychologists to find a satisfactory definition for whatever is measured by Binet's test. Some psychologists believe that the IQ as measured by the Stanford-Binet, the Wechsler Intelligence Scale for Children, and by similar tests, covers most, if not all, intellectual functions and they consider it psychology's greatest achievement; others have viewed it as a technological trap, testing only very specific mental functions unrelated to the essential nature of human development (Zigler & Trickett, 1978). The truth lies somewhere in between. The IQ is not, or is only partially, related to physical health, motivation, and emotional stability. But like no other measure, it has been found to relate to many other behaviors of practical significance, especially to occupational selections and income—important factors in our society.

How many mental capacities are there and how many does the IQ encompass? Little attention was given to the classification of mental abilities when the IQ was first constructed. At the turn of the century people were thought to be either dumb or smart. The smart ones were supposed to be able to handle any academic subject. No university student would have dared to say, "I can understand English composition, but not mathematics." The mind was considered to function as one unit, being able to handle all mental tasks equally well or equally poorly. It did not matter whether these tasks were of a verbal or an arithmetical nature. In fact, one mental activity was thought to strengthen the other one. Latin was required of all academicians because the study of it was thought to strengthen mathematical as well as all other mental capacities.

More attention was paid to the special capacities of the mind as more IQ scores, psychologists, and computers became available. Researchers, for instance, tried to find out how many of those people who score high in verbal items also score high in arithmetical items. Or, putting the question differently, whether those who score poorly on verbal items also score poorly on arithmetical items. The statistical technique used in such comparisons is called "correlation." It tells us how many people have approximately equal ranks in their scores on two or more categories. If, for instance, people would always rank equal in both verbal and arithmetical capacities, we would assume that these two capacities depend on one and the same mental function. If, on the other hand, we would find divergencies among most individuals with respect to these two functions, we would have to assume that there are two separate mental capacities or two separate IQs.

We do not have any unqualified resolutions of the above alternatives. Verbal and arithmetical abilities, for instance, are related, but only to a certain degree. Spearman (1927) described the IQ as containing a "g," or general, factor as well as an "s," or special, factor. The g, he thought, carried more weight or was more important than the s. Spearman would have been inclined to disbelieve a student who said, "I can comprehend English composition but not mathematics." The importance of the g factor would make one guess that this student would be just as good or smart in mathematics had he or she received an equal amount of classes and cultural pressure or encouragement in this area of study.

As the years went by, more IQ categories were found. Instead of dividing the IQ into verbal and arithmetical items we could, for instance, divide it into "problem solving" and "rote memory" categories. We could subdivide further and have verbal and arithmetical items for each of these categories. Thurstone (1947) examined the IQ test for many such possible categories. He found the following seven more or less unrelated factors, which he called *primary abilities*:

V = verbal comprehension
W = word fluency
N = numerical ability
S = space visualization
M = memory

P = perceptual ability
R = reasoning

Guilford (1959) suggested an even more detailed model of the IQ. His model has the following three basic categories and subcategories.

(1). *Mental operation.* Cognition, memory, divergent thinking, convergent thinking, evaluation
(2). *Task content.* Figural, symbolic, semantic, behavioral
(3). *Products.* Unit, classes, relations, systems, transformations, implications

Each mental function can be classified by three subcategories, one from each major classification. Stott (1967) has clearly described Guilford's system and has given the following example. If a baby grabs a block, his mental function for this task may be classified as "cognition-figural-unit." First, the baby had to recognize the block, which is a visual figure. The product was a unit, as it did not have to be related to other objects. Let us take a somewhat more difficult task. A child is required to select a certain square block in order to put it into one of several diversely shaped holes. In Guilford's model this action would perhaps be classified as "memory-figural-relations." In his model any action can be described in such a three-way fashion. With a total of five mental operations, four tasks, and six products, Guilford offers a total of 120 such three-way descriptions.

It is difficult to see the practical value of those IQ models that single out 100 or 200 separate factors. Recommendations can perhaps be more readily made with Thurstone's seven factors. We can visualize a school subject or a profession which requires more V (verbal comprehension) and less N (number relation) or vice versa. For a low M (memory) score we may recommend a good notebook for both names and numbers. But what can we recommend in Guilford's system if a child is low on the "divergent-symbolic-classes" factor and high on the "convergent-semantic-relations" factor? Or how many of the 120 factors are necessary for a child to bring home a good report card? It is quite possible that computer work and future research will give us the exact answers to such questions.

Another way of defining or understanding the IQ is by looking at what it can do, what it can predict, or which capacities are linked to it. Many of the controversies about the IQ stem from the misbelief that the IQ is good for everything. Tallness, for instance, is a good predictor and is in actuality very helpful for making a good score in basketball, but tallness is not helpful for entering small cars and it has nothing to do with, for instance, the number of colds one catches. Scientists would say that tallness is a valid predictor for basketball scores and for the ease in entering small cars, correlating positively with the former and negatively with the latter, but that it correlates zero with the number of colds. For the predicting validity of the IQ test we present the following list as a general guideline:

(1) There is *good* prediction that people with high IQs will be successful in general scholastic achievement, especially in English, physics, and arithmetic, and in professional occupations such as accounting, engineering, and medicine.

(2) There is *some* prediction that people with high IQs will be successful in school subjects such as chemistry and biology and in professions such as machinists, clerks, and electricians. Also, certain personality traits seem to be linked to the IQ. Introverts, for instance, learn somewhat faster than extroverts.

(3) There is *no* prediction between the IQ and accomplishment in playing musical instruments by ear, driving an automobile, football, operating an adding machine, and studying a foreign language. High, average, and low IQ people have an equal chance to become alcoholics and have health, character, mental disorders, and accidents. They also have an equal chance to be successful in such professions as machine operators, bricklayers, and carpenters.

(4) There is negative prediction, which means that we can predict that people with *low* IQs will be somewhat more successful in jobs requiring simple routine and repetitive work

It is somewhat surprising that the IQ correlates highly with aptitude in one's mother tongue, but correlates practically zero with the capacity to learn a foreign language. In spite of the seven diverse mental factors identified by Thurstone, the IQ does not seem to tap any factors related to learning a foreign language. Perhaps there is little logic and too much rote memory involved in learning a foreign language. It may also involve a musical ability for which psychologists have developed separate tests such as the *Seashore Measures of Musical Talent* or the *Wing Standardized Test of Musical Ability,* which present such musical components as pitch, loudness, rhythm, and timbre.

Considering the academic nature of the IQ test one would assume that there would be a high correlation between IQ and the grade point average (GPA) of college students. But in reality there is none. If all students took the same courses distributed over the disciplines of science, social science, and humanities, the correlation between the IQ and GPA would probably be high and positive. But as it is, students select easier and harder subject matter to fit their intellectual capacities. In other words, they form more or less homogeneous groups with respect to their IQs. For example, those students with IQs around 130 will be more likely to select physics as their major field than students with IQs around 110. Hence the student with a high IQ is likely to compete for the grade with students who likewise have high IQs. In the average American university a physics major may actually have less of a chance to receive an A than a psychology major, since fewer As are generally given in science than in social science courses.

Teachers often argue against the validity of the IQ test because they frequently encounter students with high IQs who are scholastically and professionally very unsuccessful. Such observations detract from the overall predictive power of the

IQ, but they do not make it invalid. Unfortunately, one is always less certain in predicting success than failure. One needs for example, a high IQ to become a certified public accountant. Most accountants have IQs ranging from 125 to 135, and a person with an IQ around 100 has practically no chance of becoming a CPA. Thus, one can be quite certain to predict that he or she will fail. However, our prediction will be much less certain if we predict success for a person with an IQ of 130 since other nonintellectual factors such as good health, emotional stability, orderliness, patience, money, etc., are additionally needed for successful studies in accounting. Failure in any one of these factors alone can prevent success. While important, a high IQ is not an all-inclusive blessing.

HEREDITY AND ENVIRONMENT

For generations psychologists have disagreed about the influence heredity has on our intellect. At one extreme there are those who believe that intelligence is not genetically determined, but needs to be established and cultivated by the environment, by parents, teachers, creative toys, and so on. At the other extreme there are those who maintain that intelligence is practically independent of environmental influences, that its potentials are present at birth, and that they will come to light in due time. The evidence points to an intermediate view. We do not need sophisticated studies to prove that a child raised in a neglectful and abusive family will generally not turn out as well as a child raised in a supportive one. But it is also true that human beings are not infinitely adjustable. Even in a perfect world some people will be unhappier, more hyperactive, or more capable than others. Heredity seems to establish upper limits (thresholds) of intelligence and other personality variables, but a favorable environment is needed so the upper limit can be reached. There is an interaction between heredity and environment, and as Scarr and Weinberg (1978) point out, some children thrive in a world that is rich and varied, whereas others react badly to overstimulation. Children who are skillful at sports spend more time on them; adults who cannot carry a tune are embarrassed to try out for a glee club. People often actively select the environment that suits them and reject those environmental aspects they dislike. Their choices are likely to be influenced by their genetic talents and interests. Quite often the environment also influences heredity. The pupil who is strong by nature is encouraged by his peers or coach to join the football team, and an adult who sings well is invited to sing. It is often believed that heredity and environment are opposed to each other, but more often than not they seem to complement and to support each other.

Due to the reciprocal nature of heredity and environment, it is difficult to determine to which degree either one influences our intelligence. When we hear a person play the piano we do not know how much of it was influenced by the player's native ability and how much of it was conditioned by practice. We cannot judge from the end product alone. If the quality of a person's performance would always correlate with the length of his or her preparation and practice times we would not need the term "talent." But it happens not infrequently that a person who practiced less plays much better than a person who practiced much. Not even better teachers and better motivation guarantee better performance. While this is an extreme case, Arthur Rubinstein when only three years old listened to his older sister having piano lessons. After the lessons were over and the teacher went home, Rubinstein would repeat from memory all that his sister had played during her lesson. At the age of seven he was an accomplished piano player. When person A plays better than B, not having practiced as much than B— when practice did *not* make perfect—we invoke talent, meaning that person A came into the world better prepared to learn to play the piano. Thus the genetic "talent" is inferred or deducted from the performance and practice variables. Most people can improve their performance by practicing more. But talent can only be improved by the geneticist. At present we do not know the genetic or the physiological mechanism for talent, but it is conceivable that certain neuroanatomical correlates may be discovered in the future.

Talent relates to musical abilities as the IQ relates to mental abilities. Binet designed the IQ test to test heredity. As stated previously, he was asked to design a test by which teachers could determine which pupils would profit from schooling and which would not. If learning was based solely on environment then the parents and teachers would be the first persons to know a child's abilities because they create and observe much of the environment. If additional information about a child's learning ability is needed then this information should be an indicator of heredity, something which the teacher or the parent cannot directly observe. In the following we shall enumerate several points to show that Binet's primary goal in constructing his test was an assessment of heredity.

1. *Simple Items.* Most, but not all, items are so simple that a child should know the elements necessary for the answer whether reared in an enriched or in an impoverished environment. Item 1 on the three-year level (see sample test) asks the child to point to nose, eyes, and mouth. Whether three-year-olds live on this or that side of the railroad track, there is only a remote chance that they never felt their nose, eyes, or mouth and that they have not heard the proper names for these body parts. Item 1 on the six-year level asks a child to "distinguish between morning and afternoon." Again, only in the rarest case could we assume that a seven-year-old was so culturally deprived that he has had no opportunity to notice any difference between mornings and afternoons.

2. *Familiarization Assured.* Certain tasks are demonstrated so that a child has an opportunity to learn the ingredients necessary for the correct solution as well as the correct solution itself. For instance, Item 2 on the three-year level asks the three-year-old to copy a bridge made out of three building blocks. The tester first builds this bridge from one oblong and

two square blocks while the child watches. On some items this demonstration can be repeated several times. Only after the task has been demonstrated is the child asked to perform. Thus it is difficult to claim that the child was not familiar with the subject matter.

3. *Where Practice is Unlikely.* There are other types of items on the IQ test with which very few children have any experience. The nonsense syllable is such an item. (The nonsense syllable was first used by Herrmann Ebbinghaus, whose work in testing preceded Binet's. Ebbinghaus was asked by the city fathers of Breslau, Germany, in 1896 to find the time during the five-hour school day at which the child was least efficient. His tests involved arithmetic, memory, and sentence-completion tasks.) Foreign language words or repetition of a word or sentence backward are also items for which past practice is unlikely. The task of repeating the letters of a word backward may actually favor a child from a deprived environment. Repeating the letters d-n-a, for instance, may be easier for a child with less schooling than for a child with more schooling who has practiced the sequence a-n-d more often.

4. *Where Practice Does Not Make Perfect.* The performance on certain tasks may improve with concentrated practice but the improvement will not last. The forward as well as the backward repetition of digits are such tasks. Most adults can repeat 7 or 8 digits forward. Some can only repeat 5 or 6 and equally few as many as 9 or 10. This repeating capacity is normally distributed, like the IQ in general. Perhaps only 1 in 1,000 persons will be able to remember 11 or 12 numbers. Only 1 person in 10 million may be able to repeat 70 numbers forward and backward without errors. In his book *The Mind of a Mnemonist,* Luria (1968), the Russian physician-psychologist, wrote the biography of a man who could do just that. For years, by the way, this man was unable to find a suitable job until he was hired by a circus. Psychologists do not know why one adult has this upper limit at 6, another one at 8, and a rare, rare individual at 70 numbers. From wherever one's upper limit

comes, it does not seem to come from practice, or from any other environmental factor that psychologists can pinpoint.

The reader can test this nonpractice effect. Single, random numbers should be read to him or her at the rate of one per second. One can, for instance, start with six numbers and if the repetition is errorless, then seven, eight, nine, etc., numbers could be tried. Each trial should, of course, contain a different set of numbers. We reach our upper limit, let us say at eight numbers, when we begin to make errors on the nine-number sets. Prolonged practice on this task would not alter our performance appreciably. If we practice too long we may get worse since our memory does not get better with age.

5. *Standardization.* Another attempt to minimize environmental influences was through standardization, a procedure that a test has to undergo after it is constructed in order to adjust it to the specific group in which it will be used. The Stanford-Binet has been given to various groups of children, to hundreds living in the Palo Alto, California, area, around Stanford University, as well as to canal-boat children without formal schooling in England. Averages or means are computed for each group and one can easily determine whether or how much of the test or which items favor one group or the other. In order to equalize a test for two or more groups, group-foreign items could be eliminated. Should this not be possible (if the groups are too different), then each subject tested can be compared with the average performance for his or her own group.

Many special IQ tests are designed to test and to compare children within certain handicapped groups. If a child, for instance, has hearing difficulties, he or she can be given a test standardized on a group of children with similar hearing difficulties. Such tests may consist of having the child copy a figure, point to an omission in a picture, and so forth. Children with verbal, perceptual, or reading difficulties can get tests tailored to their particular group. The Wechsler Intelligence Test, now as widely used as the Stanford-Binet, was designed to yield two separate scores: a verbal score depending on such items as word repetition, naming of objects, and so on, and a performance score based on stringing beads, completing a jigsaw puzzle, copying a mosaic pattern, and other such nonverbal items. All in all, it seems that psychologists bent over backwards to design a fair test—a test that would not favor or disfavor any particular environment. How well have the psychologists succeeded with their good intentions?

Psychologists succeded well in constructing a test that actually measures the inborn aspects of intelligence. But they did not succeed in convincing the American public to accept this fact. European psychologists were more successful in this respect. The British psychologist H. J. Eysenck (1967) has most clearly presented the evidence for the inheritance argument. Before enumerating his points, we should again emphasize that the inheritance of the IQ can never be measured directly. Environmental factors will always be present since we cannot test a child at birth, but must wait for a number of years before we can adequately test intelligence. Although we cannot eliminate environment, we can minimize much of its effect by measuring the intelligence of children who have had more or less the same environment. Here are some of Eysenck's points.

1. *Twins.* Identical twins arise from one female ovum and from one male sperm. Nature provides nothing closer with respect to human heredity. The IQ of such pairs of twins are practically equal for each set. Fraternal twins arise from two separate ova and spermatozoa. They differ genetically as much as the average brother and sister. Pairs of such twins differ in their IQ much more than identical twins. The correlation between the IQs of identical twins is .95, being on the average only 3 points apart, while the correlation between fraternal twins is .65, being on the average about 10 points apart. This difference can be demonstrated by the following hypothetical examples of five sets of identical and five sets of fraternal twins.

Pairs of twins generally have the same environment. Thus the difference found between the "IQ-likeness" of identical and fraternal pairs points to the heredity factor. Environment could

Identical twins (correlation = 0.95)	Differ-ence	Fraternal twins (correlation = 0.65)	Differ-ence
120–122	2	120–110	10
112–106	4	112–99	13
105–109	4	105–117	12
97–99	2	97–105	8
90–87	3	90–82	8
	15		51
Average Difference = 3		Average Difference = 10	

only cause these differences if parents gave identical twins a more equal home environment than they gave fraternal twins. This, however, is quite unlikely. The most telling evidence of the hereditary part of intelligence comes from studies which examined the IQ of identical twins reared apart. When compared with fraternal twins, the IQs of the identical twins reared in different families is closer than those of fraternal twins reared in the same family.

2. *Orphanages.* Another point that speaks strongly for the inherited nature of the IQ is the distribution or the scatter of IQs in orphanages. Orphanages differ much from each other in staff ratio, physical setup, pedagogical philosophies. However, we can assume that the conditions are quite similar for each child within one orphanage. The same toys, educational materials, teachers, and books are usually available to each child. If environment were the main factor influencing the IQ, then children in one and the same orphanage should have more or less similar IQs. This, however, is not the case. They differ almost as much as children reared in different parental homes on the outside.

3. *Biological curves.* There are also several statistical factors that compel us to view the IQ as mainly hereditary. Many inherited characteristics follow a normal, bell-shaped curve. For instance, when we measure and plot the height of 1,000 men, we find that most measures fall around the middle or

average, and fewer and fewer measures fall toward the extreme
short and the extreme tall ends of the distribution. Intelligence
has a similar distribution, as will be apparent from the following
two curves.

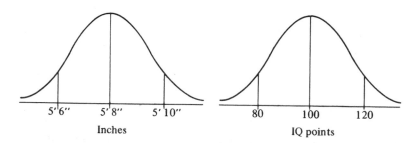

Inches   IQ points

There is also the biological phenomenon of *regression,*
which speaks for the hereditary on intelligence. It was first
observed by Galton (1822-1911), who compared height between parents and offspring, finding that tall parents tend to
have smaller children and smaller parents taller ones. This
regression towards the mean is also present when we compare
the IQ between parents and children. For example, the mean
IQ of children whose parents have IQs of 120 will be a few
points below 120 and, conversely, the children of parents with
IQs of 80 will be above 80. Only the offspring of parents with
a mean IQ (100) will, as a group, be equal to their parents, with
an average IQ of 100.

4. *Relatives.* IQ studies have been conducted for over 50
years and millions of people have been tested in England,
France, Germany, Japan, and the United States. Almost all of
these studies show that the correlations between the IQs of pairs
of individuals decrease regularly with decreases in the degree of
genetic relationship. The following list, adapted from Kimble
and Garmezy (1968), summarizes some general findings.

From the above sequences of correlation we can make the
conclusion that the IQ depends to a considerable degree on
inheritance, with the environment playing a lesser role. It is
interesting to note that the correlation between mother's and

Degree of relationship	Correlation
Same individual at successive testing	.95, very high
Identical twins reared together	.95, very high
Identical twins reared apart	.75, a great deal
Fraternal twins reared together	.65, considerably
Fraternal twins reared apart	.50, fair amount
Nontwin siblings	.50, fair amount
Parent and child	.50, fair amount
Parent and foster child	.25, some similarity
Grandparent and child	.15, slightly
Unrelated individuals	.00, none

the child's IQ is .50 and that that between father and child is also .50. This indicates again the predominant influence of heredity, since the child's environment is mostly created through the presence and the interaction with the mother, especially in the early developmental years when the father interacts with the child to a much lesser degree.

5. *Adoptions.* A number of studies compared the relationship between adopted children and their foster parents with similar relationships between children and their blood (biological) parents. Hilgard and Atkinson (1967) described a number of such studies in which children had been placed into foster homes for adoption before six months of age and had lived with their foster parents for an average of 13 years. In general, the IQ of the adopted children did not correlate with that of their foster parents ($r = .00$), but it did correlate with their biological parents ($r = .40$), almost as high ($r = .50$) as that of children who live with their biological parents. Scarr and Weinberg (1978) compared biological and adopted children within the same family who had lived together from about three months after birth until late adolescence. They found that black adopted children had an average IQ of 110, about a ten-point increase from their biological parents, but not as high as their adoptive parents (about 119) or those of the biological children (about 116). The white adopted children showed similar trends.

Their IQs were six and one-half points lower than those of the biological children, but six and one-half points higher than those of their own parents. The increase in the adoptees' IQ was mainly due to vocabulary abilities which seem to be most amenable to environmental influences.

Scarr and Weinberg also tested the degree of authoritarianism, rigidity of belief, and prejudice and they found that these attitudes are also genetically transmitted from parents to children, just as verbal ability and intelligence are. They found no correlation between adopted children and their adopted parents with regard to these attitudes, even though the adoptees had been exposed to them since infancy. Scarr and Weinberg state that they were as different as if adults and teenagers had been paired on a street corner. Moreover, the attitudes of the adoptees tended again to be very similar to those of their biological parents, whether both were highly authoritarian or both were antiauthoritarian. Authoritarianism was linked with a verbal factor: verbal family members were the least authoritarian, and vice versa. It was also found that the vocational interests of the adolescent adoptees were quite different from the parents they grew up with. Practically no modeling took place in regard to vocational interests. For all their similarity to their adoptive parents, the adopted children of teachers and engineers could have grown up with cattle ranchers or plumbers.

The above discussion on heredity and environment make a strong argument for the role of inheritance. Yet it is difficult to express the role of inheritance with any certain numerical figures. Eysenck has ventured to say that inheritance determines about 80% of the IQ, and environment 20%. He cautions, however, that these figures would not hold for countries where the educational opportunities are grossly unequal. But he believes that these percentages fit the United States and England. Other investigators support Eysenck's view. Burt (1958), in an article entitled, "The Inheritance of Mental Ability," reports that about 77% of the variance of general intelligence can be accounted for by genetic factors. Erlenmeyer-Kimling and Jarvik (1963) examined 52 IQ studies undertaken in eight different countries and found similar results.

IQ and Socialization

Be it for educational or social reasons, most parents desire that their child have a high IQ. Many have a secret hope for their child to be a genius. But only one child among 1,000 children is a genius. As assessed by Wechsler (1958), about 25% of all adults have IQs below 90, 50% score between 90 and 110, and only 25% above 110. In this latter group there will only be two people who score above 130.

Even if your child were a genius, nobody could tell you for sure until your child was six or eight years of age. It is difficult to forecast the mental development of a child because the IQ develops unevenly, especially during the early years. There is a general and an individual unevenness in its development. The general unevenness may be demonstrated by the following digit-repeating task:

> The average 2-year-old can repeat 1 digit
> The average 3-year-old can repeat 2 digits
> The average 4-year-old can repeat 3 digits
> The average 7-year-old can repeat 5 digits
> The average 12-year-old can repeat 7 digits

From age two to age four the average digit-repeating capacity seems to increase by one number per year. In the next eight years, however, it increases only by half a number per year. Other mental tasks have similar irregular patterns.

More disturbing to the forecasting efficiency of the IQ test are the individual differences that occur in mental development. They may be demonstrated by an example of child A and child B and their maximum number of words known at ages two, three, and four.

Child A	Child B
50 words at age 2	10 words at age 2
100 words at age 3	300 words at age 3
400 words at age 4	400 words at age 4

IQ tests given before the age of two have no predictive value of adult intelligence. Tests given after two years of age and before six years predict very poorly. Eysenck (1967) has surveyed over 30 studies concerned with IQ measurements repeated over various time spans. He suggests that IQ tests before the age of six should be discouraged because they are bound to raise many false hopes and unjustified fears. The development of the IQ becomes more stable from age six to age ten and its measurement during this time gains predictive value. The IQ remains fairly constant after adolescence and it rarely changes during a person's adult years. Decreases are generally reported around age sixty, but some psychologists believe that these changes are due to losses in sensory capacity, motor reaction, and changes in motivation (Horn & Donaldson, 1977).

Leona Tyler (1965), one of America's foremost psychologists, concurs with Eysenck's suggestions. She lists several reasons for the unpredictability of IQ tests given to young children and for the increasing predictability when given to older ones. During the course of a child's development IQ changes can occur in the following ways. Some children may become brighter over the years, some may become less bright, and some may fluctuate. Changes over shorter periods of time are more likely to occur than changes over longer periods. A six-year-old with an IQ of 85, for instance, will hardly ever change to an IQ of 130 at any later age. However, it is likely that a six-year-old with an IQ of 110 may reach an IQ of 125 later on.

Is there something definite a parent or child can do to increase the IQ? Tyler has examined several longitudinal studies and has found no single factor in a child's teaching or environment that could be pinpointed as the cause of such an increase. Neither can the factors be found that cause developmental decreases with the exception of certain physical or medical causes. In short, we know that changes occur, but we do not know why. During their development, about 60% of all children will change up to 15 IQ points or so. There is no use to be hopeful about this statistic because decreases occur as frequently as increases. Occasionally, extreme cases of IQ increase are cited in the literature and attributed to the effectiveness of certain teaching or childrearing methods. These cases may be misleading because increases also occur in the absence of extra training or schooling.

Certain prenatal conditions influence the IQ. These are not genetic, but are determined by the uterine environment during the gestation period. Jensen (1969) has surveyed the literature and reports that first-born children tend to have higher intelligence (4–5 points) than later-born children. Twins are slightly less intelligent than singletons (4–7 points) and the twin with the lower birth weight usually has the lower IQ (5–7 points). Deficiencies in the mother's nutrition, larger number of children, and shorter intervals between births are conditions which appear to be of further detriment to the IQ. It appears that certain uterine (chemical) conditions which favor intelligence become depleted by the frequency and the close spacings of childbirth.

The IQ can be raised, but only to a certain extent and often only with efforts yielding diminishing returns. Tyler (1965), for instance, cited much of the controversial literature about the effect of nursery schooling on future IQ. Depending on the type of school and on the socioeconomic level of its children, some studies report an increase of 10 IQ points for the group that had nursery training as compared to the control group that had none. Other studies also cited by Tyler report no differences.

The most reliable increases in IQ (10–15 points) have been reported in the studies examining adopted children. Rather constant increases (10 points) are also reported from groups of southern blacks after they have lived in the North for a number of years. More permanent IQ changes usually involve total and year-long changes in the intellectual and social environment (Munn, 1966).

Short-term programs such as day-care and Head Start have not been successful in terms of raising the IQ or scholastic accomplishment significantly, although they may have other social and physical health benefits. The children's IQ and scholastic performance is usually raised 5–10 points, but both increases are lost within a year or two after the compensatory program ends. Financially, the diminishing returns experienced in educating the intellectually and/or socially disadvantaged are quite apparent. Gallagher (1978) reports that during 1979 the federal government plans to spend $900 million for the mentally handicapped, but only $3 million for programs for the development of the gifted and talented child.

Americans have been very skeptical toward the usefulness of the IQ test. Yet it has been the IQ score, or more typically the increase in IQ, by which the usefulness of most childhood intervention programs has been evaluated in the 1960s and 1970s. Zigler and Trickett (1978) suggest that social competence, rather than IQ, should be the primary measure to evaluate aid programs. Their suggested index includes measures of physical health, IQ, school achievement, juvenile delinquency, and motivational and emotional variables such as responsiveness to social reinforcement, measures of learned helplessness, expectancy of success, etc. Whether such a test would differ greatly from the conventional IQ test and to which degree it would differentiate between individuals remains to be seen.

Many people resent any studies and suggestions indicating that the IQ is inherited. They believe mistakenly that this suggests that the IQ is totally inherited and that all educational efforts are useless. However, our genes do not teach us anything. They only give us the speed with which we can learn and certain levels we can reach. The environment must ultimately present the building blocks and the material for learning to people of all intelligence levels. It should also be noted that the intelligent person can learn "good" as well as "bad" things faster and that intelligence is not a measure of kindness, trust, or altruism. We can use our knowledge about the genetic and the environmental determinants of the IQ democratically by avoiding burdening some individuals with education in excess of their capacity and by not boring others who have higher capacities. Perhaps we will be more democratic when we can talk about our children's average and low IQs without embarrassment.

Chapter 10

PRE-CONCEPTION AND PRENATAL INFLUENCES

Whether we look at the development of a newborn, a preschool child, or an adolescent, we usually weigh their inborn capacities against the amount of knowledge and training we can offer. The interaction between heredity and environment is obvious throughout an individual's life-span. In our discussion on maturation, we presented some of the genetically determined growth processes which occur after birth and in some of the following chapters, we discussed environmental influences received through conditioning, modeling, and schooling.

In this chapter, we again will consider the interplay between heredity and environment as it pertains to human organisms before conception and birth. A very basic amount of the hereditary mechanism will be presented to show how humans can influence the heredity of their offspring. The hazards of certain prenatal conditions caused by diseases and drugs and how they can be prevented or ameliorated through prenatal examinations and counseling will be discussed.

Genotypes and Phenotypes

Genetic knowledge is difficult to obtain because the functions of our hereditary mechanisms can only be observed in retrospect. Parents may have to wait several months to see whether their daughter has inherited their brown eyes and they may have to wait for 40 years or more, to find out if their son has inherited his grandfather's premature baldness. Since our looks or our *phenotype* is often different from our genetic composition, from our *genotype*, observers may have to wait two generations to determine an individual's genetic make-up.

That genetics involve the study of successive generations can best be shown by the occurrence of hemophilia in the descendants of Queen Victoria. Her son, King Edward VII, was not a bleeder, but her son Leopold, the Duke of Albany, was. Leopold's daughter Princess Alice, again was like Queen Victoria, not a bleeder, but her son, the Viscount of Trematon, was (Fischer & Lazarson, 1984). From this and other family histories of hemophiliacs, geneticists have learned that this defect is caused by a sex-linked, recessive gene in the mother's X chromosome. This means that hemophilia only can be transmitted by the mother, who is a carrier but who is not affected by it. This, in turn, means that the mother's phenotype, a nonbleeder, is different from her genotype of transmitting bleeding.

The differences between phenotypes and genotypes depend on *dominant* and *recessive* genes first conceptualized in 1895 by the Austrian monk, Gregor Mendel. When crossing certain red- and white-flowered plants, Mendel obtained 25 percent white- and 75 percent red-flowered plants. The white-flowered ones were termed "pure" white because when crossbred with each other, they yielded only white flowers. The 75 percent red-flowered plants, however, fell into two categories: 25 percent pure red and 50 percent which were red in appearance (phenotypically) but were genetically mixed, containing one red and one white gene. The gene, which determines the phenotype, the redness in this example, is said to be dominant. When Mendel crossed these genetically mixed plants with each other, he obtained, again, 25 percent white- and 75 percent red-flowered plants. Thus, it was shown that two red-looking plants can have some pure white offspring, but that only can be predicted from knowing the plant's "grandparents!"

In principle, human heredity follows Mendel's discoveries, although it is vastly more complicated. Each human cell has 23 pair of chromosomes, one member of each pair being inherited from the mother and one from the father. It is estimated that each chromosome has approximately 20,000 genes, and each human cell contains about $23 \times 20,000$ or approximately 500,000 gene pairs. One pair of chromosomes, the 23rd pair, is of greatest interest to us: it determines our sex and provides us with much genetic information because it produces such sex-linked characteristics as hemophilia and many others.

The male sperm and the female ovum contain 23 chromosomes each. After conception, these chromosomes line up in pairs. The members of each pair are approximately equal in size and shape, except those of the 23rd pair. It consists of one X chromosome inherited from the mother and in females of another X chromosome inherited from the father. In males, this 23rd chromosome contains likewise one X chromosome inherited from the mother but receives a Y chromosome from the father. This Y chromosome received from the father is approximately one-third the length of the X chromosome inherited from the mother. This unevenness accounts for the fact that the boy inherits between 3–5 percent more genetic material from the mother than he does from the father. This maternal surplus is not always to his advantage. Besides the "good" parts he inherits from his mother's X chromosomes, he can also inherit several which are "not so good" such as some types of muscular dystrophy, diabetes, and hemophilia.

Another example which follows the Mendelian principles is red-green color-blindness. It occurs in 1 in 20 men but only in 1 of 400 women and stems from a defect on the X chromosome of which the woman has two and the man, only one. Usually, there is a 1 in 20 chance that an X chromosome has this defect. If the man inherits one of these defective chromosomes, he will be color-blind. But if a woman inherits one she will not be color-blind because the chances are that her other X chromosome is not defective. She only will be color-blind if both her X chromosomes are defective, which is a 20×20 chance, or 1 in 400.

The female ova contain only X chromosomes, while the male sperms carry X and Y chromosomes in a 50:50 ratio. The seminal fluid from one male ejaculation contains between 300 and 500 million sperm, but only one of them "wins" in the race through the uterus and the fallopian tube to meet and to fertilize the ovum. If this sperm contains a Y, the newly conceived organism will be an XY, a boy. If the sperm with an X wins, the result is XX, a girl. So oddly enough, a girl actually inherits her femaleness from her father!

The female's XX chromosome can serve to demonstrate the recessiveness as well as the sex-linkage mechanisms that play a role in the transmission of several genetic defects. Hemophilia, for example, is caused by a defective gene on the X chromosome. Females are not susceptible to hemophilia because they have two chromosomes, and their defective gene on one of the X chromosomes will have a healthy companion gene on the other X chromosome. The defective gene, in this case, is called recessive because its function is offset by its dominant, healthy companion.

When a woman like Queen Victoria has children, one half of them will inherit her defective X chromosome and the other half will inherit her healthy one. The sons who inherit her defective X chromosome will all be bleeders because in males the X chromosome has no double and the defective gene has no healthy companion gene. None of her daughters, in contrast, who inherit the defective gene, will be bleeders because they inherit a second X chromosome from their father, which will supply the dominant, healthy companion gene.

Probabilities and relationships of numbers, measures, and

accounts have long fascinated human observers. More than 2,000 years ago, the Pythagoreans were so impressed with the numerical ratios which exist between the length of the lyre strings and their pitch that they believed "that all things were numbers" (Esper, 1964). Perhaps they were not quite the mystics they were thought to be.

CHROMOSOMAL DEFECTS

Hereditary defects can be transmitted by genes but also by missing or additional chromosomes. When these aberrations involve the 23rd pair, they are described as sex-linked and when they involve any of the remaining 22 pair, they are termed *autosomal*. One of the most frequent chromosomal abnormality is *Down's syndrome* which accounts for 25 percent of the severely mentally retarded. It is called *extra-autosomal* because it is caused by an extra chromosome on the 21st pair. Down's syndrome was known as "Mongolism" because most individuals afflicted with it are unusually short, have a flat face and an eyelid fold which superficially resembles that of Asians or Mongols. Because of its negative reference to an ethnic group the term is no longer used by health care professionals. It is now called Down's syndrome or briefly, D.S., after the physician who first described it in 1866. Its chromosomal cause, however, was not proven until 1959 after the development of electron microscopy. It is also called *Trisomy 21* because in 95 percent of the cases, there is an extra chromosome 21. This extra chromosome comes from the father in one third of the cases (Merck, 1982). It causes the afflicted person to produce too much of an enzyme that breaks down the necessary protein tryptophan, which occurs in milk and is necessary to normal brain function.

Down's syndrome children develop slower physically and mentally and reach an average IQ of about 50 points. They are predisposed to cardiac complications and susceptible to infections. In 1940, the average life expectancy of a child with D.S.

was 15 years, but with advances in medicine, they live now an average of 40 years. Their long-term life expectancy is not yet known (Pueschel, 1983). Due to their retardation, they need special schooling and varying degrees of custodial care throughout their lives. They usually are placid and good-natured and seem to derive pleasures from very simple things in life, from seeing an animal, being hugged, or watching television. Their good-naturedness, however, is not immutably bound to their chromosomal condition. When scared or frightened, they can become very emotional and upset.

Although the chromosomal arrangement present in the various types of Down's syndrome is known, it is not known why the extra chromosomal condition occurs. In approximately half of the cases, both parents will have normal chromosome pairs but the syndrome will appear in their children *de nova*, meaning that it had no prior family history. The only, and most striking, predictor of Down's syndrome is the mother's age. In 15- to 19-year-old mothers, it occurs 1 in 2,400 live births but its rate rises dramatically after the mother reaches 30. By the maternal age of 40 the risk is 1 in 100, and with mothers older than 40 the risk increases to 5 in 100.

Down's syndrome is one of the most crucial issues in genetic counseling. The earliest it now can be detected is in the second trimester between the 14th to 16th week of pregnancy by amniocentesis, a surgical procedure whereby a hollow needle is inserted into the placenta in order to withdraw a sample of the amniotic fluid that surrounds the fetus. This fluid can be examined or karyotyped to determine the presence of the chromosomes which are indicative of Down's syndrome. Women older than 30 are becoming increasingly more concerned about the risk they take by having children, and an amniocentesis is now practically a routine procedure with this age group. Although it is the physician's and the laboratory technician's task to determine whether a fetus has Down's syndrome, it may be necessary for a psychologist or other genetic counselors to explain the behavioral conditions of Down's syndrome children and the life-long care they are likely to require. It may also be necessary to prepare the pregnant mother for a second trimester abortion.

A new technique called *chorionic villus biopsy* can now be used and performed in the 10th week of pregnancy, allowing the mother an option for an abortion in the first trimester of her pregnancy. This technique employs a catheter inserted through the cervix into the chorion to extract fetal cells from the amnion, the watertight bag surrounding the embryo. It can be foreseen that the detection methods for Down's syndrome will become more urgent in the future since more women have their first child at a later age now than in previous decades.

There are a number of other chromosomal defects which are sex-linked, involving abnormalities of the 23rd chromosome pair. *Turner's syndrome* is such an abnormality which is due, usually, to the complete or partial absence of one of the two X chromosomes in the female. Its incidence is low, approximately 1 in 3,000 in female births. Females who are affected by it remain small in stature and often have stubby fingers and toes, a webbed neck, a low hairline, and a wide chest. At puberty, their estrogen production is absent or deficient, causing underdeveloped breasts and the lack of menstruation. Although the administration of hormones may start menstruation and normal breast development, the Turner female will remain sterile because she either lacks the ovaries or her ovaries fail to produce ova. Rovet and Netley (1982) describe the typical Turner female as rather quiet and cheerful with female interests and activities. Fink (1984) describes her as having normal intelligence, but being somewhat below average in her nonverbal IQ.

In contrast to the Turner female who has a missing X chromosome, the *super female* has an extra female chromosome, a sex-linked triploid XXX condition involving her 23rd chromosomes. This condition was first discovered in hospitals for the mentally retarded but it was later found that the same ratio, about 1 in 1000, exists among the population in general. Although sterility sometimes occurs, several normal *XXX* females have had offspring who were both geno- and phenotypically normal (Merck, 1982).

Another sex-linked, extra chromosomal anomaly, which has received much publicity in the sports world, is *Klinefelter's syndrome*. It occurs in approximately 1 out of 700 male births with an *XXY* chromosomal condition. The typical, affected individual is tall and has male sex organs, which are usually underdeveloped. After puberty, Klinefelter males maintain their high-pitched voice and develop wide hips. They can easily pose as females and apparently have taken advantage of this in various sports competitions because in spite of their female characteristics, they are usually taller and stronger than even the average, normal male. At the Olympic Games in 1968, a female shot-putter was suspended for refusing to take a medical examination. It was suspected, as Shaffer (1985) states, that this individual would not have passed the sex test as "she" was actually a Klinefelter male. In a truly androgynous world, Kleinfelter persons would perhaps win all the Olympic Gold Medals.

Another extra chromosomal sex-linked aberration is the *supermale* or the *XYY* syndrome. It received much psychological attention in the 1960s because a number of aggressive and violent males with this syndrome were found in institutions for criminals and the mentally retarded. Similar to the history of the super female syndrome, it was later discovered that an equal proportion of *XYY* males was found in the general population.

GENETIC ABNORMALITIES

More than 2,000 conditions have been identified as single-gene defects for which the risk of producing affected offspring can be predicted. One example of this, hemophilia, has already been discussed. Other relatively frequent occurring sex-linked defects are color-blindness, two types of diabetes, and, some types of, muscular dystrophy. These sex-linked defects are due to a recessive gene on the *X* chromosome and as in hemophilia befall mostly males, since the defective gene on the *X* chromosome has no companion gene in males.

Genetic counseling and an examination of the family history is most important in all recessive conditions because they "run in families" but may skip one or two generations. Diabetes mellitus, for example, will not manifest itself if one parent is diabetic, provided the other parent is not a carrier. But should this other parent be a carrier, 50 percent of the children will have diabetes. If two diabetics have children, then all of their children will be diabetics.

Another chronic, sex-linked hereditary disease is *muscular dystrophy*, which is characterized by a progressive degeneration and weakness of the voluntary muscles. Its inheritance again is similar to that of hemophilia. Although it may occur at any age, it strikes mostly boys between the ages of two and six. Afflicted persons understandably become depressed with loss in appetite and motivation for living. Close to 50 percent of them have a lower IQ than their genetic expectation would suggest. There is no treatment, but all females on the maternal side of an affected boy should be examined for the elevations of certain muscular enzymes which would indicate whether they are carriers. If they are, they should be counseled about risks involving their offspring. The above discussion pertains mainly to the most common form of muscular dystrophy, the Duchenne type. There are several other types, which are autosomal (non sex-linked) affecting females as well as males.

Various other genetic defects such as *sickle cell anemia* are transmitted through an autosomal recessive gene, meaning that they can be transmitted to both male and female children. Approximately 1 in 400 black babies is affected by sickle cell anemia. In this disease, the red corpuscles change from a round to a sickle shape. In this form, they are more likely to cause clogging in the blood vessels, severe pain, and early death. Since the sickle cells carry less oxygen than the normal hemoglobin cells its victims are anemic, tire easily, have slow-healing wounds, and may suffer strokes. If two carriers have children, 25 percent of them will have the disease. But if one parent has the disease and the other parent is normal (not having the disease and not being a carrier) none of their children will have the disease but all of them will be carriers (Fink, 1984). This is an example where the genetic defect does not follow the simple dominant-recessive rules as Mendel's flowers did and as many other hereditary characteristics do. Here, the dominant gene fails to mask the recessive one a phenomenon termed *incomplete dominance*. In the usual dominant-recessive interplay, the Mendelian formula would predict that only half of the children would be carriers if one parent had the diseases and the other was not a carrier. A rather simple blood test can determine whether a person is a carrier of the disease.

Approximately 3 in 1,000 babies are born with a cleft spine, a condition called *spina bifida*. This condition ranges from a least severe form of a vertebrae malformation to the most serious form where the spinal cord, itself, protrudes into a fistula beyond the vertebrae. Spina bifida is caused by an autosomal recessive gene with irregular heredity due to the influence of other genes. If parents have one child with spina bifida, the odds are 1 in 20 that a second child will also be afflicted. Carriers for this defect cannot be detected. Surgery is necessary in almost all cases, but extensive neurological damage and physical handicaps may remain throughout life.

One of the most serious autosomal recessive defect is *Tay-Sachs disease*. It usually affects only Ashkenazi Jews of central and eastern European ancestry. A total of 1 in 30 American Jews is a carrier, and following the Mendelian law, two such carriers will have children with a 25 percent chance of developing the disease. An enzyme test can reveal carriers who can be cautioned against conception. The genetic defect involved causes a total absence of an enzyme *(Hex A)*, a catalyst for the breakdown of lipids in the brain. The accumulation of these lipids leads to a degeneration of the central nervous system. By 18 months, the child will become paralyzed and blind, and by age two, all voluntary movement will be lost, with death occurring by the third birthday.

Another autosomal, recessive defect is *phenylketonuria*, briefly PKU, which causes an improper breakdown and assimilation of phenylalanine, one of the essential amino acids. This creates an oversupply of phenylalanine and a deficit of tyrosine, melanin, and adrenalin. On the behavioral side, this causes mental impairment, varying from mild, borderline cases to life-long and severe retardation marked by idiocy and passiveness, with occasional outbreaks of destructiveness and seizures. PKU can be detected in the fetus by amniocentesis and, at birth, by a urine test (Guthrie Test), obligatory in most states. In most cases, PKU can be completely controlled by a low phenylalanine diet, which should begin in early infancy. It should be pointed out that a "complete cure" in PKU and other hereditary defects is only a phenotypical and not a genotypical cure. Although "cured" PKU persons will feel and act normal throughout their lives, their genetic defects will remain transmittible. This is, of course, "wonderful" for the affected individual but not quite so good for future generations. Under their ethical codes, physicians have an obligation to prevent phenotypical ailments, but they have no obligation to prevent them from occurring in future generations. Hence, this responsibility rests solely with the afflicted.

The above discussion of the chromosomal and genetic defects suggests that many inheritable diseases can be prevented by genetic counseling or ameliorated by medical technology. It should be mentioned, however, that the public does not always believe in the concept of probability. If a couple, for instance, is told that one out of four of their children will be afflicted with a certain disease, they may not opt for an abortion, hoping that their first child will not be the one. Even a probability of one healthy child in four afflicted ones may, at times, not be a warning. The reluctance of the public to accept preventative measures is apparent in many other facets of our daily lives. As will be discussed in the following section, behavioral psychology has still "a long way to go" in preparing the public to accept sound medical advice and discontinuing unhealthy habits and behavior.

PRENATAL COUNSELING

The prenatal environment, in comparison to the genetic one, is under much greater environmental influence. There is a much greater number of dos and do nots, which an expectant mother, and perhaps an expectant father, can follow to contribute to their offspring's fetal and future health. Prenatal counseling concerns the areas of age, nutrition, immunology, drugs, and living habits.

It has already been mentioned that maternal age influences the occurrence of Down's syndrome and for various, still unknown reasons, mothers younger than 15 and older than 35 experience about twice as many fetal miscarriages and neonatal death, (approximately 40 in 1,000 births) than mothers between the ages 18 and 35 who experience only 20 neonatal death in 1,000 (Kessner, 1973).

Approximately 7 percent of all babies born in the United States weigh only 5½ lbs., almost 2 lbs. less than the normal weight. The percentage of nonwhite babies with low birth weight is almost twice as high as that of white babies. Undernourishment and malnutrition are related to socio-economic class; underweight, in turn, correlates positively with neonatal death. Cross-cultural studies of various war famines indicate malnutrition affects the fetus most seriously during the last three months of pregnancy. At that time, much of the neural tissue develops which is most necessary for the full physical and mental health of the newborn. A well-balanced diet of 1,000 calories and 30 grams of protein including calcium, iron, and vitamins is necessary for both the health of the fetus and the mother. If the fetus receives insufficient nourishment, it can draw calories and calcium from the mother's fatty tissue and bones. To avoid this, detriment mothers should gain approximately 2½ lbs. during each month of pregnancy.

Certain immunological and physiological tests should be made before, during, and after pregnancy. *Rubella or German measles* is one of the most harmful diseases a woman can contract during her early pregnancy. Although it may not discomfort the mother more than a common cold, it can have severe effects on the fetus such as hearing loss, cataracts, blindness, heart defect, and mental retardation. One study (Michaels & Mellin, 1960) reports 47 percent of one or more defect when rubella occurred during the first month of pregnancy, 22 percent when it occurred during the second month, and 7 percent during the third month. These percentages are rather academic and a thing of the past since rubella can now be prevented by a reliable vaccine routinely administered during childhood immunization programs. If an adult woman is in doubt whether she had the disease or the vaccination, she should have her blood tested for the presence of the antibodies. If the vaccination is needed, it must be administered several months before the beginning of the pregnancy. The vaccine consists of live viruses and a vaccination during pregnancy would be as risky as the disease itself. In the case of rubella, one must prepare the house even before the guest's conception!

Other maternal diseases can be prevented from harming the newborn by regular medical checkups during pregnancy. *Syphillis* can be cured in most cases with antibiotics before birth so that the neonate will not be infected during delivery. Although *herpes* cannot be cured, contact with it during birth can be prevented by Caesarian section. This procedure is especially recommended if there is an active outbreak in the birth canal during delivery.

All parents should also have an *Rh compatibility* test. When an Rh-negative woman is impregnated by an Rh-positive man, at least half of their children will be Rh-positive, since the positive factor is genetically dominant. If an Rh-negative mother gives birth to an Rh-positive child it is likely that some of the child's blood cells enter the mother's blood stream, which, in turn, would stimulate the mother to produce antibodies against the Rh-positive invasion. The mother's antibodies may remain in her body and could cause damage to the Rh-positive cells of a second fetus. This damage to a second or third child can be prevented by an injection of an anti-Rh-positive preparation within 72 hours after the birth of the first and all subsequent children.

DRUGS

If at all possible, all *drugs* should be avoided during pregnancy. Almost all cross the placenta and enter the fetus' blood stream. The classic case against drugs comes from the hundreds of deformed children born to European mothers during the 1950s and 1960s. These women had taken Contagan, an over-the-counter drug to prevent nausea in pregnant women. This drug contained *thalidomide,* which inhibited the formation of limbs and other tissues during the embryonic stage. The women, who had taken the drug between the 21 and 36 days after conception, bore babies whose arms, legs, or ears were grossly deformed or absent. In the United States, Frances Kelsey, a physician employed by the Food and Drug Administration, repeatedly refused to allow the distribution of this drug (Fischer & Lazerson, 1984). She considered thalidomide unsafe because its effect on embryos had only been tested on animals where it had no detrimental effects. The European authorities were misled by this differential effect.

Another warning against new drugs can be taken from a case closer at home. In the 1950s and 1960s a synthetic estrogen, *diethylstilbestrol (DES),* was frequently prescribed to prevent miscarriages during the early months of pregnancy. It was later discovered that this hormone contributed to the development of a carcinoma involving the vagina or cervix. Herbst, et al. (1978) found that of 293 cases of this rare cancer, 182 were exposed to DES *in utero*.

The effects of drugs quite often are specific. Procaine, for example, is associated with eye and ear defects and tetracycline, with stained teeth. If drugs have to be taken during pregnancy, they should be given under close, medical supervision. Dose and duration of ingestion of the drug, developmental stage of the embryo or fetus, and the susceptibility of the individual are all factors which should be carefully examined and monitored.

TOBACCO AND ALCOHOL

In 1985, several citizens were preparing damage suits against a large tobacco company, claiming that its product caused them irreparable heart and lung damage. The claimants alleged that cigarette smoking is an incurable addiction for them and that the warning on the product should state that cigarette smoking is addictive. The defendants, the tobacco companies, will claim that smoking is not an addiction but a mere habit which can be freely pursued and willfully and freely discontinued. The fact that thousands of smokers were able to discontinue the habit and that no one has ever died from a cigarette withdrawal symptom should be in the tobacco company's favor.

There is no clear distinction between an addiction and a habit, but it is clear that smoking is, in many ways, harmful to the fetus and mother. The warnings in the ads which picture women smoking have changed in 1985 from ". . . dangerous to your health," to "Smoking by pregnant women may result in fetal injury, premature birth, and low birth weight." This sums up the results of many research studies reviewed by Stechler & Halton (1982), which examine the relationship between fetal physiology and smoking in more detailed analysis. One study found, for instance, a rapid rise in the women's pulse rate, blood pressure, and carboxyhemoglobin after the onset of smoking. After the women had smoked for 7 minutes, the fetal heart rate also began to rise, increasing as much as 23 beats per minute. Smoking is associated with various neonatal abnormalities, such as reduced head circumference, cleft lip, cleft palate, and lower-than-average birth weight. An examination of 50,000 pregnant women found that mothers who smoked more than 30 cigarettes per day had more than twice as many low birth weight babies as nonsmoking women.

Although the neonatal weight deficiencies are reported quite consistently, the long-term effect on the children of women who smoked during pregnancy is less clear. A British study tested children at ages 7 and 11 whose mother had smoked during pregnancy found that the children were shorter and poorer readers with slightly lower IQs. An American study, on the other hand, examining 4- and 7-year-olds in New York reported no such differences. Looking at our life span, the detrimental effects of smoking have been unmistakenly proven, although it is difficult to assess the effects on shorter periods. It is also difficult to pinpoint the harmful effects of malnutrition, alcohol, and drugs, which often accompany the smoking habit.

In many ways, the alcohol habit is similar to the smoking habit, and we can ask similar questions. How much, for example, constitutes a social drinker, a habit, or an addiction? In relation to pregnancy, 2 cocktails per day or more than 45 per month have been defined as "heavy" drinking because some detrimental effects such as mental retardation, a flattened face, and smaller eyes have been found in children of these women. Much depends on the trimester in which the drinking occurs. While thalidomide is most damaging when taken in the first trimester when the limbs form, alcohol is most damaging in the last trimester when the neural tissue develops. Babies born to very heavy alcohol consumers will be born with the *fetal alcohol syndrome*, signified by nerve damage, mental and physical retardation, microcephaly, irritability in infancy, and hyperactivity in childhood. Mothers who drink or smoke seem to double the risk of bearing a growth-retarded infant. Mothers who do

both, drink and smoke, quadruple this risk (Stec
1982).

The Surgeon General's Report, *Healthy Peop*
shows that at the beginning of this century influenza, p
nia, diphtheria, and tuberculosis accounted for a yearly
rate of 580 people from a population of 100,000. This figure
now reduced to only 30 deaths per year. The major health hazards are now heart attacks, cancer, cirrhosis of the liver, accidents, violence, and poisoning. Approximately 50 percent of
these fatalities can be traced back to life-styles, including the
habits of drinking and smoking.

The many possible pre- and neonatal defects discussed in
this chapter sound overwhelming, even to those who do not plan
to have children. It should be pointed out, however, that each
defect mentioned has only a very limited chance of occurring,
perhaps less than 1 in 1,000 and that this risk can still be reduced through proper counseling and precautions. To end this
chapter on a more hopeful note, it should be stated that the infant mortality rate in the United States has been steadily declin-
ing. Although it is not quite as low as the rates for Sweden and
Japan, in the United States only 13 infants out of 1,000 die during the first year of their life.

Chapter 11

'E SOCIAL SELF

The effects, which different childrearing practices have in shaping a child's personality and behavior, have already been discussed in a previous chapter. In this chapter, the causes and types of attachments, which infants and parents form with each other, will be examined as well as the implications which these attachments have for the child's later social and emotional development. It has been estimated that by 1990 more than half of all children in the United States will be reared in single-parent families. Consequently, special emphasis will be given to attachments formed with working mothers and fathers. Prosocial behavior and antisocial behavior such as aggression and child abuse in family, day-care, and preschool settings will also be discussed.

ATTACHMENT

Almost a hundred years ago, the "father of child development" G. Stamly Hall (1844–1924) wrote that adolescence is the most crucial stage of the life cycle for the development of personality. Most subsequent developmental pscyhologists challenged this idea. Freud believed that the process of personality development begins the moment the baby is handed to the parents and continues for 5 to 6 years. The neo-Freudian, Eric Erikson (1963) also believes that the early years are of utmost importance for the establishment of a basic trust when children learn whether the world is a satisfying or frustrating place to live. Although usually at opposite poles, the behaviorists, likewise, emphasize the importance of the early developmental years. Watson's famous statement, "Give me a dozen healthy infants. . . . ." has already been quoted (see p. 24).

The first social interaction between a newborn and a parent is often defined as attachment or bonding. It is expressed in behaviors that promote proximity and contact such as signaling, clinging, approaching, and following. To a large degree, the success or the failure of this bonding is a two-way street. The temperament of newborns may contribute much to the attachment process and determine in general whether a newborn is liked by others. Horowitz (1980) asked different examiners to test newborn babies and to comment whether they liked the babies. There was considerable agreement among the different examiners—some babies were generally liked, others were not. Responsive, alert babies who did not cry easily tended to be most popular, but other factors such as physical appearance also probably influenced the examiners. As one might expect, there were some indications that caregiver-infant interactions were most successful with the likable babies who were spoken to more often and held for longer periods. Their mothers seemed to find it fairly easy to feed them, while the mothers of the less popular babies had more problems during feeding sessions.

Alexander Thomas and Stella Chess (1977), both psychiatrists at New York University Medical Center, previously had found that some of the unique temperaments babies show at birth persist throughout childhood. In a longitudinal study, Thomas and Chess rated babies every three months on such temperament dimensions as cheerful-fussy, distractibility-steadiness, sensitivity to visual and auditory stimuli, and intensity of emotional reactions. Based on these ratings, they were able to classify 40 percent of the babies as "easy" babies being cheerful, adaptable, and regular in their habits. On the opposite end, there were the "difficult" babies, about 10 percent, whose biological cycles were irregular and whose reactions to new people and situations tended to be more negative and intense. Thomas and Chess identified 15 percent of the babies as "slow to warm up" who, like the "difficult" babies, reacted negatively to anything new, but their reactions tended to be milder.

It is not surprising that "easy" and likable babies develop more secure attachments to their caregiver than "difficult" babies. Even when they have less responsive mothers, easy babies seem to be less affected than are difficult babies by their mothers' behavior by virtue of their easy temperaments. Furthermore, easy babies are less likely to demand as much of their caretakers as do difficult babies (Crockenberg, 1981). But there is also hope for those babies who are not in the easy category. Awareness of their baby's temperament can help parents to develop a style of interaction that is satisfying for all, parents and baby. For example, the parents of a difficult or slow-to-warm-up baby can introduce new experiences gradually. Such a baby, if given time to adjust, may eventually accept new people and new situations. In a supportive environment, a difficult baby is less likely to turn into a problem child. In sum, both factors, environment and temperament, interact to shape the child personality.

CAREGIVERS' ATTACHMENT

The concept of bonding as introduced by Klaus and Kennell in 1976 has already been discussed (see p. 149). These two pediatricians maintained that a togetherness of mother and child right after birth sets up a linkage which is beneficial to both of them. Since 1976, a number of studies have been conducted in Sweden, Germany, and the United States to examine the nature of this bonding and its alleged benefits for mother and child. Grossmann and her colleagues (1981) measured the amount of "tender touches" mothers would execute during a 20-minute feeding time. They observed mothers who had different amounts of contact with their babies right after birth, mothers whose contact was delayed, and mothers whose contact was delayed for several days. The early contact group, 30 minutes after birth, had the highest touching rate. Another early contact group, which had 30 minutes touching plus 5 hours of additional rooming-in, touched their babies much less often. If there is a special attachment due to early bonding as Klaus and Kennell claim, it was undone within a few subsequent hours. A little absence, even from a baby, may make the heart grow fonder! Furthermore, Grossmann found that mothers who had no initial contact with their babies increased their tender touches, while those with early contact decreased them, so that the amount of touching was equal in all groups after 9 days. Bee and Mitchell (1984) cite several other studies which found no lasting effect of early contact on specific maternal caregiving.

Infants' Attachment

Schaffer and Emerson (1964), the experimenters already mentioned in the discussion on contact-love (see p. 19), studied the development of attachment in 60 Scottish infants over their first 18 months of life. They conducted monthly interviews with each infant's mother concerning her child's responses to a variety of separation situations as, for example, being left in a crib or being left in the presence of strangers. They also observed the child's reaction on being approached by the interviewer, a stranger, at various distances and found their infants to pass through four stages of social responsiveness. The first stage is the *asocial stage* from birth to six months, when infants are largely asocial creatures who are aroused by all parts of their environment by people as well as objects.

The second stage, that of *indiscriminate attachment* lasts until about the seventh month when infants prefer human company and are apt to protest when an adult puts them down or leaves them alone. Near the seventh month, the third stage of *specific attachments* begins when infants begin to protest only when separated from one particular individual, usually the mother. At this time, many infants also begin to show fear of strangers. Schaffer and Emerson interpret these data as an indication that the infants have formed their first genuine attachment, although it can be argued that the degree by which one fears person X is not a valid indicator of how well one likes person Y. Many children form attachments to their parent without ever showing any fear of strangers. They seem to skip Schaffer and Emerson's final stage, that of *multiple attachments*, which usually starts within weeks after the specific attachment began. About half of the children in Schaffer and Emerson's study did become attached to several people, to members of the household and to frequent visitors. Each attachment may serve a different function. Mothers may primarily satisfy the infant's daily needs, fathers the need for play, and grandparents the need for spoiling!

THEORIES OF ATTACHMENT

Attachment plays an important part in an infant's social and emotional development, and, for years, theorists have questioned why babies become enamored of their caregivers. According to Freud (discussed in Chapter 8) infants are pleasure-seeking and lustful creatures who become attached to their parents, usually the mother, by seeking or fantasizing sexual relations with her. For a secure attachment, Freudians would recommend that the parents should not frustrate their children in these efforts. In the same Freudian vein, Erik Erikson believes that the feeding situation is a major determinant of social attachment trust and aversive feeding conditions will promote distress and frustrations.

Theorizing somewhat differently, learning theorists consider the mother a logical attachment object for her baby. Not only do mothers feed their infants, they also change them when wet or soiled, provide warmth, tender caresses, and reassuring vocalizations. According to Pavlovian generalization (see Chapter 3), an infant eventually will associate the mother with pleasurable feelings and sensations, so that she becomes a conditioned stimulus for positive outcomes or expectations. The learning theorists consider this status of a conditioned or secondary reinforcer the basis of attachment.

Proponents of Jean Piaget's cognitive development theory believe that an infant's ability to form social attachments depends, in part, on his or her intellectual development.

Before an attachment can occur, however, the infant must be able to discriminate between the potential attachment person and the stranger. Furthermore, the infant must be able to keep the attached person in mind during her or his absence and to recognize that person on return. Piaget termed this ability *object permanence*, although it involves objects as well as persons. As early as 1926, the German psychologist Oswald Kroh had both object-permanence and person-permanence in the nomenclature of his system of developmental periods, but Piaget disregarded the research of other developmental psychologists usually. In any event, object permanence appears in Piaget's system during the "sensorimotor" period in the stage of "Coordination of Secondary Schemata" (8 to 12 months) discussed in Chapter 8. Presumably, infants who recognize that objects or persons have a permanent existence will develop a stable schemata for people with whom they interact. They should then prefer these people to all others and may even protest the presence of others.

The ethologists, who study animals and humans in their natural surrounding rather than in the laboratory, offer still another explanation for the causes of social attachment. They maintain that animals as well as humans are born with certain "signals" or behaviors that attract and promote social interaction (Ainsworth, et al., 1974; Bowlby, 1973). Considering the infants' actions Bowlby points to such *executive functions* as sucking, grasping, crawling, and walking, which infants execute to keep their caregivers in sight. The infants also produce *signaling functions*, such as smiling and vocalizing, to engage the caregiver to approach the infant. In summary, the ethological theory maintains that infants are biologically programmed to signal to their caregivers who, in turn, are also programmed to respond. Freud and Bowlby's theories are essentially instinct theories, which, in so many different words simply say, the infant comes born that way.

The difference among the various theories are mainly differences in emphasis. Freud, Watson, and especially Piaget would all agree with the ethological view that the human baby is biologically predisposed to attachment and bonding, meaning that he or she has the physiological mechanism to do so. These theorists, however, would not assume that this is automatic. They view attachment as the result of an interaction in which each participant has learned to respond, in a meaningful way, to the social signals of his or her partner—not too different from all other love affairs.

FEARFUL REACTIONS

Many good things may also have a negative side. Love often begets jealousy and a fondness for coffee may effect a dislike for tea. Childhood is not exempt from these dichotomies. After the seventh month when infants have formed their first genuine attachment many of them also develop a fear of strangers often called *stranger anxiety*.

In marked contrast to the friendly smiles and babblings by which infants greet familiar people, they may stare, turn away, whimper, cry, and hide when a stranger approaches. This stranger anxiety emerges in the stage which Schaffer and Emerson have called the specific attachment stage. It peaks at about the 10th month and declines gradually during the second year. As mentioned earlier, many infants never develop it, and much depends on the setting in which the stranger is met. Sroufe, et al., (1974) found that few 10-month-old infants reacted negatively when strangers were met in the family home but that many reacted with anxiety meeting a stranger in an unfamiliar laboratory setting. If the stranger waits until the infant makes some overtures, the baby's anxiety may never be aroused.

Stranger anxiety is rarely observed in large or extended families and it rarely exists in communal living situations as in the kibbutzim or in China's agricultural communes. It appears stranger anxiety is an environmentally conditioned phenomenon rather than an innate, developmental milestone (Shaffer, 1985).

At about the same time when infants begin to fear strangers, they also begin to show *separation anxiety*. This anxiety manifests itself by signs of discomfort, protest, or acute fear reactions when the child is separated from the mother or other familiar companions. Separation anxiety peaks a few months later than stranger anxiety, usually at 14–18 months whereafter it subsides gradually in frequency and intensity (Weintraub & Lewis, 1977).

Types of Attachments

Infants differ in the type or the quality of the attachments they have with their caregivers. Mary Ainsworth (1978) and her associates measured the quality of attachment in one-year-olds by exposing them to a number of strange situations which contained an increasing amount of strangeness and stress. Measuring the child's crying, exploring, and reunion behavior, she found that 70 percent of her subjects were "securely attached," meaning that the infants in this category were visibly upset by separation, but explored and were outgoing with strangers while the mothers were present. The other infants, about 30 percent, were "insecurely attached." Some infants in this category did not explore while the mother was present and became distressed when the mother departed. When the mother returned, they were likely to resist contact initiated by the mother. Ainsworth termed these infants anxious-resistant. Other infants in the insecurely attached group showed little distress when separated from the mother and usually did avoid contact with her when she returned. These infants were not wary particularly of strangers but avoided or ignored them sometimes in much the same way they avoided their mothers.

As would be expected, Ainsworth (1979) found that mothers of securely attached infants are more attentive caregivers enjoying their daily interactions with their infants, while mothers of insecurely attached infants find it less enjoyable and have more difficulties interpreting their children's desires. In certain cases, however, the problem may be attributable to a "difficult" infant. Studies have found that infants resistant to attachment at 1 year of age often had been rather irritable and unresponsive as neonates (Waters et al., 1980). As will be discussed later, sickly and irritable infants are more prone to child abuse than healthy and calm ones. It has also been found that the caregiver's inconsistency, impatience, and self-preoccupation lead to the avoidance, if not to the resistance, of attachment (Belsky, et al., 1984; England & Faber, 1984).

ALTRUISM: BEING PROSOCIAL

As pointed out previously (p. 176), Americans value sociability and are concerned when a child is inner-directed, or worse, asocial. Attachment can be viewed as the earliest social interaction forecasting sociability in day-care, preschool, and later life. The term *altruism* was coined by Auguste Compte (1798–1857) to indicate the selfless concern for others. Along the Darwinian line of thought it was believed, rather optimistically, that altruistic behavior improved the chance for survival of the group and the species, although it may be detrimental, or perhaps even fatal, for the individual. Today, we seem to practice altruism for an entirely different purpose. Few parents and developmental psychologists would advocate altruism if they thought it might be to the individual's disadvantage. In our reward-oriented society, we believe that rewarding others will be rewarding to ourselves, sooner or later. Be this as it may, the topic of altruism has become of great interest to developmental psychologists. Research and applied interests in altruism, also called *prosocial behavior*, primarily arose to counteract antisocial behavior, especially aggression discussed subsequently.

Developmental psychologists have studied prosocial behavior at all age levels. It usually is observed that infants interact with objects rather than with other infants during their first year. Thereafter, their interests in other children increase steadily while those in objects decrease. Toddlers can perform acts of kindness and are able to show empathy toward others, but close friendships are rarely formed before age three (Bee & Mitchell, 1984). Youngsters who had formed secure attachments in infancy, as compared to those who had not, are reported by Sroufe, et al. (1977, 1983) to be more in leadership roles, more curious, and more sensitive to the needs of others in both kindergarten and elementary school settings. Preschoolers can recognize and explain an emotional perspective that differs from their own in a given situation, indicating that they can understand the feelings of others although they may be different from their own (Smith, et. al., 1983).

Parents can promote altruistic behavior regardless of sex by encouraging their child to perform acts of kindness, by reinforcing the child's prosocial deeds, and by practicing what they preach (modeling). Working with 4- and 5-year-olds, Cathleen Smith and her associates (1983) have shown that prosocial behavior can be greatly increased when adults provide verbalizations of need such as "Oh! I spilled the sticks," or "I don't know how to make a glitter picture," or by more direct commands such as "When I play with you, I want you to help." Prosocial behavior was also increased through rehearsal and practice.

As pointed out in the discussion on play (p. 176), all cultures do not share the American enthusiasm about infant and childhood sociability. French parents, for instance, consider toy sharing more an invasion of privacy than a cultural asset. The dangers of being too social and too responsive to peers are rarely mentioned by developmental psychologists, although many acts of delinquency and the usage of drugs and alcohol in adolescence are frequently blamed on "peer pressure." It is important, therefore, that along with prosocial behavior we teach our children to discriminate when they should and should not be cooperative.

AGGRESSION

Even a mere cursory look at a preschool playground will show that not all children are prosocial. Some will show little cooperation and others, usually just a few, will be outright aggressive. Thousands of experiments, books, conferences, and symposia have attempted to determine the causes of aggressiveness in children, adolescents, and adults as well as aggression by groups, governments, and nations. In spite of the 240 different definitions of aggression which are in the pscyhological literature, it usually is agreed that an aggressive act is any form of behavior designed to harm or injure another living being who is motivated to avoid such treatment (Baron & Byrne, 1981).

Aggressive acts are often divided into a *hostile aggression* category where it is the aggressor's major goal to injure a victim, and into *instrumental* aggression in which one person harms another as a means to an end to coerce or to take an object away. Both types of aggression are shown by two- and three-year olds. They are likely to be hostile aggressive after parents have thwarted or angered them by exerting authority, and they are also likely to exhibit instrumental aggression by kicking an adversary in confrontations concerning toys and other possessions.

Infants do become angry and may occasionally strike out at people, and it is difficult to think of these actions as having an aggressive intent. But things begin to change and it often becomes difficult to discern between play, horseplay, and aggression. Most children begin to hit, push, and bang objects, animals, and people as soon as they are physically able to do so. But unless a hostile or instrumental intention is involved such behavior may be totally fortuitous. Some youngsters learn this very fast and quickly say, "it was an accident!"

Many psychologists believe that aggression begets aggression, that children hit because they, themselves, are hit. Although a fair number of such cases can be found, there are also many other children who hit though they, themselves, have never been hit. Who do these children model? Bandura's Bobo doll discussed previously, (p. 133) or similar scenes? Aggression can be vicariously rewarding through television, and comic books, and it also "works" quite often in reality. If Johnny grabs a toy from another child by pushing or hitting, his aggression will be rewarded unless it has an immediate, aversive consequence. This would mean that the toy has to be taken away immediately. In practice, however, there usually will be a delay. The victim cries, the teacher comes to investigate, the toy will be taken away, etc. We have discussed the intricacies of reward and punishment in Chapter 4 and have seen that even a delay of a few minutes can negate the effect of punishment. It can be assumed that most parental punishment is misapplied if it does not curb a child's aggression. Goldstein (1984) summarizes Bandura's social learning theory in relation to aggression and states "when aggression pays, it tends to persist: when unrewarded, it tends to be extinguished" (p. 37).

Everyday aggression causes an immeasurable amount of pain and suffering among Americans. Hostile aggression is evident in wanton beatings, stabbings, and shootings, and instrumental aggression occurs in many robberies and coercions.

More indirectly, aggression causes much suffering since it is a contributing factor, if not the cause, to many automobile accidents. In the hope of curbing aggression, psychologists have searched for its causes, but have, unfortunately, not been able to reduce it. In developmental psychology, it has been found that aggression is a rather stable attribute from the preschool period through early adolescence to early adulthood. It is stable for males, but not for females, a finding which has already been mentioned in connection with modeling aggression shown on television (see p. 133). Perhaps due to socially expected "sex typing," aggressive adolescent females are more likely to become assertive rather than aggressive adults.

As the research on aggression continues, an increasing number of its causes are being isolated. Some of those which relate to the parental milieu and to the types of rewards and punishment received in early childhood already have been discussed. Moreover, a variety of hereditary, social, and economic factors are being delineated. But in spite of the fact that psychologists were able to gain more detailed knowledge about the cause of aggression, they have not been able to stem the tide of the various environmental factors which cause aggression. This is most evident in the epidemic occurrence of child abuse discussed in the following section.

CHILD ABUSE

In 1985, the Scientific Council of the American Medical Association reported that more than a million children in the United States are abused every year and that between 2,000 and 5,000 die as a result of their injuries. Another study by Starns and his coworkers (1980), based on a nationwide survey, estimated the number of abuse cases close to two millions, indicating the large number of abuse cases which are not reported to the authorities. Starns' study, appropriately titled, "Behind closed doors: Violence in the American family," shows that marriage partners, relatives, and neighbors fearing reprisals often do not report the abuse cases they have experienced or witnessed. There are indications that even mandated professionals report only 20 percent of the cases of which they are aware, giving the lack of short-term intervention and the possible detrimental effect on the relationship between the client and the child care worker as reasons (Faller, 1985). In the words of one physician (Sargent, 1985) there is "our lack of trust in the caretakers' ability to refrain from further violence. Unfortunately, we also lack confidence if the alternative to parental care is a child protection system with a reputation for ineffectuality" (p. 803).

The very definition of child abuse presents an additional difficulty in determining the number of cases. The Federal Child Abuse Prevention and Treatment Act of 1974 defines child abuse and neglect as the "physical or mental injury, sexual abuse, negligent treatment, or maltreatment of a child under the age of 18. . . ." The language of this Act is rather general, and there is much interpretive leeway in each abuse category the Act enumerates. Individuals, social, and cultural groups have often divergent ideas on what type of punishment constitutes abuse. Physical injuries and the presence of hand, stick, or belt marks which compromise about 50 percent of all abuse cases (Johnson & Showers, 1985) are easily identifiable as abuser inflicted. The causes of the other half of the injuries, however, such as broken bones, burns, or injuries received from being thrown or pushed, or from thrown objects, are difficult to determine. These types of injuries could be caused by an abuser, but also by the child's own actions. This, perhaps, explains that more than half of the cases which are reported are not legally substantiated as involving abuse (Faller, 1985).

Child neglect is even more difficult to define than physical abuse. Aside from the more obvious cases of malnutrition and the denial of medical aid, neglect is difficult to detect and still more difficult to prove. Most evasive, however, is the category of mental or psychological abuse. The current controversies about media violence shows that there is little consensus on what constitutes psychological damage to children. There is little concern about the cruelties in the "good old" fairy tales, but there is much uncertainty about the effects of seeing torture and killings on the screen. A frightening story or television program may not have the same effect as frightening the child directly. At times, it appears that children enjoy being frightened before, perhaps, their fears have been associated with specific pains. It has already been mentioned in the discussion on punishment (see p. 84) that psychologists differ in their opinion on how much, if any, fear and pain a child should experience.

THE ABUSER

Although there are still many unknowns about the frequency and the definition of child abuse, it is known that the percentage of Americans who consider child abuse a serious national problem has increased from only 10 percent in 1976 to 90 percent in 1983 (Harris Poll, 1983). This increased concern has stimulated a tremendous amount of research. The international journal *Child Abuse and Neglect* was founded in 1977, and much additional research is reported in various medical, sociological, and psychological journals. Much of the psychological research has centered on the personality profile of the child's abuser. A decade or so ago, this research centered on a *psychiatric model* based on the assumption that the abuser suffers from a distinct parental psychopathology with symptoms of depressions, loss of self-esteem, and inadequate impulse control. But empirical studies revealed that only about 10 percent of the abusers suffer from a psychosis or mental sickness (Kempe & Kempe, 1978) and that the remaining 9 percent do not fit any single psychological pattern but become abusers when specific family, social, and economic conditions arise. Psychologists have now adopted the more recent *social interactional model* of child abuse.

The people who abuse their children come from all races,

ethnic groups, and social classes, and many of them appear to be rather typical, loving parents—except for their tendency to become extremely irritated with their children and to do things they may later regret. Wolfe (1985) has reviewed close to 100 studies which examine these predisposing and situational variables by comparing the personality and the family circumstances of abusers with nonabusers. He summarizes that child abuse is more likely to occur if the abuser had a history of aggression with poor impulse control, immaturity, anger, rigidity, and if he or she had received harsh physical punishment as a child. These predisposing factors, in themselves, do not produce abusive behavior. In a multicausal fashion, they are likely to interact with the following averse conditions: financial difficulties, adolescent age at birth of child, having a premature or sickly child, improper education, and distorted perceptions of a child's capacities.

The family situation presents further contributing factors. Child abuse is likely to occur in families under stress. Situational stresses such as marital problems, loss of job, social isolation, and poverty contribute to abusive and neglectful parenting. For example, the battered child often comes from a large family in which overburdened caregivers have many young children. Almost one half of all sexual abuse victims come from families with four or more children (Pierce & Pierce, 1985). These families often live in "high risk" deteriorating neighborhoods in which families "go it alone" without interacting much with their neighbors or making use of community services (Garbarino & Sherman, 1980). Comparing abusive with nonabusive families, it was found that the families in which the abuser lives have a higher rate of abusive behavior toward other family members besides the abused child. Usually, there is more hitting, overt conflict, and disharmony in the family than in any other social group. Gelles & Straus (1979) consider ascribed roles, lack of privacy, high levels of stress, and the legitimate acceptance of physical aggression as the main contributing factors.

Comparing the reward-punishment patterns between abusive and nonabusive families several developmental studies found no difference between the number of negative or restrictive statements used. There were just as many "don'ts" in the nonabusive families as there were in the abusive ones. There was a great difference in the number of positive or reinforcing statements, however, with the child in the nonabusive family receiving many and the child in the abusive family rarely. Moreover, in the abusive family the parents often responded negatively to their child's prosocial behavior (Wolfe, 1985).

Child abuse in the United States is more prevalent than in other Western and in many non-Western countries. The fatalities from abuse, for example, are three to five times higher in the United States than in the Scandinavian countries (Gregersen & Vesterby, 1984).

Looking at the world in general, there are wide differences in the concept of what constitutes child abuse. Okeahialam (1984) reports that many traditional practices in some rural African areas are abusive to children. He lists the abandonment and death of newborns with gross physical abnormalities and, likewise, that of twins and triplets who are believed to be a throwback to animalism. He further lists severe corporal punishment for minor offenses and scalding of the feet as a method of controlling convulsions. These occasional practices coexist with extended family life which provides much love and protection to the child. As the result of urbanization in Nigeria, there is a high rate of abandonment of babies in the cities by single mothers. Another consequence of urbanization in Nigeria is the "childminder" who comes from the country to take care of a baby when both parents work. Unlike the nanny of the Western countries, the childminder is usually a girl between the ages of 7 and 12. The childminders, themselves, are beaten, at times, by the women of the household, and Okeahialam believes that they, in turn, abuse the babies. Some babies in urban Nigeria have as many as four different childminders within the first year of their life.

A totally different picture of child abuse is given by Jill

Korbin (1981) who studied the conditions in the People's Republic of China and states that child abuse in the Chinese cities does not exist. As the major reason for its absence, she stresses the communal attitudes where the biological parent and the society, as a whole, entrust much of the child's care to communal institutions and where the individual can always depend on social, medical, and economic support, although primitive by American standards. On the technical side, Korbin mentions semi-annual medical checkups and that "accident prone" is not an excuse for an injury. The parent in China is held responsible whether an injury is accidental or intentionally inflicted. For example, if a child is burned from falling against a heater, the parent would be reprimanded or punished for not putting a screen around it.

Cross-cultural comparisons can give us additional information regarding the etiology of child abuse. Korbin considers the Chinese experience as a contradiction to the most consistently reported cause of child abuse, namely cyclical nature, that the abused child will be an abusive parent. Although there is some correlation between these two factors in the United States, China seems to have made a complete turnabout within one generation, from an abusive "bitter past" to a nonabusive present. Although the developmental psychologists cannot change the many social factors which contribute to child abuse in the United States they can and have been instrumental in working at helping agencies such as "hot lines" and Parents Anonymous. In spite of the research and public concern the abuse problem is by no means solved. The frustrations which still exist are succinctly expressed by Sargent (1985) a physician on the advisory council of the American Medical Association, who writes that one is "hardly able to believe that parents could savage their children yet bring them to us for repair" (p. 803).

Chapter 12

COGNITION

In human development as in psychology in general, different theoretical viewpoints are predominant at different times. As the Freudian assumptions influenced the 1940s and 1950s and the behavioristic methods the 1960s and 1970s, 1980 is clearly the decade of "cognition." From the four volumes of Mussen's (1983) *Handbook of Child Psychology,* one entire volume, nearly 1,000 pages, is devoted to the topic of "cognitive" development. Cognition is as old as psychology. A century ago, most psychologists believed cognition, affect, and conation (knowing, feeling, and wanting) were the three categories under which all mental processes can be classified. Over the decades, its meaning broadened considerably to include such concepts as sensing, perceiving, judging, reasoning, and understanding (English & English, 1958). More recently, developmental psychologists generally define cognition as the process by which a person acquires knowledge and understanding (Fischer & Lazerson, 1985). Needless to say, the cognitive process, whatever it is, is poorly understood and perhaps never solvable entirely. It is influenced by the capacities to sense, perceive, categorize, and organize, and these functions, in turn, are influenced by many genetic, physiological, and environmental variables.

In this chapter, the current research on cognition and some of its application will be discussed. A brief history of cognition will be followed by a summary of the renewed efforts to examine the cognitive processes of sensing and perceiving in infancy. The cognitive processes relating to the acquisition of language in early childhood will also be examined as well as the cognitive skills and cognitive styles which affect the learning process. Furthermore, emphasis will be given to social cognition and the application of cognitive behavior modification.

Binet's Beginnings

Questions and experimentations concerning the acquisition of knowledge and the ability to reason permeate nearly all of Piaget's developmental periods and stages. Perhaps for this reason, many psychologists believe Piaget was the first cognitive psychologist, although most cognitive concepts such as the conservation of numbers and cognitive styles were introduced by Alfred Binet in 1890, four years before Piaget was born. Binet's IQ test, his quantitative measurement of the mental process, has almost totally overshadowed his quest for cognition—the qualitative understanding of the developing mind (Wolf, 1961, 1966). The following description of Binet's early work may serve to introduce the concept of cognition.

Binet earned a law degree and a doctorate degree in neurophysiology. Psychology was his hobby, and he became an ardent associationist, seeking to explain mental phenomena by the stimulus-response model. After his daughters were born, however, Madelaine in 1885 and Alice in 1887, he became less enthusiastic about associationism and more intrigued with the different cognitive styles by which his daughters learned. Madelaine concentrated firmly, was silent, and cautious, while Alice was compulsive, gay, and exuberant. These differences in-creased with age, greatly influencing their modes of learning and the material they preferred to learn. This aroused Binet's interest in the learning process, especially in its qualitative aspects caused by individual differences and by age.

Observing his daughters, Binet found, for instance, that they could not differentiate between dreams and reality at age three, but could do so at age four. He also noticed that children can recognize the picture of a complete figure, such as a horse, by the age of two, while at age four, they were still unable to recognize parts of this figure, an eye or nose. To further investigate the developmental aspects of the mind, Binet asked his daughters the same questions at different ages. For example, the answers to the question "What is a knife?" were different at different ages. At two years and six months the reply was: "cuts little children," a month later it was: "That means to cut," and a year later, "to cut meat." From this and other observations, Binet suggested that the development of our thoughts proceeds from the general to the specific (Binet, 1890).

Binet found his most surprising results in his studies on the visual discrimination of lines of different length. He found that 2-year-old and 4-year-old children, as well as adults, could all differentiate between two lines when one was 40 mm long and the other 36 mm or less. Neither children nor adults, however, could differentiate correctly above chance between a line of 40 mm and a line 38 mm. Children seem to have a sense of distance as acute as adults. Commenting on the functional aspects of this capacity, Binet pointed out that very young children get around as fast as adults and have to be as sensitive to distance as adults in order to avoid bumping into objects.

Binet found further that the distance perception of children supersedes their number concept. He put two rows of beans equal in number and length on the table which were perceived as equal in number by his 4-year-old daughter. But when he pushed the beans in one row closer together, his daughter insisted that there were fewer beans in the shorter row. Experimenting with various comparisons he found that his daughter could not conceive that the number of objects remained the same (was conserved) if both rows had more than five objects, but if one of them was shorter. This was apparently the first experiment on *conservation* for which Piaget has falsely received credit as its originator.

Binet's ideas and experiments on cognition formed the basis for much of Piaget's work, and for the present, investigation in the area of cognition. As mentioned in a previous chapter, Americans have never been too accepting of the IQ, especially not of low IQs and their inherited determinants. Something which is fixed at birth does not seem to fit into the land of unlimited opportunities! Scarr (1981) suggests, for instance, that motivational insufficiencies and adjustment difficulties are more important determinants of the poor learning histories of children than their IQs. Perhaps for this, and other reasons, there is a renewed emphasis on cognition, on exploring which learning method is optimal for a given individual in a given subject matter.

INFANTS' COGNITION

Developmental psychologists, like Kroh (1926a, 1926b) and Piaget (1952, 1953), have labeled the first two years of life the sensori-motor period. By this, they meant infants begin their lives by sensing and reacting. But the purely reflexive *stimulus-response* pattern seems to disappear soon after birth, if it ever existed. The sucking reflex discussed in Chapter 3, for example, becomes evokable through auditory and visual stimuli in addition to the original touch stimulus. Simple engrams or neurological pathways grow into an interconnecting circuitry and certain cognitive processes begin to appear several months after birth. Memory becomes evident when infants begin to recognize their mother or other familiar faces. The word recognize means being again cognizant of something which was previously experienced. Infants also react to familiar voices and words by head turning, arm stretchings, and other movements. Memory is perhaps always influenced by bodily states of well-being and distress. At about six months after birth, choice-behavior is more clearly demonstrated when infants can reach for wanted objects and withdraw from unwanted ones, guiding their actions by previous physiological experiences.

The cognitive processes such as symbolization and organization become apparent by the age of one when the infant's motor development such as crawling or walking are advanced enough to carry out their intentions. At that age, infants may search for a toy which has rolled under a couch, and they may refuse to accept another toy as a substitute (Sophian & Sage, 1985). This requires a symbolization or a mental image of the absent object—a cognitive process which has been called *object permanence* when referring to an object and *person permanence* when the absence involves a person (Kroh, 1926; Piaget, 1954). The beginnings of the mind as an organizing mechanism also can be observed around age one when a child may remove all objects from a purse and also, more hopefully, when all toys on the floor are thrown back into the toy box.

By 18 months, or so, almost all rudimentary forms of the adult cognitive processes are present. At that age, children begin to tease. When they mean "yes" they may say "no" and smile, or vice versa. They are also capable of supplying missing objects. For example, seeing a parent sweep the livingroom floor, an 18-month old may run into the kitchen to fetch the dust pan. This apparently simple action requires a combination of various cognitive processes, such as an initial association, an encoding or discrimination between the present and the missing object, a symbolization of the missing object, a memory of its storing place, and an intention to fetch it.

INFANTS' SENSATIONS

For better or worse, developmental psychologists in the 1980s examine and reexamine infants' sensations and perceptions. The journal, *Infant Behavior & Development,* founded in 1978, reports almost exclusively research findings involving infants in their first year of life. Studies in sensation examine mostly visual and auditory threshold—how early and how sharply infants can see faces, objects, colors, and movements, and how early can they hear certain tones and detect loudness thresholds.

As already discussed in chapter 3, the ophthalmologist Raehlmann in 1891 showed rather conclusively that 3-month-old infants can discriminate between the major colors, and hence, can sense them. This capacity has been reaffirmed, almost 100 years later, by Werner and Wooten (1985), although there is some doubt whether infants can discriminate shades of a specific hue as acutely as adults (Banks & Salapatek, 1983). At birth, the infant's vision is poor, approximately 20/600, far worse than the legal criteria for blindness, 20/200. Their visual mechanism is also deficient in fixation, accommodation, and convergence. They do not seem to scan a figure extensively, but halt their gaze on a single part of it. Month by month, the newborn's vision improves and by the end of the first year the acuity, in many respects, is equal to an adult's. Compared to vision, the newborn's auditory mechanism is further developed at birth, although there seems to be a hearing loss of 10–20 decibel (Aslin, et al., 1983). This may protect them somewhat against their own screaming! Between the sixth and twelfth month, babies can make rather fine pitch and loudness discrimination and they can also localize sound as evidenced by head turning (Bower, 1982).

INFANTS' PERCEPTIONS

For the investigation of cognition, perceptual functions are more indicative than the basic sensory capacities. In perceptual studies, psychologists try to examine the meaning evoked by a sensation. They try to discover how sensations are influenced by previous sensations, mental patterns, and other bodily states. In the 1980s, the infant's perceptual development is one of the "hottest" areas in developmental psychology (Flavell, 1985).

One of the new techniques which has made it possible to investigate the perceptual capacities of infants more accurately involves the fact that humans, and even infants, become bored when repeatedly seeing or hearing the same thing again and again. This boredom, called *habituation*, manifests itself in a loss of arousal and a decrease in attention, which can be measured by changes in heart and brain waves. Working with lower animals, Kandel (1985) detected that the action potentials of involved neurons become smaller and smaller during habituation until they are no longer detectable. Not all repetitive stimuli cause habituation. Noted exceptions can be found in foods and sexual attractions which satisfy reoccurring tissue needs. But even here, a new stimulus, at times, can increase the arousal! In any event, when infants see the same picture repeatedly, they habituate, but when the picture is altered they recover from this habituation, they *dishabituate*. With this technique Stauss & Curtis (1981) have shown, for instance, that 6–9 month-old infants can discriminate or perceive the difference between 2 and 3 objects. Their attention as measured by eye, heart, and brain activities decreased during repeated exposures to pictures showing three objects, but increased again when a two-object picture was presented. The pictured objects differed in type, size, and arrangement, assuring discrimination by the cognition of numbers. In another study, it was shown that even 3-day old neonates habituated on a simple geometrical design and dishabituated on a different one (Antell & Carson, 1985).

A number of studies testing auditory perceptions also have shown certain cognitive capacities in the neonate. Molfese & Molfese (1985), for example, tested neonates 36 hours after birth for their auditory-evoked responses by placing electrodes over their temporal regions of the left and right hemispheres of the brain. To varying degrees, some of their subjects could discriminate between consonants, consonant and vowel combinations, and speech and nonspeech stimuli. Furthermore, it was found that those neonates who responded more vigorously had slightly better scores when retested with the verbal subscale of the McCarthy Scale of Children's Abilities at 3 years of age. At 6 months of age, infants begin to show rather sophisticated auditory discrimination abilities. Trehub et al. (1985) presented their 6- to 8-month-old subjects a standard, 6-tone melody. Using operant-conditioned head turning as a response criterion, they found their infants could discriminate between the standard melody and transformations of it in which only one of the notes was changed by 10 semitones.

Some relationships between vision and sound can already be perceived by 4-month-old infants. Spelke & Cortelyou (1981) presented their subjects simultaneously two film strips showing talking adult females. Each film had its own sound track but only one of them was switched on during a given time. The infants looked predominantly at the woman whose sound track was switched on. When "on," the sound of the left and the right film strips came through one and the same speaker located in the middle. Hence, the infants must have been able to detect the temporary synchrony between speech sounds and facial movements.

In general, the investigations of the more recent years show that infants by the age of 6 months have certain sensory acuities nearly equal to those of adults and have perceptions which show the beginnings of various cognitive processes. Flavell (1985) in his text, *Cognitive development*, states repeatedly that Piaget and other early investigators underestimated the infant's information-processing capabilities to sense, perceive, and memorize complex and abstract patterns. By 18 months, for sure, the child already resembles an adult more than it does an infant (the child is more of an adult than an infant.)

Cognition in Early Childhood

The most important cognitive accomplishment of childhood is the acquisition of language. There seems to be a supporting reciprocity between cognition and language. Cognitive processes such as memory, symbolism, and understanding further the learning of words and sentences and these, in turn, reinforce one's problem-solving and reasoning ability as they aid one in forming abstract concepts and in dealing with ideas (Brown, 1958).

Because language separates the human species from the subhuman ones, it has always been of great interest how it originates. Long before the event of psychologists, it is said that Frederick II (1194–1250), Holy Roman Emperor, King of Sicily, Germany, and Jerusalem, and among many other occupations, author of a falcon-training manual, ordered 20 babies to be reared in linguistic isolation in order to find out which language they would innately speak. The Greeks thought it would be Greek, the Romans believed it would be Latin, and the theologians were convinced it would be Hebrew. Unfortunately, all the babies died and the problem has never been solved.

LANGUAGE THEORIES

More than 800 years and hundreds of publications later, the psycholinguists are still unable to agree on the innateness issue. Some follow B. F. Skinner's idea presented in his book, *Verbal behavior* (1957), in which he proposes that children learn to talk through classical and operant conditioning, sometimes called the "babble-luck" theory (Crain, 1985). For example, when a baby happens to babble "da" the parent reinforces it by smiles or repetitions. This will cause the "da" to be uttered more frequently and soon there will be "dada" and, of course, more smiles, etc. French and German parents would neither knowing or unknowingly react to the "da-sound" because in their languages fathers are called "papa," never dada or daddy.

Quite different from Skinner's idea is Noam Chomsky's (1972) "innateness" hypothesis and his suggestions of a "universal grammar." Chomsky maintains that the linguistic environment primarily triggers the construction of grammatical systems by a genetic blueprint (Chomsky, 1980). He believes that without "innateness" children would encounter greater difficulties to perform grammatical transformations, for example, transforming the statement, "You watched the movie" to the question, "Did you watch the movie?" There is, however, nothing universal with respect to this transformation. In Russian, for instance, the words and their order remain identical in both the statement and the question. There is only an intonation change. "Vui buil ve kino" (You were in movie) is a statement. It becomes a question when the voice is raised slightly on the word "buil" (were). Americans who study Russian usually are surprised, if not disturbed, that there are, for instance, no words, "the" and "am." To say, "I am in the university" the Russian simply says, "I in university" (Ja ve universitaetje). This is not baby talk. Even Tolstoy and Solzhenitsyn said it that way!

The heredity-environment controversy in linguistics is rather academic. It has never been as fierce as that which befell the IQ. Even the most ardent behaviorists realized that all learning is based on innate capacities, which increase with maturation. They merely disbelieve these innate capacities are bound to a specific knowledge, be it to a specific word, its meaning, or a specific grammatical rule. The behaviorists also realize the human physiological mechanism is attuned to certain sensory input more than to others. For example, newborns prefer tones in the frequency range around 500 Hz to those near 100 Hz. That is why they prefer "motherese" or high intonations to a flat or monotone voice (Fernald, 1985).

Language, as a whole, is a rather illogical business. In French, the conjugations are illogical, (even to the French), in Russian there are the declentions, and in English the incongruency between spelling and pronunciation are well known. One can marvel, as Chomsky does, how fast children can learn a language, but one can also be dismayed how long it takes adults to learn a second language. The mother tongue is learned when one's logic is not fully developed. A second language is much harder to learn because one's logic and one's mother tongue will often cause more of a negative than positive transfer of learning.

In Russian, for example, there are 13 different words for the pronoun "my" and there are 24 different rules relating to cases and genders which need to be learned in order to select the correct "my." Even if these rules are well known, there is no time during the normal speech tempo to scan through 24 of them. The learning of a foreign language seems to relate closer to musical talent than to logical ability. This may explain as shown by Tyler (1956) why the IQ correlates only negligibly with high school grades in both music and foreign languages (r - .74).

Although there are still many unknowns about our linguistic development, it has long been recognized that language is one of our most important cognitive events. In 1933, the Kellogs, a husband and wife psychologist team, adopted a 7-month-old chimpanzee, Gua, and raised her together with their 9-month-old son, Donald. The chimp's voice box and speech centers in the brain are anatomically similar to those of humans and the Kellogs wanted to know if it was merely the lack of being spoken to which prevented apes from talking. Hence, for almost a year they gave Don and Gua equal opportunities. They clothed, kissed, cuddled, and spoke to them in equal fashion. The ape was ahead in all of her cognitive and behavioral functions. She had good table manners, was toilet-trained, and could fulfill a variety of commands better than Don. All these advantages, however, were lost around the age of 18 months when Don began to learn and to use the meaning of words. Another experiment was undertaken by the Hayes (1952). They lived with their chimp "Vicki" for six years, but were only able to teach her three words (papa, mama, and cup).

LANGUAGE ACQUISITION RATES

There is much agreement among psycholinguists on the vocabulary acquisition rate. By 18 months, most toddlers know a dozen or more words, by the end of the second year they have a command of almost 200, and by the end of the third year they can produce approximately 1,000 words, 80 percent of which are intelligible to strangers. By the age of six, children can master about 90 percent of their native language (Lenneberg, 1967; Berger, 1984).

Psycholinguists usually are interested in the four following aspects of language development: phonology (sound); syntax (the underlying structure); semantics (meaning of words and phrases); and pragmatics (practical communication skills). Phonologically, infants laugh and "coo" by 3 months. By 12 months, they babble consonant-vowel combinations having a particular preference for *d, m, p, n,* and *b.* Verbal semantics appear at about 1 year when toddlers begin to understand the meaning of some words and when one-word utterances may express entire sentences. For example, depending on the situation the word "mama" may mean, "mother come here," or perhaps, "glad you are back."

By 18 months or so, two-word utterances are formed expressing possession (my ball), repetition (more juice), negation (all gone), etc. By the age of two, children begin to ask "what" and "why" using language to increase their knowledge and understanding. At that age, they also begin to use syntax correctly saying "more juice" and "go play" rather than "juice more" and "play go" (Berger, 1984). The pragmatics of language or the ability to communicate begin with nonlinguistic gestures and body language during the first months after birth, and after the first year of life they receive additional impetus through words and sentences. Communicative skills develop throughout life—in high school in forensic teams and in college, we hope through speech and English composition courses!

COGNITIVE STYLES

After children acquired the basic linguistic skills during their preschool years, they enter school to be taught additional skills in reading, writing, and arithmetic. At this time, it becomes apparent that different children have different ways or modes of learning—something which psychologists call *cognitive style*. Binet's daughter, Madelaine, as may be recalled, had a totally different learning style than her sister Alice. Madelaine was reflective and slower in her *cognitive tempo* than Alice, who was impulsive and faster. In more recent years, psychologists have tried to observe and categorize different cognitive styles and have attempted to design measuring instruments which would indicate an individual's preferred style of learning.

Ehrhardt (1984) has compiled a list of various cognitive styles and their respective measuring instruments. Among others, she lists *scanning vs. focusing* during the acquisition of relevant information. Scanners look for the attributes and proceed in a constraint-seeking, broad-to-narrow fashion, while focusers try to generate a more global all-encompassing hypothesis, often proceeding in a trial-and-error fashion. These two styles can be observed in a "Twenty Questions Game." Another style is *broad vs. narrow categorizing,* with the former preferring a small number of categories with a large number of items, while the narrow categorizers prefer the reverse, a large number of categories with a small number of items as can be observed in object-sorting tasks. There is also the *leveling vs. sharpening* style, the leveler showing greater readiness to assimilate new information than the sharpener who tends to differentiate more clearly new instances from old ones. There are other cognitive styles which relate perhaps more to personality variables and emotions, such as *impulsive vs. reflective responsing, risk-taking vs. caution* observable in cost-payoff games, and *systematic vs. intuitive* style.

As the research on cognitive styles multiplies, so do the problems relating to them. Similar to the question surrounding intelligence, one may ask in to how many different styles can the cognitive process be divided. One may further ask how consistently does an individual use a certain cognitive style. Can one individual be a risk-taker when learning to converse in a foreign language and a non-risk-taker while playing chess? Furthermore, it is still poorly understood how emotions (and drugs) influence our cognitive style, how they alter or perhaps obviate it. Zajonc (1980), for instances, believes that there is a separation between emotion and cognition.

Unemotional or "cold" judgments such as comparing two distances, seem to involve more cognition than judging likes and dislikes concerning aesthetics and preferences which are usually made with a great deal of certainty. The emotional decisions are not subject to immediate sensory experiences, but stem from previously learned perceptions of "good" and "bad." Hence, Zajonc theorizes that they need not undergo cognitive evaluation and are effortless as far as cognition is concerned. Our cognition can recognize the effect of our emotion and can appraise them, but cannot change them. Zajonc believes that emotional changes may be produced by corrective experiences, but rarely by reflection or persuasion. Corrective experiences brought about through shaping and reinforcement are, of course, the essence of behavior modification. More recently, however, the cognitive behavior modification techniques, discussed subsequently, emphasize reflection and persuasion as much as corrective experiences.

Most researchers consider cognitive styles to be value-free, having no good or bad judgments (Arnold, 1984). But there are indications that certain cognitive styles facilitate the learning of certain cognitive skills. Kagan, et al. (1978), for example, have found that reflective children are more attentive and less distractable than impulsive ones and may have an easier time learning to read. In the same vein, Brodzinsky (1982) found that more reflective adolescents usually outperform impulsives on tests of recall memory, taking the perspective of others, and in certain problem-solving tasks. In spite of these performance differences, there seem to be no IQ differences when comparing reflectives with impulsives. Messer (1976) found no difference in the IQ scores between impulsive "retainees" and their classmates who were promoted. This indicates that the deficit lies in their cognitive style, rather than in their general intelligence. In the long run, the cognitive styles may not offer a value-free alternative for the value-laden IQ.

COGNITIVE BEHAVIOR MODIFICATION

The teaching of acceptable behaviors and the dissuasion from unacceptable ones is an ongoing process in human development. It was pointed out in previous chapters how behavior can be modified through classical and operant conditioning methods using successive approximation, modeling, reinforcement, punishment, etc. These techniques, called *behavior modification*, have changed slightly and in keeping in trend with the "cognitive decade" are now called *cognitive behavior modification*, or briefly, CBM. The change represents mainly a renewed emphasis on the verbal instructions which accompany the conventional behavior modification procedures. The cognitive procedures are not entirely new, however. Behavioral interventions usually have been accompanied by words. Seldom would one punish or physically restrain a child without verbalizing, "don't run into the street," or "let sister have the toy for a while," etc.

What is novel about the cognitive procedures is their pronounced emphasis on linguistic self-instructional and reasoning procedures. As summarized by Meichenbaum & Genest (1980), cognitive-behavioral procedures are applied in the management of hyperactivity, impulsiveness, stress, anger, aggressions, etc. They are also used to facilitate skills training, problem solving, and scholastic performance in general. A typical, cognitive behavior modification procedure involves *cognitive modeling,* an adult who performs the desired task while talking to him- or herself out loud. Then, the child performs the same task and verbalizes alongside the adult. The child then performs alone while talking out loud, and lastly, the child begins to whisper the self-instructions until they become inaudible or covert.

Much of the theoretical background of CBM was provided

by several Soviet psychologists. Luria (1961) thought that there
are three stages by which the imitation and inhibition of a
child's behavior comes under his or her verbal control. At first,
the child is controlled by the speech of others. Then, a child's
overt speech becomes the controller, and last, overt speech
transforms into covert speech. Very lastly, Luria might have
added, the child begins to control others through language.
Vygotsky (1962) in *Thought and language* adds that the child's
covert speech is not a mere faded vocalization, but rather, a
transformation into an interpersonal thought system.

The CBM technique can be used in conjunction with im-
agery. Robin et al. (1976), for example, trained some hyperactive and disruptive school children to imagine and to subsequently self-instruct, "I will not go faster than a slow turtle,
slow turtle." Their procedure included reading a turtle story,
imitating a turtle withdrawing into its shell, and to self-instruct
to "do turtle" whenever the children felt they were losing control. The teacher spent 15 minutes each day for about three
weeks in training and practicing "turtle" with the class and experienced a decrease in aggression and disruptions.

The CBM method is also used to reduce stress in adults by
giving them such phrases as: "I can do it," "Relax, you are in
control," etc. Meichenbaum and Genest employ it also to alleviate academic problems. Such self-statements as, "Be creative,"
"be free-wheeling," "be unique," are suggested to train students
to be more creative and possibly raise their grades in the arts
and letters. Obviously, quite a different set of self-instructions
would be needed to improve one's grade in physics or chemistry.

Behavior modification procedures do not always require
the giving of correct advice. Over the last decade, *paradoxical*
techniques have received increasing attention, although the
method was first introduced by Knight Dunlap in 1932. He tried
to stop children from biting their nails by telling them to bite
even harder every time he saw them biting their nails. The subjects in this procedure experience pain as a consequence of their

bad habit. Dunlap called this method of breaking a bad habit *negative practice*; today, much fancier, it is called *response-contingent aversive stimulation* (Karoly, 1980). As reported by Wilson and Bornstein (1984), the more recent paradoxical procedures do not apply aversive stimuli. To control absenteeism from school, a student is repeatedly told to stay away from it. In several experiments concerned with the amelioration of sleep-onset insomnia, the subjects were instructed to stay awake as long as possible and were offered a seemingly appropriate rationale for it, namely, that they will discover their disturbing thoughts. With this paradoxical intervention, their being-awake-time decreased on the average from 30 to 10 minutes.

SOCIAL COGNITION

There never has been a clear, dividing line between psychology and social psychology and this demarcation has not become any clearer in the 1980s when much of psychology is called cognition and much of social psychology, social cognition. Under the heading of *social cognition,* psychologists study an individual's awareness and understanding of the actions, thoughts, and feelings of others. In the human species, however, the self can hardly be distinguished from "other," since human infants are totally dependent on their caretaker for the first years of their lives. Infants are fed and clothed by others and they see and use objects provided by others. Our language was "made" and is taught to us by others and so is our entire school curriculum, mores, and values. The development of our "self," whatever is left of it, supports our social cognition, and our social cognition in turn furthers our self-cognition, a reciprocity similar to that found between cognition and language.

Despite the difficulties which are encountered to separate our own understanding from our social understanding, psychologists have made some interesting observations and have proposed several theories concerning the development of social cognition. It has already been pointed out that certain studies have shown that the newborn's senses are attuned to the range of the human voice and to the perception of faces and gestures. Flavell (1985) in his chapter on social cognition describes the normal development of social attachment. At first newborns show no detectable attachment to humans nor nonhumans, then they show interest to any person, and next, when they are able to discriminate, they begin to show an increasingly intense and pleasurable attachment to their caretaker(s).

From questioning school-age children about the characteristics of their peers, Barenboim (1981) found that 6- to 8-year-olds described their classmates by behavioral comparisons such as "Billy runs faster than Johnny." During the ages 8 to 10 peers usually are described by psychological traits or attributes such as "She is nice," "He is stingy," etc. By the beginning of adolescence, the majority of judgments are made by psychological comparisons as, for instance, "Bill is much more shy than Ted." The degree of empathy and how well children can assess and understand the perspectives of others have also been used as criteria in examining the development of social cognition (Selman, 1980). Many recent studies continue to examine the effect which birth order, parental milieu, and nursery and school environments have on the developing person. In general, the environment which Baumrind (1971) described as "authoritative," not too strict and not too permissive, is most conducive to a mature, social adjustment.

METACOGNITION

One of the primary researchers in the area of *metacognition*, John Flavell (1985), defines it as "cognition about cognition." Metacognition signifies the knowledge and the understanding we have about our own thought processes, covering a broad spectrum of cognitive functions, including communication, comprehension, reading and writing skills, memory, social cognition, self-instruction, and self-control. In short, metacognition applies to any endeavor for which we use our mind.

An experiment conducted by Flavell, et al. (1970) may serve to illustrate the "meta" concept. Preschool and elementary school children were instructed to study a list of a few items until they were sure they could recall them. When the older children said they were ready they could usually recall every single item correctly. But when the younger children reported their readiness, they could not recall the list. The older children had a better self-assessment of their memory functions. Experiments which examine how well we can assess our own memory capacities fall into the subcategory called *metamemory*. Knowledge about metamemory can further our schooling and is useful throughout our entire life. B. F. Skinner (1984) at age 80 described certain aspects of his failing memory, its decrease during fatigue, and its specific detriment in recalling names. He lists a number of ameliorative aids such as notes, outlines to strengthen intraverbal connections, and refrainment from digression.

Metacognitive explorations are not entirely new to psychology. Many classical introductory texts contained a chapter on the management of learning presenting useful metacognitive knowledge telling the reader when and how to study best for a given subject. Cognitive techniques such as whole vs. part learning, distributed vs. massed practice, and the advantages and disadvantages of reading vs. recitation were frequently discussed. Most of this metacognitive advice pertained to short and long-term memory while the more recent studies attempt to investigate a broader variety of cognitive aspects.

Another subcategory of metacognition is *metacommunication*, referring to the knowledge of why one is or is not understood when giving instructions or explanations, and conversely, why we do or do not understand others when they give us instructions. Meichenbaum and Genest (1980) point to the advantage of *metacognitive manipulation* during cognitive behavior modification. In this combination technique, they teach their pupils how to assess their own learning skills in addition to the task-specific self-instruction. It seems very useful to monitor the success of our own self-control strategies, to know, for instance how often we will plan to go to the library after class and how often we wind up in the coffee shop instead. Mischel (1979) found, however, depressed people tend to evaluate themselves more realistically than normal subjects. Thus, when it comes to ourselves, a little metacognitive enhancement might not hurt!

ENCODING AND RETRIEVING

Concurrent with the research on cognition our memory has also been examined by an information processing approach. Using computer metaphor psychologists refer to establishing, holding, and remembering information, respectively as encoding, storing, and retrieving. *Encoding* requires first that a stimulus is noticed and selected from the many events which impinge on us. It must then be assorted and connected to already existing categories of knowledge or desires. During the encoding process, the incoming information may have to be translated or transformed so that it fits an already established idea or a network of ideas. New information is more readily remembered if it can be related to several, rather than to one, bit of information.

Some developmental psychologists distinguish between semantic and nonsemantic levels of encoding (Gross, 1985). Attending to the sound of a word or to its spelling are examples of *nonsemantic encoding*, while thinking about its meaning constitutes *semantic encoding*. Geis and Hall (1976, 1978) examined the recall ability of grade school children who heard stimulus words presented to them under acoustic and orthographic (spelling) nonsemantic conditions and also under semantic conditions. To obtain these different encoding conditions, different groups of pupils were asked different questions while being shown the same stimulus word. For example, when the word "arm" was shown, the acoustic group was asked whether the word rhymed with "larms"; the orthographic group was asked whether it is in big letters; and the semantic group was questioned whether it is part of the body. It was found that semantically encoded words compared to nonmeaningfully encoded ones are remembered best across a wide range of grade levels, particularly from grade 3 upward. There seems to be a relationship between nonsemantic and semantic encoding as most children show *multiattribute encoding*. It has been found that children who remember the semantic attributes of an item, for instance, that a goldfish is an animal which lives and swims in water, are also likely to remember its nonsemantic or physical attributes such as its color or shape.

After encoding, information is stored in as yet mainly unknown biochemical and neurophysiological processes—in the billions of neurons and trillions of variable strength synapses. Psychologists differentiate between *short-term memory*, the initial storage and *long-term memory* for more permanent storage. It is believed that all memory traces that are successfully encoded or attended to are permanently stored in the long-term memory, but that only a fraction of them are retrievable (Kintsch, 1983).

The efficacy of encoding and storing information can only be assessed by its retrieval. Retrieval from short-term memory seems to proceed differently than it does from long-term memory. It is of developmental interest that the short-term retrieval processes in children are similar to those of adults. When given a series of numbers for immediate recall like 4, 9, 3, 5, for instance, the recall time, about 40 milliseconds per number, is equal for both children and adults. There are, however, some age and individual differences when information is recovered from long-term storage. Retrieval from long-term memory depends much on how successfully the context of encoding is reinstated at the time of retrieval. Recognition is simpler than recall since it can be accomplished with fewer and, perhaps, only partial retrieval cues. A number of studies using recognition tests, where the memorized information is provided as in multiple choice tests, have shown that there are few age differences in memory performance. But when retrieval requires recall, different retrieval strategies such as "where did I hear this word?" or "who explained it to me?" must be used. Children are much less proficient than adults in producing such retrieval cues, although they are able to use them if they are provided (Gross, 1985).

The research on memory is not new in psychology. Ebbinghaus' work *Über das Gedächtnis* (*On memory*) published in 1885 is considered one of the founding stones of experimental psychology. The more recent work, clad in computer language, has merely given renewed emphasis to memory research, especially in the developmental area. As throughout the entire area of cognition, much attention has been paid to how preschool and grade school children process and retrieve information. And again, similar to Binet's qualitative findings, it has been shown that children function much like adults when retrieving information from short-term memory, but are less proficient in the use of strategies involving long-term recall.

COGNITION OR REPETITION

In assessing the developmental literature of the last decade, it becomes apparent that we are in a "cognitive revolution." Psychologists are beginning to put the words "cognition" and "metacognition" in front of every term and concept they had previously developed. Skills are becoming cognitive skills, speed changes to cognitive tempo, learning techniques to cognitive styles, BM to CBM, etc. Skinner (1984) in his article, "Intellectual self-management in old age" states that he could have doubled his audience by calling his article, "Cognitive self-management in old age," because cognitive means so many things. There is certainly a loss in precision when everything is given the same name and it is often confusing if one expects a new concept but finds only a new name. But revolutions usually are confusing, although a few may have some beneficial effects.

The major benefit of the "cognitive revolution" may be realized in the breakdown of specific schools, diminishing prejudicial viewpoints among psychologists. In the future there may no longer be Freudians, Piagetians, and Skinnerians, but only "Cognitians!" Another advantage of the recent cognitive trend is the increase in the quantity and the quality in research which it brought about. The journal, *Cognitive Psychology* was founded in 1970, reporting studies in sensation, perception, and memory. The international journal, *Cognition,* appeared in 1972 dealing with cognitive aspects in psychology, linguistics, computer science, ethology, philosophy, and music, and the quarterly, *Imagination Cognition and Personality* was established in 1981. The cognitive work has been quite prolific in developmental psychology. The outstanding results in this area are the new, experimental findings that even very young infants possess the beginnings of many cognitive functions such as organization, numerosity, and figural and speech perceptions—something mothers may have known all along!

REFERENCES

Adams, R. L., & Phillips, B. N. (1972). Motivational and achievement differences among children of various ordinal birth positions. *Child Development, 43,* 155–164.

Ainsworth, M. D. S. (1979). Attachment as related to mother-infant interaction. In J. S. Rosenblatt, R. A. Hinde, C. Beer, & M. Busnel (Eds.), *Advances in the study of behavior* (Vol. 9). New York: Academic Press.

Ainsworth, M. D. S., Bell, S. M., & Stayton, D. J. (1974). Infant-mother attachment and social development: Socialization as a product of reciprocal responsiveness to signals. In M. P. M. Richards (Ed.), *The integration of the child into a social world.* London: Cambridge University Press.

Ainsworth, M. D. S., Blehar, M., Waters, E., & Wall, S. (1978). *Patterns of attachment.* Hillsdale, NJ: Lawrence Erlbaum Associates.

Aldrich, C. A. (1928). A new test for hearing in the newborn. *American Journal of Diseases of Children, 35,* 36–37.

Alexander, T. (1969). *Children and adolescents.* New York: Atherton Press.

Altus, W. D. (1965). Birth order and academic primogeniture. *Journal of Personality and Social Psychology, 2,* 872–876.

Ames, E., & Randeri, K. (1965). Some differences in the child rearing practices of Indian and Canadian mothers. *Indian Psychological Review, 2* (1), 15–18.

Antell, S. E. G., & Carson, A. J. (1985). Neonatal perception of spacial relationships. *Infant Behavior and Development, 8,* 15–23.

293

Apgar, V., & Beck, J. (1972). *Is my baby all right? A guide to birth defects.* New York: Trident Press.

Armentrout, J. A., & Burger, G. K. (1972). Children's reports of parental child rearing behavior at five grade levels. *Developmental Psychology, 7,* 44–48.

Armstrong, L. (1967). *Louis Armstrong: People of destiny.* Chicago: Children's Press.

Arnold, M. B. (1984). Cognitive learning styles. In R. J. Corsini (Ed.), *Encyclopedia of psychology.* New York: John Wiley & Sons.

Aslin, R. N., Pisoni, D. P., & Jusczyk, P. W. (1983). Auditory development and speech perception in infancy. In M. M. Haith & J. J. Campos (Eds.), *Handbook of child psychology: Infancy and developmental psychobiology* (Vol. 2), New York: John Wiley & Sons.

Azrin, H. N., & Foxx, R. M. (1977). *Toilet training in less than a day.* New York: Pocket Books.

Bailey, P. S. (1964). Sigmund Freud: Scientific period (1873–1897). In J. Wolpe, A. Salter, & L. J. Reyna (Eds.), *The conditioning therapies.* New York: Holt, Rinehart & Winston, 83–95.

Bakeman, R., & Brown, J. V. (1977). Behavioral dialogues: An approach to the assessment of mother-infant interactions. *Child Development, 48,* 195–203.

Baker, B. (1969). Symptom treatment and symptom substitution in neuresis. *Journal of Abnormal Psychology, 74,* 42–49.

Bandura, A. (1965). Influence of models' reinforcement contingencies on the acquisition of imitative responses. *Journal of Personality and Social Psychology, 1,* 589–595.

Bandura, A. (Ed.). (1971). *Psychological modeling: Conflicting theories.* Chicago: Aldine-Atherton Press.

Bandura, A. & Walters, R. H. (1959). *Adolescent aggression.* New York: Ronald Press.

Bane, M. J. (1976). Marital disruption and the lives of children. *Journal of Social Issues, 32,* 103–117.

Banks, M. S., & Salapatek, P. (1983). Infant visual perception. In M. M. Haite & J. J. Campos (Eds.), *Handbook of child psychology: Infancy and developmental psychobiology* (Vol. 2). New York: John Wiley & Sons.

Barenboim, C. (1981). The development of person perception in childhood and adolescent: From behavioral comparisons to psychological constructs to psychological comparisons. *Child Development, 52,* 129–144.

Baron, R. A., & Byrne, D. (1981). *Social psychology: Understanding human interaction.* Boston: Allyn & Bacon.

Baumrind, D. (1966). Effects of authoritative parental control on child behavior. *Child Development, 37,* 887–907.

Baumrind, D. (1971). Current patterns of parental authority. *Developmental Psychology Monographs, 4*, 1–103.

Baumrind, D. (1972). Socialization and instrumental competence in young children. In W. W. Hartup (Ed.), *The young child* (Vol. 2). Washington, DC: National Association for the Education of Young Children.

Bayley, N. (1968). Behavioral correlates of mental growth: Birth to 36 years. *American Psychologist, 23*, 1–17.

Becker, W. C. (1964). Consequences of different kinds of parental discipline. In M. L. Hoffman & L. W. Hoffman (Eds.), *Review of child development research*. New York: Russell Sage Foundation.

Beckmann, H. V. (1923). Die entwicklung der zahlleistung bei 2–3 jährigen kindern (development of number capacity in 2–3 year olds). *Zeitschrift für Angewandte Psychologie, 22*, 1–72.

Bee, H. L. (1978). *The developing child.* New York: Harper & Row.

Bee, H. L., & Mitchell, S. K. (1984). *The developing person*. New York: Harper & Row.

Belsky, J., Rovine, M., & Taylor, D. G. (1984). The Pennsylvania infant and family development project, III: The origins of infant-mother attachment: Maternal and infant contributions. *Child Development, 55*, 718–728.

Bem, S. L. (1975). Sex role adaptability: One consequence of psychological androgyny. *Journal of Personality and Social Psychology, 31* (4), 634–643.

Bem, S. O. (1976). Die harten und die zarten (the tough and the gentle ones). *Psychologie Heute, 3* (2), 54–59.

Berger, K. S. (1984). Language development. In R. R. Corsini (Ed.), *Encyclopedia of psychology*. New York: John Wiley & Sons.

Berger, R. J. (June 4, 1970). Morpheus descending: Sleep, unease and dreams. *Psychology Today*, pp. 33–36, 70.

Bernard, L. L. (1924). *Instinct.* New York: Holt.

Bernstein, A. (1955). Some relations between techniques of feeding and training during infancy and certain behavior in children. *Genetic Psychology Monographs, 51*, 3–44.

Bijou, S. W. (1957). Patterns of reinforcement and resistance to extinction in young children. *Child Development, 28*, 47–54.

Biller, H. B. (1971). *Father, child and sex roles*. Lexington, MA: Heath Lexington Books.

Biller, H. B. (1974). The father-infant relationship: Some naturalistic observations. Unpublished manuscript, University of Rhode Island.

Biller, H. B. (1976). The father and personality development: Paternal deprivation and sex role development. In M. E. Lamb (Ed.), *The role of the father in child development*. New York: John Wiley & Sons.

Biller, H. B., & Meredith, D. (1974). *Father power*. New York: McKay.

Binet, A. (1890). La perception des longueurs et des nombres chez quelques petits enfants (the perception of lengths and numbers in small children). *Revue philosophique, 30,* 68–81.

Binet, A., & Simon, T. (1908). Le dévelopment de l'intelligence chez les enfants (the development of intelligence in children). *L'Année Psychologique, 14,* 1–94.

Bishop, D. W., & Chace, C. A. (1971). Parental conceptual systems, home play environment, and potential creativity in children. *Journal of Experimental Child Psychology, 12,* 318–338.

Blanchard, R. W., & Biller, H. B. (1971). Father availability and academic performance among third grade boys, *Developmental Psychology, 4,* 301–305.

Book, H. M. (1932). A psychological analysis of sex differences. *Journal of Social Psychology, 3,* 436.

Bossard, J. H., & Boll, E. S. (1960). *The sociology of child development.* New York: Harper Brothers.

Bostock, J., & Shakelton, M. (1951). Enuresis and toilet training. *Medical Journal of Australia, 2,* 110–113.

Bower, T. G. R. (1977). *A primer of infant development.* San Francisco: W. H. Freeman.

Bower, T. G. R. (1982). *Development in infancy.* San Francisco: W. H. Freeman.

Bowlby, J. (1973). *Attachment and loss.* Vol. 2: *Separation.* London: Hogarth Press.

Brandwein, R. A., Brown, C. A., & Fox, E. M. (1974). Women and children last: The social situation of divorced mothers and their families. *Journal of Marriage and the Family, 36,* 498–514.

Bransby, E. R., Blomfield, J. M., & Douglas, J. W. B. (1955). The prevalence of bed-wetting. *The Medical Officer, XCIV* 5–7.

Breland, H. M. (1974). Birth order, family configuration and verbal achievement. *Child Development, 45,* 1011–1019.

Brodbeck, A. J. (1950). The effect of three feeding variables on the nonnutritive sucking of new-born infants. *American Psychologist, 5,* 292–293.

Brodzinsky, D. M. (1982). Relationship between cognitive style and cognitive development: A 2–year longitudinal study. *Developmental Psychology, 18,* 617–626.

Bronfenbrenner, U. (1978). The changing American family. Paper presented at Oregon Psychological Association, Eugene.

Broussard, E. R., & Hartner, M. S. (1971). Further considerations regarding maternal perception of the first born. In J. Hellmuth (Ed.), *Exceptional infant: Studies in abnormalities* (Vol. 2). New York: Brunner-Mazel.

Brown, J., Bakeman, R., Snyder, P. A., Fredreckson, W. G., Morgan, S., &

Hepler, R. (1975). Interactions of black inner city mothers with their newborn infants. *Child Development, 46,* 677–686.

Brown, R. (1958). *Words and things.* Glencoe, IL: Free Press.

Budin, P. C. (1907). The feeding and hygiene of premature and full-term infants. *The Nursling,* London: Caxton.

Burchinal, L. G. (1964). Characteristics of adolescents from unbroken, broken and reconstituted families. *Journal of Marriage and the Family, 26,* 44–51.

Burt, C. (1958). The inheritance of mental ability. *American Psychologist, 13,* 1–15.

Campbell, D. (1968). Adaptations to the environment by the newborn child. *The Canadian Psychologist, 9,* 467–473.

Caplan, F. (Ed.). (1978). *Parents' Yellow Pages: A directory by the Princeton Center for Infancy.* New York: Doubleday.

Carlsmith, J. M., Lepper, M. R., & Landauer, T. K. (1974). Children's obedience to adult requests. *Journal of Personality and Social Psychology, 30,* 822–828.

Carmichael, L. (1926). The development of behavior in vertebrates experimentally removed from the influence of external stimulation. *Psychological Review, 33,* 51–58.

Centers, R. (1972). The completion hypothesis and the contemporary dynamic intersexual attraction and love. *Journal of Psychology, 82,* 111–126.

Cherry, F. F., & Eaton, E. (1977). Physical and cognitive development in children of low income mothers working in the child's early years. *Child Development, 48,* 158–166.

Cheyne, J. A., & Walters, R. H. (1969). Intensity of punishment, timing of punishment and cognitive structure as determinants of response inhibition. *Journal of Experimental Child Psychology, 7,* 231–244.

Child abuse. (September 6, 1976). *U.S. News and World Report,* pp. 45–62.

Chomsky, N. (1972). *Language and mind.* New York: Harcourt Brace Jovanovich.

Chomsky, N. (1980). *Rules and representations.* New York: Columbia University Press.

Cicirelli, V. G. (1973). Effects of sibling structure and interaction on children's categorization style. *Developmental Psychology, 9,* 132–139.

Clarke-Stewart, A. (1978). Popular primers for parents. *American Psychologist, 33,* 359–369.

Clausen, J. A. (1966). Family structure, socialization and personality. In W.L. Hoffman & M. L. Hoffman (Eds.), *Review of child development research, 2.* New York: Russell Sage Foundation.

Clifford, E. (1959). Discipline in the home: A controlled observational study of parental practices. *Journal of Genetic Psychology, 95,* 45–82.

Cowan, P. A. (1978). *Piaget with feeling*. New York: Holt, Rinehart & Winston.

Crain, W. C. (1985). *Theories of development*. (2nd Ed.). Englewood Cliffs, NJ: Prentice-Hall.

Crockenberg, S. B. (1981). Infant irritability, mother responsiveness, and social support influences on the security for infant-mother attachment. *Child Development, 52*, 857–865.

Dallenbach, K. M. (1939). Pain: History and present status. *American Journal of Psychology, 52*, 331–347.

Davis, D. J., Cahan, S., & Bashi, J. (1977). Birth order and intellectual development. The confluence model in the light of cross-cultural evidence. *Science, 196*, 1470–1472.

Davis, H., Sears, R. R., Miller, H. C., & Brodbeck, A. J. (1948). Effects of cup, bottle, and breastfeeding on oral activities on newborn infants. *Pediatrics, 3*, 549–558.

Dennis, W. (1934). A description and classification of the response of the newborn infant. *Psychological Bulletin, 31*, 5–22.

Dennis, W. (1960). Causes of retardation among institutional children. *Iran Journal of Genetic Psychology, 96*, 47–59.

Dennis, W., & Dennis, M. G. (1940). The effect of cradling practices upon the onset of walking in Hopi children. *Journal of Genetic Psychology, 56*, 77–86.

Dennis, W., & Dennis, M. G. (1951). Development under controlled environmental conditions. In W. Dennis (Ed.), *Reading in child psychology*, Englewood Cliffs, NJ: Prentice-Hall.

Despert, J. L. (1953). *Children of divorce*. Garden City, NY: Doubleday.

Digest of Education Statistics 1977–1978. Washington, DC: U.S. Government Printing Office.

Diven, K. (1937). Certain determinants in the condition of anxiety reactions. *Journal of Psychology, 3*, 291–308.

Dunlap, K. (1932). *Habits: Their making and unmaking*. New York: Liveright.

Ebbinghaus, H. (1885). *Über das Gedächtnis* (on memory). Leipzig: Dunker & Humbolt.

Egeland, B., & Farber, E. A. (1984). Mother-infant attachment: Factors related to its development and changes over time. *Child Development, 55*, 753–771.

Ehrhardt, H. B. (1984). An overview of cognitive style. In R. J. Corsini (Ed.), *Encyclopedia of psychology* Vol. 1. New York: John Wiley & Sons.

Elias, M. F., Elias, P. K., & Elias, J. W. (1977). *Basic processes in adult developmental psychology*. St. Louis: C. V. Mosby.

Elkind, D. (1970). *Children and adolescents: Interpretive essays on Jean Piaget*. New York: Oxford University Press.

Elkind, D. (1979). *The child and society*. New York: Oxford University Press.

Elkind, D., & Flavell, J. M. (Eds.). (1969). *Studies in cognitive development: Essays in honor of Jean Piaget*. New York: Oxford University Press.

Engen, T., Lipsitt, L. P., & Kaye, H. (1963). Decrement and recovery of responses to olfactory stimuli in the human neonate. *Journal of Comparative and Physiological Psychology, 56*, 73–77.

England, S. (December 8, 1974). Birth without violence. *New York Times Magazine*, pp. 113–125.

English, H. B., & English, A. C. (1958). *Psychological and psychoanalytical terms*. New York: Longmans, Green.

Epstein, A. S., & Radin, N. (1975). Motivational components related to father behavior and cognitive functioning in preschoolers. *Child Development, 46*, 831–839.

Erikson, E. H. (1960). Youth and life cycle. *Children, 7*, 43–49.

Erikson, E. H. (1963). *Childhood and society*. New York: Norton.

Erlenmeyer-Kimling, L., & Jarvik, L. F. (1963). Genetics and intelligence: A review. *Science, 142*, 1477–1479.

Esper, E. (1964). *A history of psychology*. Philadelphia: Saunders.

Essex, D., Parrott, G., & Barnes, P. (1971). Horizontality training at three to nine years. Paper presented at Western Psychological Association, San Francisco, April.

Etaugh, E., Collins, G., & Gerson, A. (1975). Reinforcement of sex-typed behaviors of two-year-old children in a nursery school setting. *Developmental Psychology, 11*, 255.

Eysenck, H. J. (1967). *Uses and abuses of psychology*. Baltimore: Penguin Books.

Eysenck, H. J. (Ed.). (1971). *Readings in extraversion-introversion*. New York: Wiley Interscience.

Eysenck, H. J. (1976). *Sex and personality*. Austin, TX: University of Texas Press.

Fagot, B. I. (1974). Sex differences in toddlers' behavior and parental reaction. *Developmental Psychology, 10*, 554–558.

Faller, K. C. (1985). Unanticipated problems in the United States child protection system. *Child Abuse or Neglect, 9*, 63–69.

Fein, G., Johnson, D., Kosson, N., Stork, L., & Wasserman, L. (1975). Sex stereotypes and preferences in toy choices of 20-month-old boys and girls. *Developmental Psychology, 11*, 527–528.

Feldman, S. M. (1961). Differential effects of shock in human maze learning. *Journal of Experimental Psychology, 62*, 171–178.

Fernald, A. (1985). Four-month-old infants prefer to listen to motherese. *Infant Behavior and Development, 8,* 181–195.

Ferster, C. B., & Skinner, B. F. (1957). *Schedules of reinforcements.* New York: Appleton-Century-Crofts.

Fink, H. K. (1984). Genetic disorders. In R. J. Corsini (Ed.), *Encyclopedia of psychology.* New York: John Wiley & Sons, 50–54.

Fischer, K. W., & Lazerson, A. (1985). *Human development.* New York: W. H. Freeman.

Fisher, S. (1973). *The female orgasm: Psychology, physiology, fantasy.* New York: Basic Books.

Flavell, J. H. (1963). *The developmental psychology of Jean Piaget.* Princeton, NJ: Van Nostrand.

Flavell, J. H. (1983). *Cognitive development* (2nd Ed.). Englewood Cliffs, NJ: Prentice-Hall.

Flavell, J. H., Friedrichs, A. G., & Hoyt, J. D. (1970). Developmental changes in memorization processes. *Cognitive Psychology, 1,* 324–340.

Florman, S. C. (1978). Engineering and the female mind: Why women will not become engineers. *Harper's, 256,* 57–63.

Ford, L. H. (1970). Predictive versus perceptual responses to Piaget's water-line task and their relation to distance conservation. *Child Development, 41,* 193–204.

Fort, J. (1961). Secondary reinforcement with preschool children. *Child Development, 32,* 755–764.

Foulkes, W. D. (1966). *The psychology of sleep.* New York: Scribner.

Franks, C. M. (1953). Conditioning and personality: A study of normal and neurotic subjects. *Journal of Abnormal and Social Psychology, 52,* 143.

Fredeen, R. C. (1948). Cup feeding of newborn infants. *Pediatrics, 3,* 544–548.

Freeman, J. (1973). The origins of the women's liberation movement. *American Journal of Sociology, 78,* (4), 792–811.

Freud, S. (1949). *An outline of psychoanalysis.* New York: Norton, (first published in German in 1940).

Friedan, B. (1963). *The feminine mystique.* New York: Dell.

Fuchs, V. R. (1975). A note on sex segregation in professional occupations. *Explorations in Economics Research, 2,* 105–111.

Gallagher, J. (1978). Government expenditures. *APA Monitor, 9,* 1.

Garbarino, J., & Sherman, D. (1980). High-risk neighborhoods and high-risk families: The human ecology of child maltreatment. *Child Development, 51,* 188–198.

Gasser, R. D., & Taylor, C. M. (1976). Role adjustment of single parent fathers with dependent children. *Family Coordinator, 25,* 397–401.

Gecas, V., & Nye, F. I. (1974). Sex and class differences in parent child interaction: A test of Kohn's hypothesis. *Journal of Marriage and the Family, 36,* 742–749.

Geis, M. F., & Hall, D. M. (1976). Encoding and incidental memory in children. *Journal of Experimental Child Psychology, 22,* 58–66.

Geis, M. F., & Hall, D. M. (1978). Encoding and congruity in children's incidental memory. *Child Development, 49,* 857–861.

Gelles, R. J., & Straus, M. A. (1979). Determinants of violence in the family: Toward a theoretical integration. In W. R. Burr, R. Hill, F. I. Nye, & I. L. Reiss (Eds.), *Contemporary theories about the family.* New York: Free Press.

Gesell, A. (1925). *The mental growth of the preschool child.* New York: Macmillan.

Gesell, A. (1954). The ontogenesis of infant behavior. In L. Carmichael (Ed.), *Manual of child psychology* (2nd Ed.). New York: John Wiley & Sons.

Gesell, A., Halverson, H. M., Thompson, H., Ilg, F. L., Costner, B. M. Ames, L. B., & Amatura, C. S. (1940). *The first five years of life: A guide to the study of the preschool child.* New York: Harper & Row.

Gilbert, S. D. (1975). *What's a father for?* New York: Parent's Magazine Press.

Ginott, H. (1969). *Between parent and child.* New York: Avon Books.

Ginsburg, H., & Opper, S. (1978). *Piaget's theory of intellectual development.* London: Prentice-Hall.

Glass, D. C., Neulinger, J., & Brim, O. G. (1974). Birth order, verbal intelligence, and educational aspiration. *Child Development, 45,* 807–811.

Glass, S. J., & Johnson, R. W. (1944). Limitations and complications of organotherapy in male homosexuality. *Journal of Clinical Endocrinology, 4,* 540.

Glueck, S., & Glueck, E. (1950). *Unraveling juvenile delinquency.* New York: Commonwealth Fund.

Goldberg, S. (1973). *The inevitability of patriarchy.* New York: Morrow.

Golding, W. (1962). *Lord of the flies.* New York: Coward-McCahn.

Goldstein, A. P. (1984). Aggression. In R. J. Corsini (Ed.), *Encyclopedia of psychology.* New York: John Wiley & Sons, 34–39.

Goldstein, K. M., Caputo, D. U., & Taub, H. B. (1976). The effects of prenatal and perinatal complications on development at one year of age. *Child Development, 47,* 613–621.

Goode, W. J. (1956). *Women in divorce.* New York: Free Press.

Gregersen, M., & Vesterby, A. (1984). *Child Abuse & Neglect, 8,* 83–91.

Gross, T. F. (1985). *Cognitive development.* Monterey, CA: Brooks/Cole.

Grossmann, K., Thane, K., & Grossmann, K. E. (1981). Maternal tactile contact of the newborn after various postpartum conditions of mother-infant contact. *Developmental Psychology, 17,* 158–169.

Grusec, J. E., & Ezrin, S. A. (1972). Techniques of punishment and the development of self-criticism. *Child Development, 443,* 1273–1288.

Guilford, J. P. (1959). Three faces of intellect. *American Psychologist, 14,* 469–479.

Guilford, J. P. (1962). Factors that aid and hinder creativity, *Teachers College Record, 63,* 380–392.

Haimowitz, N., & Haimowitz, M. L. (1960). What makes them creative? In N. Haimowitz & M. L. Haimowitz (Eds.), *Human development: Selected reading.* New York: Thomas Y. Crowell.

Halford, G. S., & Fullerton, R. J. (1970). A discrimination task which induces conservation of number. *Child Development, 41,* 205–213.

Hardy, J. D., Wolff, H. G., & Goodell, H. (1947). Studies on pain: Discrimination of differences in intensity of a pain stimulus as a basis of a scale of pain intensity. *Journal of Clinical Investigation, 26,* 1152–1158.

Hayes, K. (1951). *The ape in our house.* New York: Harper.

Heidbreder, E. (1928). Problem solving in children and adults. *Journal of Genetic Psychology, 35,* 522–545.

Heinstein, M. I. (1963). Behavior correlates of breast-bottle regimes under varying parent-infant relationships. *Monographs of the Society for Research in Child Development, 28* (4), Serial No. 88.

Herbst, A. L., Scully, R. E., Robboy, S. J., & Welch, W. R. (1978). Complications of prenatal therapy with diethylstilbestrol. *Pediatrics, 62,* 1151–1159.

Hersen, M., Eisler, R. M., & Miller, P. M. (Eds.) (1975–1977). *Progress in behavior modification.* New York: Academic Press, Vols. 1–4.

Hetherington, E. M. (1972). Effects of father absence on personality development in adolescent daughters. *Developmental Psychology, 7,* 313–326.

Hetherington, E. M., & Cox, R. (1976). Divorced fathers. *Family Coordinator, 25,* 417–427.

Hetherington, E. M., & Cox, M. (1977). Divorced fathers. *Psychology Today, 10* (April), 42–46.

Hilgard, E. R., & Atkinson, R. C. (1967). *Introduction to psychology* (4th ed.). New York: Harcourt Brace Jovanovich.

Horn, H. L., & Donaldson, G. (1978). Faith is not enough: A response to the Baltes-Schaie claim that intelligence does not wane. *American Psychologist, 32,* 369–373.

Horowitz, F. D. (1980). Intervention program. In A. W. Brann & J. J. Volpe (Eds.), *Neonatal neurological assessment and outcome.* Report of the

77th Ross Conference on Pediatric Research. Columbus, OH: Ross Laboratories.

Hull, C. L. (1920). Quantitative aspect of the evolution of concepts: An experimental study. *Psychological Monographs, 28,* (No. 123).

Hunt, J. McV. (1961). *Intelligence and experience.* New York: Ronald Press.

Hunt, J. McV. (1963). Piaget's observations as a source of hypotheses concerning motivation. *Merrill-Palmer Quarterly, 9,* 263–275.

Hurlock, E. (1925). An evaluation of certain incentives used in school work. *Journal of Educational Psychology, 16,* 145–159.

Ilg, F. L., & Ames, L. (1955). *Child behavior.* New York: Harper & Row.

Inhelder, B. (1969). Memory and intelligence in the child. In D. Elkind & J. M. Flavell (Eds.), *Studies in cognitive development: Essays in honor of Jean Piaget.* New York: Oxford University Press.

Jacobs, B. S., & Moss, H. A. (1976). Birth order and sex of sibling as determinants of mother infant interaction. *Child Development, 47,* 315–322.

Jensen, A. R. (1969). How much can we boost IQ and scholastic achievement? *Harvard Educational Review, 39* (1), 1–123.

Johnson, C. F., & Showers, J. (1985). Injury variables in child abuse. *Child Abuse and Neglect, 9,* 207–215.

Jones, E. (1953). *Life and works of Sigmund Freud* (Vol. 1). New York: Basic Books.

Jones, M. C. (1924). The elimination of children's fears. *Journal of Experimental Psychology, 7,* 382–390.

Jones, M. C., & Bayley, N. (1950). Physical maturity of boys as related to behavior. *Journal of Educational Psychology, 41,* 129–148.

Jost, A. (1897). Die assoziationsfestigkeit in ihrer abhangigkeit von der verteilung der wiederholungen (association strength and its dependence on the time of repetition). *Zeitschrift für Psychologie, 14,* 436–472.

Kagan, J. (August 1978). The parental love trap. *Psychology Today,* pp. 54–61.

Kagan, J., Kearsley, R., & Zelazo, P. (1978). *Infancy: Its place in human development.* Cambridge, MA: Harvard University Press.

Kagan, J., & Klein, R. E. (1973). Cross cultural perspectives in early development. *American Psychologist, 28,* 947–961.

Kagan, J., Lapidus, D. R., & Moore, M. (1978). Infant antecedents to cognitive functioning: A longitudinal study. *Child Development, 49,* 1005–1023.

Kagan, J., & Moss, H. A. (1962). *Birth to maturity: A study in psychological development.* New York: John Wiley & Sons.

Kandel, E. (1985). Brain structure effects what, how we know. *APA Monitor, 16* (9), 6.

Karoly, P. (1980). Operant methods. In F. H. Kanfer & A. P. Goldstein. *Helping people change*. Elmsford, NY: Pergamon Press.

Kellogg, W. N., & Kellogg, L. A. (1933). *The ape and the child: A study of environmental influence upon early behavior*. New York: McGraw-Hill.

Kempe, R. S., & Kempe, C. H. (1978). *Child abuse*. Cambridge, MA: Harvard University Press.

Kennedy, W. A. (1975). *Child psychology* (2nd ed.). Englewood Cliffs, NJ: Prentice-Hall.

Kessen, W., Leutzendorff, A-M, & Stoutsenberger, K. (1967). Age, food deprivation, nonnutritive sucking, and movement in the human newborn. *Journal of Comparative and Physiological Psychology, 63,* 82–86.

Kessner, D. M. (1973). *Infant death: An analysis by maternal risk and health care*. Washington, DC: National Academy of Sciences (2).

Kimble, G. A., & Garmezy, N. (1968). *Principles of general psychology* (3rd ed.). New York: Ronald Press.

King, W. H. (1960). The development of scientific concepts in children. *British Journal of Educational Psychology, 31,* 1–20.

Kinsey, A. C., Pomeroy, W., Martin, C., & Gebhard, P. (1953). *Sexual behavior in the human female*. Philadelphia: W. B. Saunders.

Kintsch, W. (1983). Memory. In R. Harre & R. Lamb (Eds.), *The encyclopedic dictionary of psychology*. Cambridge, MA: MIT Press.

Klaus, M. H., & Kennell, J. H. (1976). *Maternal infant bonding*. St. Louis: C. V. Mosby.

Kleitman, N. (1939). *Sleep and wakefulness*. Chicago: University of Chicago Press.

Kleitman, N., & Englemann, T. G. (1953). Sleep characteristics of infants. *Journal of Applied Physiology, 6,* 269–282.

Koch, H. (1956). Sissiness and tomboyishness in relation to sibling characteristics. *Journal of Genetic Psychology, 88,* 231–244.

Kohn, M. (1969). *Class and conformity*. Homewood, IL: Dorsey Press.

Korbin, J. E. (1981). "Very few cases": Child abuse and neglect in the People's Republic of China. In J. E. Korbin (Ed.), *Child abuse and neglect*. Berkeley: University of California Press.

Korner, A. F. (1971). Individual differences at birth: Implication for early experience and later development. *American Journal of Orthopsychiatry, 41,* 608–619.

Krestoffnikoff, A. H. (1913). An essential prerequisite for the process of conditioning. *Society of Russian Physicians, 80,* 35–41.

Kroh, O. (1926a). Die Anfänge der kindlichen entwicklung in allgemein psychologischer beleuchtung (child development from a psychological view). *Zeitschrift für Psychologie, 100,* 325–343.

Kroh, O. (1926b). Die phasen der jugendentwicklung (developmental phases). *Würtembergische Schulwarte, 4,* 185–208.

Lamaze, F. (1958). *Painless childbirth: Psychoprophylactic method.* London: Burke.

Lamb, M. E. (1977). Father infant and mother infant interactions in the first years of life. *Child Development, 48,* 167–181.

Lavoie, J. C., & Looft, W. R. (1973). Parental antecedents of resistance to temptation behavior in adolescent males. *Merrill Palmer Quarterly, 19,* 107–116.

Leboyer, F. (1975). *Birth without violence.* New York: Alfred A. Knopf.

Lenneberg, E. H. (1967). *Biological foundations of language.* New York: John Wiley & Sons.

Lessing, E. E., Zagorin, S. W., & Nelson, D. (1970). WISC subtest and IQ score correlates of father absence. *Journal of Genetic Psychology, 117,* 181–195.

Leventhal, G. S. (1970). Influence of brothers and sisters on sex-role behavior. *Journal of Personality and Social Psychology, 16,* 452–465.

Levin, G. R., & Kaye, H. (1964). Nonnutritive sucking by human neonates. *Child Development, 35,* 749–758.

Levy, D, M. (1928). Fingersucking and accessory movements in early infancy: An etiological study. *American Journal of Psychiatry, 7,* 881–918.

Levy, D. M. (1934). Experiments on the sucking reflex and social behavior of dogs. *American Journal of Orthopsychiatry, 4,* 203–224.

Lewis, M. (February 1977). The busy, purposeful world of a baby. *Psychology Today,* pp. 53–56.

Lipsitt, L. P., Kaye, H., & Bosack, T. N. (1966). Enhancement of neonatal sucking through reinforcements. *Journal of Experimental Child Psychology, 4,* 163–168.

Long, A. (1941). Parents' reports of undesirable behavior in children. *Child Development, 12,* 43–62.

Longstreth, L. E. (1968). *Psychological development of the child.* New York: Ronald Press.

Lovaas, O. I. (1976). *The autistic child.* New York: Halstead Press.

Lovibond, S. H. (1964). *Conditioning and enuresis.* Oxford, England: Pergamon Press.

Luria, A. R. (1961). *The role of speech in the regulation of normal and abnormal behavior.* New York: Liveright.

Luria, A. R. (1968). *The mind of a mnemonist.* New York: Basic Books.

Maccoby, E. E. (1961). The taking of adult roles in middle childhood. *Journal of Abnormal and Social Psychology, 63,* 493–503.

Maccoby, E. E., & Jacklin, C. N. (1974). *The psychology of sex differences*. Palo Alto, CA: Stanford University Press.

Maccoby, E. E., & Masters, J. C. (1970). Attachment and dependency. In P. H. Mussen (Ed.), *Carmichael's manual of child psychology* (3rd ed.). New York: John Wiley & Sons.

Madigen, F. C. (1957). Are sex mortality differentials biologically caused? *Millbank Memorial Fund Quarterly, 35* (2), 202–223.

Malparenting. (1978). *APA Monitor, 9* (8), 2.

Marchall, H. K., & Kennel, J. H. (1976). *Maternal-infant bonding*. St. Louis: C. V. Mosby.

Margolin, G., & Patterson, G. (1975). Differential consequences provided by mothers and fathers for their sons and daughters. *Developmental Psychology, 11*, 537–538.

Marquis, D. (1931). Can conditioned responses be established in the newborn infant? *Journal of Genetic Psychology, 39*, 479–492.

Martin, M. K., & Voorhies, B. (1975). *Female of the species*. New York: Columbia University Press.

Matussek, P. (1971). Funktionelle sexualstörungen (functional sex dysfunction) In H. Giese (Ed.), *Die sexualität des menschen*. Stuttgart: Enke.

McCall, R. B. (1974). Exploration manipulation and play in the human infant. *Monographs of the Society for Research in Child Development, 39*, (2).

McCandless, B. R. (1967). *Children: Behavior and development* (2nd ed.). New York: Holt, Rinehart & Winston.

McCandless, B. R., & Evans, E. D. (1973). *Children and youth: Physiological development*. Hinsdale, IL: Dryden Press.

McClelland, D. C. (1978). Managing motivation to expand human freedom. *American Psychologist, 33*, 201–210.

McCord, W., McCord, J., & Zola, I. K. (1959). *Origins of crime*. New York: Columbia University Press.

McEwen, B. S. (1976). Interaction between hormones and nerve tissue. *Scientific American, 235* (1), (July), 48–58.

McGraw, M. B. (1940). Neural maturation as exemplified by the achievement of bladder control. *Journal of Pediatrics, 16*, 580–590.

McGraw, M. B. (1943). *The neuromuscular maturation of the human infant*. New York: Columbia University Press.

Meichenbaum, D., & Genest, M. (1980). Cognitive behavior modification: An integration of cognitive and behavioral methods. In F. H. Kanfer & A. P. Goldstein (Eds.), *Helping people change*. Elmsford, NY: Pergamon Press.

Mendes, H. A. (1976). Single fathers. *Family Coordinator, 25*, 439–444.

Merck Manual, (The). (1982). 14th ed. Rahway, NJ: Merck & Co.

Messer, S. B. (1976) Reflection-impulsivity: A review. *Psychological Bulletin, 83,* 1026 -1052.

Michaels, R. H., & Mellin, G. W. (1960). Prospective experiences with matern? rubella and the associated congenital malformations. *Pediatrics, 26, 200–209.*

Mischel, W. (1979). On the interface of cognition and personality: Beyond the person-situation debate. *American Psychologist, 34,* 740–754.

Molfese, D. L., & Molfese, V. J. (1985). Electrophysiological indices of auditory discrimination in newborn infants: The bases for predicting later language development? *Infant Behavior and Development, 8,* 197–211.

Montemayor, R. (1974). Children's performance in a game and their attraction to it as a function of sex-typed labels. *Child Development, 45,* 152–156.

Moss, H. A. (1967). Sex, age, and state as determinants of mother-infant interaction. *Merrill Palmer Quarterly, 13,* 19–36.

Mowrer, O. H. (July 1961). Psychiatry and religion. *The Atlantic,* pp. 88–91.

Mowrer, O. H., Mowrer, W. M. (1938). Enuresis: A method for its study and treatment. *American Journal of Orthopsychiatry, 8,* 436–459.

Muellner, S. R. (1960). Development of urinary control in children: A new concept in cause, prevention and treatment of primary enuresis. *Journal of Urology, 84,* 805–810.

Muller, P. F., Campbell, H. E., Graham, W. E., Brittain, H., Fitzgerald, J. A., Hogan, N. A. Muller, V. H., & Ritterhouse, A. H. (1971). Perinatal factors and their relationship to mental retardation and other parameters of development. *American Journal of Obstetrics and Gynecology, 109,* 1205–1210.

Munn, N. L. (1966). *Psychology* (5th ed.). Boston: Houghton Mifflin.

Murray, E. J. (1965). *Sleep, dreams, and arousal.* New York: Appleton-Century-Crofts.

Mussen, P. H., & Conger, J. J. (1969). *Child development and personality.* New York: Harper & Row.

Nash, J. (1978). *Developmental psychology: A psychobiological approach.* Englewood Cliffs, NJ: Prentice-Hall.

Neill, A. S. (1960). *Summerhill: A radical approach to child rearing.* New York: Hart Press.

Newton, N. (June 1968). Breast feeding. *Psychology Today,* pp. 68–70.

Nye, F. I. (1957). Child adjustments in broken and in unhappy unbroken homes. *Marriage and Family Living, 19,* 356–361.

O'Donnell, T. (October 3, 1972). Divorced fathers: When a home is home only on weekends. *San Francisco Chronicle.*

Okeahialam, R. C. (1984). Child abuse in Nigeria. *Child Abuse and Neglect, 8,* 69–73.

O'Leary, K. D., Kaufman, K. F., Kass, R. E., & Drabman, R. S. (1970). The effects of loud and soft reprimands on behavior of disruptive students. *Exceptional Children, 37,* 145–155.

Ormerod, M. B. (1975). Subject preference and choice in co-educational and single-sex secondary schools. *British Journal of Education Psychology, 45,* 257–267.

Orthner, D. K., Brown, T., & Ferguson, D. (1976). Single parent fatherhood: An emerging family life style. *Family Coordinator, 25,* 429–437.

Paris, S. G., & Cairns, R. B. (1972). An experimental and ethological analysis of social reinforcement with retarded children. *Child Development, 43,* 719–729.

Parke, R. E. (1969). Effectiveness of punishment as an interaction of intensity, timing, agent nurturance, and cognitive structuring. *Child Development, 40,* 213–235.

Parmelee, A. H., Schulz, H. R., & Disbrow, M. (1961). Sleep patterns of the newborn. *The Journal of Pediatrics, 58,* 241–250.

Pedersen, F. A., & Robsen, K. S. (1969). Father participation in infancy. *American Journal of Orthopsychiatry, 39,* 466–472.

Piaget, J. (1929). *The child's conception of the world.* London: Routlege & Paul.

Piaget, J. (1930). *The child's conception of physical causality.* London: Routlege & Paul.

Piaget, J. (1952). *The origins of intelligence in children.* New York: International University Press.

Piaget, J. (1954). *The construction of reality in the child.* New York: Basic Books.

Piaget, J., & Inhelder, B. (1956). *The child's conception of space.* New York: Humanities Press.

Piaget, J., & Inhelder, B. (1968). *Memoire et intelligence* (memory and intelligence). Paris: Presses Universitaires de France.

Pierce, R., & Pierce, L. H. (1985). The sexually abused child: A comparison of male and female victims. *Child Abuse and Neglect, 9,* 191–199.

Pinard, A., & Laurendeau, M. (1969). "Stage" in Piaget's cognitive-developmental theory: Exegesis of a concept. In D. Elkind & J. M. Flavell (Eds.), *Studies in cognitive development: Essays in honor of Jean Piaget.* New York: Oxford University Press.

Pines, M. (1978). Head head start. In B. B. Glanville (Ed.), *Readings in human development 77/78.* Guilford, CT: Dushkin.

Pollack, R. H., & Brenner, M. W. (Eds.) (1969). *The experimental psychology of Alfred Binet: Selected papers.* New York: Springer.

Pratt, K. C. (1954). The neonate. In L. Carmichael (Ed.), *Manual of child psychology* (2nd ed.). New York: John Wiley & Sons.

Pueschel, S. M. (1983). The child with Down's syndrome. In M. D. Levine,

W. B. Carey, A. C. Crocker, R. T. Gross (Eds.), *Developmental behavioral pediatrics.* Philadelphia: W. B. Saunders.

Raehlmann, E. (1890–1891). Physiologische-psychologische studien über entwicklung der gesichtswahrnehmung bei kindern und bei operierten blindegeborenen (physiological-psychological studies of children and adults born blind who regained their vision through operations). *Zeitschrift für Psychologie und Physiologie der Sinnesorgane, VI* (2), 51–96.

Raehlmann, E. (1903). Über den farbsinn des kindes. (color perception in children). *Opthalmologische Klinik, VII* (2), 221–224.

Read (Dick-Read), G. (1944). *Childbirth without fears: The principles and practice of natural childbirth.* New York: Harper & Row.

Rebelsky, F. G. (1967). Infancy in two cultures. *Nederlands Tydschrift voor de Psychologie, 22,* 379–385.

Rebelsky, F. G., & Hanks, C. (1971). Fathers' verbal interaction with infants in the first three months of life. *Child Development, 42,* 63–69.

Reese, H. W., & Lipsitt, L. P. (Eds.). (1970). *Experimental child psychology.* New York: Academic Press.

Roberts, E. (1944). Thumb- and fingersucking in relation to feeding in early infancy. *American Journal of Diseases of Children, 68,* 7–8.

Robin, A., Schneider, M., & Dolnick, M. (1976). The turtle technique: An extended case study of self-control in the classroom. *Psychology in the Schools, 13,* 449–453.

Rosenbaum, J., & Rosenbaum, V. (1978). *Stepparenting.* New York: E. P. Dutton.

Rosenberg, B. G., & Sutton-Smith, B. (1960). A revised conception of masculine-feminine differences in play activities. *The Journal of Genetic Psychology, 96,* 165–170.

Rosenblatt, P. C., & Skoogberg, E. H. (1974). Birth order and cross-cultural perspective. *Developmental Psychology, 10,* 48–54.

Rovet, J., & Netley, C. (1982). Processing deficits in Turner's syndrome. *Developmental Psychology, 18,* 77–94.

Rutter, M. (1974). *The qualities of mothering.* New York: Jason Aronson.

Ryan, T. J., & Moffitt, A. R. (1966). Response speed as a function of age, incentive value, and reinforcement schedule. *Child Development, 37,* 103–113.

Sage, W. (1978). Violence in the children's room. In B. B. Granville & A. Gilpin (Eds.), *Readings in human development 78/79.* Guilford, CT: Dushkin.

Santrock, J. W. (1972). Relation of type and onset of father absence to cognitive development. *Child Development, 43,* 455–469.

Sargant, W. (1961). *Battle for the mind: The mechanics of indoctrination, brainwashing, and thought control.* Baltimore: Penguin.

Sargent, D. A. (1985). Child Abuse. *JAMA, 254* (6), 803.

Sauls, J. M., & Larson, R. C. (April 1975). *Exploring national assessment data using singular decomposition.* Denver: Education Commission of the States.

Scanlon, J. M., & Alper, M. H. (1974). *Perinatal pharmacology and evaluation of the newborn.* Boston: Little, Brown.

Scarr, S. (1981). Testing for children: Assessment and the many determinants of intellectual competence. *American Psychologist, 36,* 1159–1166.

Scarr, S., & Weinberg, R. A. (April 1978). Attitudes, interests, and IQ. *Human Nature,* pp. 29–36.

Schachter, F., Shore, E., Hodapp, R., Chalfin, S., & Bundy, C. (1978). Do girls talk earlier? Mean length of utterances in toddlers. *Developmental Psychology, 14,* 388–392.

Schaefer, E. S. (1959). A circumflex model for maternal behavior. *Journal of Abnormal and Social Psychology, 59,* 226–235.

Schaefer, E. S. (1965). A configurational analysis of children's reports of parent behavior. *Journal of Consulting Psychology, 29,* 552–557.

Schaffer, H. R., & Emerson, P.E. (1964a). Patterns of response to physical contact in early development. *Journal of Child Psychology and Psychiatry, 5,* 1–13.

Schaffer, H. R., Emerson, P. E. (1964b). The development of social attachments in infancy. *Monographs of the Society for Research in Child Development, 29* (3).

Schlaegel, J., Schoof-Tams, K., & Walczak, L. (1975). Sexuelle sozialization in vorpubertät und früher adolezenz (sexual socialization in pre-puberty and adolescence). *Sexualmedizin, 4,* 4–6.

Schmidt, G., & Sigusch, V. (1972). Changes in sexual behavior among young males and females between 1960–1970. *Archives of Sexual Behavior, 2,* 27–45.

Schofield, M. (1965). *The sexual behavior of young people.* London: Longmans Green.

Sears, R. R. (1977). Sources of life satisfaction of the Terman gifted men. *American Psychologist, 32,* 119–128.

Sears, R. R., Maccoby, E. E., & Levin, H. (1957). *Patterns of child rearing.* New York: Harper & Row.

Sears, R. R., & Wise, G. W. (1950). Relation of cup feeding in infancy to thumbsucking and the oral drive. *American Journal of Orthopsychiatry, 20,* 123–138.

Selman, R. L. (1980). *The growth of interpersonal understanding.* New York: Academic Press.

Shaffer, D. R. (1985). *Developmental psychology.* Monterey, CA: Brooks/Cole.

Sigusch, V. (1971). Sexuelle reaktionen bei der frau (female sexual reactions). In H. Giese (Ed.), *Die sexualität des menschen.* Stuttgart: Enke.

Singer, J. L. (1973). *The child's world of make-believe: Experimental studies of imaginative play.* New York: Academic Press.

Skinner, B. F. (1938). *The behavior of organisms: An experimental analysis.* New York: Appleton-Century-Crofts.

Skinner, B. F. (1957). *Verbal behavior.* Englewood Cliffs, NJ: Prentice-Hall.

Skinner, B. F. (1963). Reflections on a decade of teaching machines. *Teachers College Record, 65,* 168–177.

Skinner, B. F. (1974). *About behaviorism.* New York: Alfred A. Knopf.

Skinner, B. F. (1984). Intellectual self-management in old age. *American Psychologist, 38,* 239–244.

Smith, C. L., Leinbach, M. D., Stewart, B. J., & Blackwell, J. M. (1983). Affective perspective-taking, exhortations, and children's prosocial behavior. In D. L. Bridgeman (Ed.), *The nature of prosocial development.* New York: Academic Press.

Smith, J. R., & Smith, L. G. (1970). Co-marital sex and the sexual freedom movement. *Journal of Sex Research, 6,* 131–142.

Smith, L. H. (1969). *The children's doctor.* Englewood Cliffs, NJ: Prentice-Hall.

Snow, E. (1971). *Red China today.* New York: Random House.

Sophian, C., & Sage, S. (1985). Infants' search for hidden objects: Developing skills for using information selectively. *Infant Behavior and Development, 8,* 1–14.

Spearman, C. (1927). *The abilities of man: Their nature and measurement.* New York: Macmillan.

Spelke, E. S., & Cortelyou, A. (1981). Perceptual aspects of social knowing: Looking listening in infancy. In M. E. Lamb & L. R. Sherrod (Eds.), *Infant social cognition: Empirical and theoretical considerations.* Hillsdale, NJ: Lawrence Erlbaum Associates.

Sroufe, L. A. (1977). Wariness of strangers and the study of infant development. *Child Development, 48,* 1184–1199.

Sroufe, L. A., Fox, N. E., & Pancake, U. R. (1983). Attachment and dependency in developmental perspective. *Child Development, 54,* 1615–1627.

Sroufe, L. A., Waters, E., & Matas, L. (1974). Contextual determinants of infant affectional response. In M. Lewis & L. A. Rosenblum (Eds.), *The origins of fear.* New York: John Wiley & Sons.

Stechlev, G., & Halton, A. (1982). Prenatal influences on human development. In B. Wolman (Ed.), *Handbook of developmental psychology.* Englewood Cliffs, NJ: Prentice-Hall.

Stein, Z., Susser, M., Saenger, G., & Moralla, F. (1975). *Famine and human development: The Dutch hunger winter of 1944–1945.* New York: Oxford University Press.

Steuer, F. B., Applefield, J. M., & Smith, R. (1971). Televised aggression and the interpersonal aggression of preschool children. *Journal of Experimental Child Psychology, 11,* 442–447.

Stone, L. J., & Church, J. (1968). *Childhood and adolescence: A psychology of the growing person.* New York: Random House.

Stott, L. (1967). *Child development.* New York: Holt, Rinehart & Winston.

Straus, M. A., Gelles, R. J., & Steinmetz, S. K. (1980). *Behind closed doors: Violence in the American family.* Garden City, NY: Doubleday/Anchor.

Strauss, M. S., & Curtis, L. E. (1981). Infant perception of numerosity. *Child Development, 52,* 1146–1152.

Sutton-Smith, B., & Rosenberg, B. F. (1970). *The sibling.* New York: Holt, Rinehart & Winston.

Szalai, A. (Ed.). (1972). *The use of time.* The Hague: Mouton.

Tanner, J. M. (1968). Earlier maturation in man. *Scientific American, 218,* 21–28.

Tanner, J. M. (1970). Physical growth. In P. H. Mussen (Ed.), *Carmichael's manual of child psychology* (3rd ed.), vol. 1. New York: John Wiley & Sons.

Tanner, J. M. (1975). Growth and endocrinology of the adolescent. In L. J. Gardner (Ed.), *Endocrine and genetic diseases of childhood* (2nd ed.). Philadelphia: W. B. Saunders.

Terman, L. M., & Merrill, M. A. (1937). *Measuring intelligence.* Boston: Houghton Mifflin.

Terman, L. M., & Oden, M. H. (1925–1959). The gifted group at midlife: Thirty-five years' follow-up study of the superior child. In Vol. 5 *Genetic studies of genius.* Stanford, CA: Stanford University Press.

Thomas, A., & Chess, S. (1977). *Temperament and development.* New York: Brunner/Mazel.

Thurston, J. R., & Mussen, P. H. (1951). Infant feeding gratification and adult personality. *Journal of Personality, 19,* 449–458.

Thurstone, L. L. (1947). *Multiple-factor analysis: A development and expansion of "The vectors of mind."* Chicago: University of Chicago Press.

Todd, T. W. (1937). *Atlas of skeletal maturation.* St. Louis: C. V. Mosby.

Trehub, S. E., Thorpe, L. A., & Morrongiello, B. A. (1985). Infants' perception of melodies: Changes in a single face. *Infant Behavior and Development, 8,* 213–223.

Tyler, L. (1956). *The psychology of human differences* (2nd ed.). New York: Appleton-Century-Crofts.

Tyler, L. (1965). *The psychology of human differences* (3rd ed.). New York: Appleton-Century-Crofts.

Vroegh, K. (1971). The relationship of birth order and sex of siblings to gender role identity. *Developmental Psychology, 4,* 407–411.

Vygotsky, L. S. (1962). *Thought and language* (Trans. & Ed. E. Haufmann & G. Vakan.), Cambridge, MA.: MIT Press.

Walters, G. C., & Grusec, J. E. (1978). *Punishment.* San Francisco: W. H. Freeman.

Waters, E., Vaughn, B. E., & Egeland, B. R. (1980). Individual differences in mother-infant attachment relationships at age one: Antecedents in neonatal behavior in an urban, economically disadvantaged sample. *Child Development, 51,* 208–216.

Watson, J. B. (1919). *Psychology from the standpoint of a behaviorist.* Philadelphia: Lippincott.

Watson, J. B. (1924). *Behaviorism.* New York: People's Institute.

Watson, J. B. (1926). Experimental studies in the growth of emotions. In C. Murchinson (Ed.), *Psychologies of 1925.* Worcester, MA: Clark University Press.

Watson, J. B., & Rayner, R. (1920). Conditioned emotional reactions. *Journal of Experimental Psychology, 3,* 1–14.

Watson, R. I. (1968). *The great psychologists: From Aristotle to Freud* (2nd ed.). Philadelphia: Lippincott.

Wechsler, D. (1958). *The measurement and appraisal of adult intelligence* (4th ed.). Baltimore: Williams & Wilkins.

Weintraub, M., & Lewis, M. (1977). The determinants of children's responses to separation. *Monographs of the Society for Research in Child Development, 42,* (4, Serial No. 172).

Werner, J. S., & Wooten, B. R. (1985). Unsettled issues in infant color vision. *Infant Behavior and Development, 8,* 99–107.

Wesley, F. (1961). The number concept: A phylogenetic review. *Psychological Bulletin, 58,* 420–428.

Wesley, F. (1968). Was Raehlmann the first behaviorist? *Journal of the History of the Behavioral Sciences, 4,* 161–162.

Wesley, F. (1971). Testing Piaget's horizontality concept. Paper: Western Psychological Association, San Francisco.

Wesley, F., & Karr, C. (1968). Vergleiche von ansichten und erziehungshaltungen Deutscher und Amerikanischer mütter (comparing childrearing practices and opinions between German and American mothers). *Psychologische Rundschau, 19* (1), 35–46.

Will, J. A., Self, P. A., & Datan, N. (1976). Maternal behavior and perceived sex of infant. *American Journal of Orthopsychiatry, 46* (1), 135–139.

Williams, J. E., & Bennett, S. (1975). The definition of sex stereotypes via the adjective check list. *Sex Roles, 1* (1), 327–337.

Wilson, G. L., & Bornstein, P. H. (1984). Paradoxical procedures and single-case methodology: Review and recommendations. *Behavior Therapy and Experimental Psychiatry, 15* (3), 195–203.

Wilson, G. L., & Nias, D. (1979). *The mystery of love.* New York: Times Book Co.

Wolf, T. H. (1961). An individual who made a difference. *American Psychologist, 16,* 245–248.

Wolf, T. H. (1966). Intuition and experiment: Alfred Binet's first efforts in child psychology. *Journal of the History of the Behavioral Sciences, 2* (3), 233–239.

Wolf, T. M. (1973). Effects of live modeled sex-inappropriate play behavior in a naturalistic setting. *Developmental Psychology, 9,* 120–123.

Wolfe, D. A. (1985). Child-abusive parents: An empirical review and analysis. *Psychological Bulletin, 97* (3), 462–482.

Wolfenstein, M. (1955). French parents take their children to the park. In M. Mead & M. Wolfenstein (Eds.), *Childhood in contemporary cultures.* Chicago: University of Chicago Press.

Wylie, L. (1957). *Village in the Vaucluse.* Cambridge, MA: Harvard University Press.

Yang, R. K., Zweig, A. R., Douthit, T. C., & Federman, E. J. (1976). Successive relationships between maternal attitudes during pregnancy, analgesic medication during labor and delivery and newborn behavior. *Developmental Psychology, 12,* 8–14.

Yarrow, L. J. (1954). The relationship between nutritive sucking experiences in infancy and nonnutritive sucking in childhood. *Journal of Genetic Psychology, 84,* 149–162.

Yarrow, L. J., Rubenstein, J. L., Pederson, F. A., & Jankowski, J. J. (1972). Dimensions of early stimulation and their differential effects on infant development. *Merrill Palmer Quarterly, 18,* 205–218.

Zajonc, R. B. (1976). Family configuration and intelligence. *Science, 192,* 227–236.

Zajonc, R. B. (1980). Feeling and thinking: Preferences need no inferences. *American Psychologist, 35,* 151–175.

Zigler, E., & Trickett, P. K. (1978). IQ, social competence, and evaluation of early childhood intervention programs. *American Psychologist, 33,* 789–798.

AUTHOR INDEX

SUBJECT INDEX